ANNIE LE BRUN

SADE

A Sudden Abyss

Translated by Camille Naish

City Light Books
San Francisco

©1990 by City Lights Books

This book was first published as *Soudain un bloc d'abîme, Sade* ©1986 by Jean-Jacques Pauvert et Société Nouvelle des Éditions Pauvert.

Cover design by John Miller, Black and White Design.

Library of Congress Cataloging-in-Publication Data

Le Brun, Annie.
    [Soudain un bloc d'abîme, Sade. English]
    Sade—a sudden abyss / by Annie Le Brun : translated from the
French by Camille Naish.
       p.   cm.
    Translation of : Soudain un bloc d' abîme, Sade.
    Includes bibliography.
    ISBN 0-87286-250-X : $12.95
       1. Sade, marquis de, 1740-1814—Criticism and interpretation.
I. Title
PQ2063.S3L3713   1991
843'.6—dc20   90-38764 CIP

City Lights Books are available to bookstores through our primary distributor: Subterranean Company. P.O. Box 168, 265 S. 5th St., Monroe, OR 97456. 1-503-847-5274. Toll-free orders 1-800-274-7826. FAX 503-847-6018. Our books are also available through library jobbers and regional distributors. For personal orders and catalogs, please write to City Lights Books, 261 Columbus Avenue, San Francisco, CA 94133.

CITY LIGHTS BOOKS are edited by Lawrence Ferlinghetti and Nancy J. Peters and published at the City Lights Bookstore, 261 Columbus Avenue, San Francisco, CA 94133.

CONTENTS

This freedom
For which fire itself became a man
For which the Marquis de Sade defied the centuries
   with his great abstract trees
With tragic acrobats
Clinging to the thread spun by the Virgin of desire
                    André Breton, from *L'Air de l'eau,* 1934

A paradoxical woman, "vaguely and willfully hermaphrodite:" thus did Annie Le Brun describe herself at the age of twenty-four in a poetic self-portrait published by the surrealist André Breton. She was, as this same text of 1967 tells us, a rebel: "already militant in elementary school," she would be denounced in her twenties as a traitor to her sex. Refusing the "colonized situation" which, as dutiful and docile citizens, we mostly inherit, she insisted on signing official documents with a name "that differed every time," but which always began with one of two formulas: the "Laughing Cavalier" or the "Lubricious Asp."

Provocative, irreverent, respectful of no authority save that of desire, this auto-depictive poem marks Annie Le Brun as a worthy descendant of surrealism. Ever noted for its celebration of the imagination, of erotic love and individual revolt, this movement was more than a little beholden to the literary experiments of the Marquis de Sade. Although Breton remarked in 1929 that "as far as revolt is concerned, none of us needs ancestors," he had earlier affirmed, in his *Manifesto* of 1924, that "Sade is surrealist in sadism," and most histories of Surrealism include Sade among the movement's antecedents. Thus, when in 1985 Jean-Jacques Pauvert came to reissue Sade's complete works, it was in no way odd that he should choose as his co-editor Annie Le Brun, who by this time had emerged not only as a poet but as a controversial critic of French neofeminism and the author of a penetrating study on Sade and the castles of the Gothic novel.

But Pauvert also chose Annie Le Brun to write a long, historically significant introduction: *Sade: A Sudden Abyss.* For Pauvert, who had already published Sade's major works — a venture interrupted by frequent trials and charges of obscenity and introduced by several brilliant prefaces — now decided to remove all previous introductions to Sade's texts, banishing them to a separate, final volume. Distinguished as they were, they seemed to Pauvert to promote the theory that Sade was unreadable — unreadable unless one read him through the eyes of Bataille or Klossowski, Blanchot or Paulhan. Blanchot wanted a new presentation, one which would cut through all the learned nonsense written about Sade in the past two hundred years and restore him to his pristine self; one which would support Pauvert's claim that Sade was France's greatest writer. No minor task, this; but one for which an irreverent surrealist was well suited.

While normally linked to the body of texts destined to follow them, some introductions rapidly acquire a stature of their own. At first sight *Sade: A Sudden Abyss* would seem to invite comparison with *Saint Genet, Actor and Martyr,* J.-P. Sartre's monumental introduction to the works of Jean Genet: the scope of Pauvert's mission, Annie Le Brun's own passionate intellection, the superficial parallels between Sade and Genet — both authors who shock, who did much of their writing in prison — all justify the rapprochement. Yet *Sade: A Sudden Abyss* differs absolutely from the Sartrian procedure. For one thing, it refuses to speak of Sade to illustrate a theory, unlike *Saint Genet,* whose 700 pages explaining "the choice a writer makes of himself, of his life and the meaning of the universe, even in the formal characteristics of his style and composition" exemplify Sartre's theories of existential psychoanalysis as much as they illumine Genet's books. For another, it constitutes a poetic undertaking in its own right. Refusing to present obsessive problematics as objective criticism, Annie Le Brun adopts a deliberately subjective point of view, approaching her topic on the nervous steed of poetry, clad in the armor of passionate conviction and questing after concrete, individual truth.

Knightly and idealized, this image might not please the author, deeply mistrustful as she is of anything that hints of ideology. Nonetheless it is important to realize that Annie Le Brun draws no essential distinction between a poetic enterprise and a critical one; for her, the process of writing is organic, deriving from a deep connection between body and mind. This attitude is admirably suited to the points she will make about Sade. For if Sade's lucid materialism, visionary gifts, opposition to traditional values and unrelenting search for the absolute in pleasure all "complete the portrait of man" as the surrealists conceived him — the terms are Maurice Nadeau's — it must not be forgotten that Sade also presented the edifying example of one who had spent twenty-seven years in prison *on account of his ideas.* A vital point, since it illustrates in high degree the Surrealist refusal to separate art from life. And so one finds Annie Le Brun directing some of her most incisive attacks against those critics, including Roland Barthes, who attempt to rehabilitate Sade through textual analysis based on the contemporary literary notion of discourse: ". . . when, no longer invoking the monotony of Sadian eroticism, but more frankly the 'monstrous turpitudes' of an 'abominable author,' we censure Sade, as does the law, for moral reasons, it's because we refuse to enter into the sole universe of Sade, which is the universe of discourse" — as Barthes would have us think. Annie Le Brun considers this approach quite tragically misleading. How, she inquires, can one base one's whole analysis on the "properly *literary* nature" of Sade's work, when Sade's whole work is a manifestation of his way of thinking? Of a way of thinking which brought him imprisonment under three different régimes, and which he consistently refused to abandon? For similar reasons she considers Michel Foucault's evocation of "Sade's calm and patient language" an impertinence. Time and again in *Sade: A Sudden Abyss* she does battle with the hydra heads of Writing and of Discourse, as with any literary theory that tends to sever poetry from concrete personal experience.

On the other hand, the poets who have commented on Sade receive high praise, particularly Breton, Eluard, Apollinaire, and Mandiargues. Thus, Sade's sense of the "innocent ferocity" of childhood, which Breton points to in his *Anthology of Black Humour,* features prominently in *Sade: A Sudden Abyss*; Annie Le Brun describes *Juliette* as a fairy tale, imbued with savage wonder. Again, her emphasis on Sadian machines — erotic machines, optical machines — probably owes something to the construc- tions of Duchamp and those paintings by Picabia which illustrate the repetitive and reproductive capacities of human bodies; rhetoric itself will be examined in terms of a machine, in the chapter where she analyses the effects of revolutionary discourse on real human bodies via the guillotine. More striking still, a predatory image from the opening chapter presents affinities with the Found Object. True to her subjective critical method, the author has been describing the physical and mental disorientation — the nameless desires and loss of erotic identity — resulting from a reading of *The One Hundred and Twenty Days of Sodom.* These imprecise obsessions continue to hold her in thrall until a visit, some weeks later, to New York. Walking through the Bronx Zoo she experiences a shock of unexpected recognition, and feels herself suddenly at home: "The birds of prey were what I'd recognized. Luxury, indifference, cruelty, magnificence: they had it all. It was that same fine animal elegance enjoyed by Sade's four libertines at Silling." After all, she continues, Sade had been demonstrating "as never before the sumptuous and savage nature of desire." Thus he had endowed each of his four libertine overlords "with amorous tastes no less astounding than the white eyes of the King Vulture, ringed with colors of fire"; tastes as troubling "as the condor's mossy ruff, its owner strutting with restrained indecency." This sudden discovery of the most savage possible objective correlative suggests that ideal coincidence between the workings of objective chance and the unconscious, which the surrealists perceived in the Found Object. In the context of *Sade: A Sudden Abyss* this sumptuous encounter is emblematic of the organic link between literature and life. It also functions as a key passage in the author's essentially personal contention that theoretical and technical readings of *The One Hundred and Twenty Days* do not and cannot adequately explain its peculiarly disturbing effect; for having ignored the projective element in any will to objectivity they unconsciously fall victim to "that horrid gorgeousness whose prey I had become for having failed to recognize it."

Poetry, therefore, is inseparable from Annie Le Brun's approach to Sade; and she credits her surrealist formation with her vigorous, lifelong opposition to any form of ideology. Thus, explaining the ideological "stripping" Sade undertakes in *The One Hundred and Twenty Days*, she points out that among the many reasons for the offense this text may cause us is our own tendency to fall into the ideological trap of justifying the unjustifiable: "In laying bare the most unjustifiable passions in the heart of Silling Sade foils that questionable play of justifications which can be made to serve *any* feeling, especially the loftier ones. . . ." Any attempt to identify Sade with a totalitarian ideology of any kind "only ends up passing judgment on the person who attempts it," for it seems as if the person making that attempt "has been simultaneously terrified and fascinated by the feelings that Sade's text awakens in him, and has hastily repressed these criminal urges by dumping them into that area still known as absolute historical evil." Thus, our disgust at reading parts of Sade derives as much from our emotion at the revelation of our criminal tendencies as from our aversion to Sade; there is always a moment, she concludes, when "the mind cannot bear to be confronted with its latent criminality."

No one who has accepted some "noble" idea — patriotism, anticommunism, antifascism — is spared in this analysis, for it would seem we all tend to fall back on ideology to legitimize concrete acts of horror. According to Annie Le Brun this ideologizing tendency is found even in such noble causes as women's liberation, a tendency she situates in neofeminism, a movement whose ideological self-righteousness she criticizes in earlier works and at which she takes incidental aim in *Sade: A Sudden Abyss* in the chapters devoted to *Juliette*. Reevaluating Juliette as a precursor of such liberated heroines as young Ellen in Jarry's *The Supermale* Annie Le Brun suggests that if feminists had anything in view beyond the promiscuity of womanhood they would perhaps have been able to read *Juliette* as a "searching reflection on the liberty of women." As she explains in an interview given to *Roman* in June 1986, "the body is the link" between her interest in Sade and her struggle against neofeminist ideology, for "it is in the nature of ideologies to produce ideas without bodies, ideas that only develop at the expense of the body." This devaluation of the body — analogous to the tendency of post-Lacanian criticism to reduce literature to discourse — is what most exasperates her in French neofeminist texts from Simone de Beauvoir to Julia Kristeva. But, as she adds in the same interview in *Roman,* Sade provides us with some of the most potent thinking imaginable, in that he "tries to think out the relationship between the mind and the body as no one else has done." And since, in her opinion, "poetry speaks of nothing else, it was normal that I should encounter Sade, and *a fortiori* through surrealism, whence I come."

Thus we confront in *Sade: A Sudden Abyss* a book which can well be termed a poetic venture, since its deliberately subjective approach — so in touch with its organic impulse as to avoid the projective traps of objectivity — denudes and deconstructs ideology almost as rigorously as does Sade himself. As Annie Le Brun remarks in her book on the Gothic novel, "Poetry always begins with this perilous operation of tracking lies to their sensory roots. . . ." Or, as one of the characters observes in *Justine* in the quotation that begins *Sade: A Sudden Abyss,* "Philosophy, Justine, is not the art of consoling the weak . . . I do not console, Justine; I am true." Not to console, but to tell the truth. For this is what we find in Annie Le Brun: a sensibility of disconcerting honesty.

—Camille Naish

But philosophy, Justine, is not the art of consoling the weak; it has no other aim but to bring soundness to the mind and to uproot its prejudices. I do not bring consolation, Justine; I bring truth.

Sade, *The New Justine*

I do not know, for all that, what was attractive about this person; but I immediately felt it was a very simple matter to love such a man.

Sade, *The Story of Juliette*

INTRODUCTION

When I accepted the disturbing honor of opening this edition of the complete works of the Marquis de Sade, I did not know in what vague manner I should live, during that period of daily contact with this shadowy mass. How could I imagine at that time the persistent dizziness which, all too often, drove me back just when I thought I'd gained a foothold? How could I imagine, before living through it, this very real dizziness, whose power, I soon thought, derived from its brutal way of reconducting thought to its organic origin? The fact remains that the horizon suddenly became confused, taking on the colors of a violent passion. So, at least, it seemed, especially as the violence which possessed me initially found food in my distraction. For several seasons, I was somewhere else.

It was not that I was unfamiliar with Sade's work. When first I read it, twenty years before, I received such a shock I would never have imagined that re-reading it could cause, in anyone at all, an agitation of such scope. What was it that had changed?

No doubt part of it was that I found myself in the alarming position of having to re-read *all* of Sade. We know how emphatically Maurice Blanchot believed this was the only way to grasp the enigma of this work. Many others had subsequently followed his injunction, so as to gain an idea of that excessiveness which constitutes Sade's singularity. But there again, I had the feeling that I couldn't get away from an almost physical diversion. It was as if, long after I thought I had crossed the various bridges which give access to

Sade's thought, I suddenly found myself bereft of that relative degree of mastery which normally results from being well acquainted with an author's work. I came to prefer emotions and sensation to ideas, convinced that ideas would lead nowhere. I began to look for signs, traces, settings left along Sade's path, without really worrying if these might prove deceptive or illusory. And against all expectations, Gilbert Lely's monumental biography, far from soothing my peculiar impatience, whetted it intolerably.

So, there were the usual Parisian thunderstorms closing their shells of sea-green light upon the Place de Victoires. There was the brisk air of the Rue Saint-Roch, etching out a spring "devoid of sentiment." There was the beginning of a white and frenzied summer, trembling against the empty sky of Sade's Château La Coste. There were late afternoons sinking into shades of battered flesh and spattered taffeta. There was all of that, and I began to think I caught some glimpse of a response to all those questions posed by the very fact of setting out to write — again — about Sade. Hadn't it all been said already? Hadn't it all been very well said? Hadn't too much, perhaps, been said by now?

Most certainly. So much so that the climate of the day had been changed. It had taken only forty years for an author quite beyond the pale to become a classic — the favored classic of our impudent modernity, which found in Sade an ideal object of resistance for trying out a critical equipment of hitherto unequaled scope, and which did not hesitate in applying its full investigative powers to so exceptional a case. It was a matter of two birds with one stone: by establishing an ever-denser network of interminable psychological, literary, medical, psychoanalytical and linguistic analyses, criticism made Sade socially acceptable, while at the same time it defused him. After an example like this, anything at all negative ran the risk of suffering the same treatment, since the figure of Sade loomed at the very spot where perversion, unreason and seclusion had marked a place of shadow which triumphal rationality aimed only to appropriate. Also, the impression that complacency, bad faith and even stupidity had played a part in this deliberately progressive and progressist normalization added further unease to my increasingly troubled state. The modern era could be proud of its virtuosity in making us familiar with Sade's peculiarity. Critics were practically jostling one another in his castle grounds. All this could well have become hateful — except that Sade was no longer there, and I knew it.

There again, something had changed, at least as far as I was concerned. When I was twenty, and disconcerted by so violent a thought as that of Sade, I had more or less consented to follow paths which others had already opened. These others seemed to me then far better armed than I was, and I thought to penetrate more easily thereby into these dangerous regions. Years had passed; had the guides grown older, or had I discovered a taste for solitary explorations? I don't know. Whatever the case, I would have been annoyed with myself for sharing the questionable assurance of most of my contemporaries, who seemed more or less convinced that Sade had brought about the transmutation of the century; namely, the transformation of a monumental darkness into a monument of paper. This splendid result had been obtained thanks to the notion of "writing"; twenty years of textual analysis had finished up by excluding Sade from his own self, whereas two centuries of dire opprobrium had simply resulted in his being excluded from the company of other men. Undeniably, progress had been made in dispossessing a way of thinking no longer protected even by the aura of its scandal. Especially as critics seemed increasingly to please others and themselves by speaking of Sade as an absolute. A literary absolute, that is. How sad! How ludicrous! Would they end up catching "The Eagle, Mademoiselle . . ." in this trap?

Of course, for our era to reach such a pass — by which I mean for it to instigate, as if in self-defense, this blind erudition — something in Sade must have been continuing to shake our foundations, something more than just the manifest outrage, the unacceptable words, the intolerable vision. Something still evaded not only the devout followers of "writing," but also those who had become most attentive to Sade's enterprise. I am thinking most particularly of Maurice Blanchot, whose celebrated analyses seemed to have the undeniable merit of revealing, once and for all, the intellectual wager of Sade's work. The intellectual wager, certainly; but what about the rest?

The rest, which turns Sade's correspondence into a stupefying seismograph of flesh and nerves, equally capable of transmitting express requests for "a very young puppy dog," or "a dozen cakes from the Palais-Royal, six of which to be flavored with orange-water." It could express an extreme need for "a little box, which I beg you to have made in the same style as the one you sent me," or "the box, then, at least the box, since you reduce me to illusions," and also this wrenching remark: "I doubt there has ever been a dizziness such as one gets in prison." It could indicate extreme lucidity: "But I was free then, I was a man, and at present I'm *an animal in the menagerie at Vincennes,*" or else the simple, sudden wish for a coat "the color of Parisian mud."

Yes, all the rest, including this question from a note to the poem *La Vérité (Truth):* "It has been estimated that more than fifty million persons have lost their lives in the wars and massacres of religion. Is there a single one among them worth even the blood of a sparrow?" Or this sudden apparition of Aline in a letter written by her mother to Valcour:

> But what is this little head drawing close to mine? . . . Did you ever see such behavior? . . . Because I was seen going to my writing desk, a face appears at once above my shoulder . . . and bursts into merriment, because I catch this little head and scold it? . . . And then suddenly, the laughter stops; for it is a singular being, a little girl whose heart is engaged.

There is also Sade's manner of addressing "Carteron, known as La *Jeunesse,* known as Martin Quiros," his manservant:

> What! you good-for-nothing monkey, you grass-face daubed with blackberry juice, you vine-prop from Noah's vineyard, you bone from Jonah's whale, you old bordello matchstick, you rancid candle that cost twenty-four cents a pound, you rotting girth from my wife's donkey . . . you dare to tell me that you've not found me any islands, you and your four shipmates from that frigate all awash, clinging to the coastline off the port of Marseilles . . .

Or there are the orders he gives Mademoiselle de Rousset in a letter of 1779, written "this Sunday evening, upon receiving yours:"

> . . . Go to La Coste in August, I absolutely condemn you, you will sit down on the bench . . . you know which bench I mean? . . . and when you are there, you will say: "A year ago, he was here beside me . . ." You will think you see me, and it will just be your shadow . . . You will think you hear me, and it will simply be the voice of your own heart. . . .

Or there is the way he makes solitude seem to last forever in *The One Hundred and Twenty Days of Sodom:* "He was in his own home, outside France, in a safe country, in the depths of an uninhabitable forest, in a clearing in this forest which, owing to his precautions, only birds of the air could approach, and he was buried in the bowels of the earth."

All this is acted out via the mad insolence of a twenty-year-old body, then a thirty-year-old body, a body which functions frenetically well but which, weakened by imprisonment and time, will slowly petrify and turn into a no less threatening inert mass. It is a formidable tragedy of living which has only been recorded by Sade — deliberately so. For in Sade there is a physical immensity that re-endows the relationship of mind and body with its original, naturally catastrophic dimension. It is certainly because he refuses, with all his might, the traditional allegiance of the organic and the spiritual that Sade simultaneously allows himself the redoubtable privilege of conceiving what goes on inside him in terms of earthquakes, the orbit of the sun, volcanic eruptions or continental drifts. Nothing could be more monstrous, since humanity is thereby confused with a possible form of energy, and since man becomes one mere probability of being, no better than another. But also, by the same token, nothing could be more banal: even if we have forgotten it, wasn't everybody's childhood haunted by a violent impression of physical dominion on a universal scale?

The causes of the continuing fascination exercised by Sade — even over those who thought they knew him well — had to be found somewhere in this indeterminate region between monstrosity and banality. In time, I grew convinced that this fascination was strengthened by the fact that Sade's extreme singularity reflected constantly upon a universality. However, this universality had nothing abstract about it, being simply the physical universality of people and things. It resembled a ground swell, carrying off one ridiculous concept of mankind and bringing back another, far more profound. Sade never stopped expropriating man from within himself and giving him back to the world. He did not realize this was the work of all great poets, giving everyone back his sense of physical sovereignty — one of the greatest privileges of childhood, which we are in such a hurry to forget. I began to wonder if this constant refusal to let go if it, like other men, might not be Sade's veritable crime, the fundamental crime which justified all those committed after.

In any case, it was the only crime that modern criticism — eager to understand and forgive his slightest deviation — continued obstinately to keep quiet about. The obvious reason for this was that it was not a deviation; it was neither perversion nor anomaly, quite the reverse. While the innumerable figures of Sadian criminality continued to be spotted, while criticism drew comfort from having penetrated the labyrinths of Sadian exception, something in Sade resisted — and seemed likely to go on resisting — this checkerwork, determining the hidden center of the landscape. That is, the point to which everything else led. The point on which converged all "sands of love," both old and new; you know the ones I mean. When one knows, when nothing else remains.

I had read too many prefaces and commentaries — all shrinking into the penumbra of their systems, like suburban apartments in the blinding height of summer — not to guess the significance of their stubborn silence on this point. Nothing in the whole of Sade had ever walked into this hall of half-measure. How could anyone still take Michel Foucault seriously, referring, in his *Madness and Civilization,* to "Sade's calm and patient language"? Did no one even see how impudent it was to praise the expressive patience of a man who had spent twenty-seven years of his life in eleven different prisons, under three different régimes? Yes indeed, Sade was far away. Once he had been a prisoner in the Bastille, then, of his opprobrium; today, criticism held him in its clasp. Yet he remained outside all that, outside in the wind and sun, thinking hell for leather, writing the same way that one might ride a horse to death, that one might ride time itself to death. Critics strove not to speak of this. A silence of this sort clearly showed the best point of departure: this physical revolt — mentioned by none of these analyses since it threatened their coherence, the coherence of all thought — was the actual foundation of Sade's thought. Perhaps it was also the starting point of that "new lucidity" whose effects Blanchot had studied in *L'Inconvenance majeure* without, however, being able to state clearly what it was. I was beginning to discern more clearly what was causing the kind of agitation I seemed unable to shake off: if I was right, wouldn't a new view of Sade make me see the world itself in a new light?

It was then that an urgent need appeared to *take absolutely literally* those parts of Sade which generation after generation kept in the dead letter rack. At the same time, I could not forget that Georges Bataille had advised a contrary procedure in *La Littérature et le mal (Literature and Evil):* "Nothing is more useless than to take Sade seriously, word for word. However one approaches him, he shies away beforehand. Of the different philosophies he lends his characters, it's impossible to recall a single one." But if his ideas shied away from one, if theories skedaddled in his thought, wasn't this because no logical system could get a grip on Sade? Because any philosophical interpretation ended up shattering against his thought? In that case, wouldn't one do better to try to read Sade, for the first time, "literally and in every sense" — like poetry?

Everything in Sade invited this approach. First of all, an excessive manner of proceeding, evidently more metaphorical than philosophical. Totally at loggerheads with all systems of control, Sade began by showing man held prisoner within the theater of his body: "All that depends upon our structure, our organs and the distress they feel; we can no more change our tastes than we can change the shape of our bodies," he declares in *The One Hundred and Twenty Days of Sodom*. At the same time, he shows the extraordinary spectacle of the steps taken by this corporeal theater in order to defeat fatality: as he also writes in *The Story of Juliette:* "Man's whole happiness lies in his imagination."

I decided to take as my departure point this contradiction which so haunted me. I was sure of very little, except that Sade was neither the madman, revolutionary, saint, fascist, prophet, man of letters, butcher, fellow creature or even the thinker he was made out to be.

I knew only that he was alone, mercilessly alone, with a solitude we try to forget can be possible.

That on his side, therefore, was the withering efficiency such solitude can bring.

Part One

CHAPTER ONE

A Major Omission and Its Repercussions

That Sade's isolation strikes daggers to the heart is something every generation has done its utmost to deny. To contend — as many do today — that his interminable works are monotonous is just one more sign of ignorance dressed up as cultural pretention. Whoever reads Sade, as opposed to his commentators, cannot emerge from that experience unscathed. I would even say that one comes out of it with one of those huge bruises of the soul whose unexpected hues can cause the far horizon to turn pale. Even then, one still has to recover from the first assault. One still has to make sure that the defense mechanisms, activated in an almost inevitable surge of panic, do not block the exits. Haven't we all read scholarly exegeses in which the author unwittingly substitutes his own problematics for those of Sade? Nor is that the smallest danger to be met in dallying with such a mind, offering its every reader the type of prison which best suits him — as one needs often to recall.

But since everything begins with *The One Hundred and Twenty Days of Sodom,* and since Sade has thus chosen to begin with something that defies all justification, I shall begin by recalling this work — and recalling it insistently.

For it is with this text, written exactly two hundred years ago during the autumn of 1785, that there first appears that stupefying crystallization of the blackest possible perspectives which constitutes the universe of Sade. Everything that Sade would subsequently write has elements of this, although nothing previously predicted the appearance, in mid-Enlightenment, of this block of abyss, even in the intellectual trajectory of the rebellious young Marquis.

We do know that in 1785, Sade had already been in prison for seven years — and for the second time — for reasons of "extreme debauch." We also know that, as early as 1782, he had already given violent expression and firm exposition to his atheistic views in his *Dialogue between a Priest and a Dying Man (Dialogue entre un prêtre et un moribond)*. But none of this can adequately explain the sudden advent of a world which would henceforth disrupt the field of human consciousness, and disrupt it absolutely. Nor does it explain the extraordinary discretion of Sade's critics as to the significance of this event. Maurice Heine mentions it, of course; so does Gilbert Lely. They mention it more often, and much better, than the others. But as one gets to know Sade's thought, as one sees it developing — if only chronologically around the mysterious kernel of *The One Hundred and Twenty Days,* one cannot help but wonder about the reluctance shown by *all* his critics when evaluating the real importance of this text in the overall body of his work. There is one exception: Jean-Jacques Pauvert, though not himself a critic, has told me several times how shatteringly significant this text has always been for him. So important was it that at the age of twenty-one, and wholly unaware of the possible repercussions, he decided to publish it. That was in 1947. At the last moment, he was overcome with panic and printed it anonymously. All the same, the deed changed his life, for he was then to undertake something nobody had dared to do before: he published the complete works of Sade, paying for his audacity with successive trials and convictions.

Otherwise, even Maurice Heine — to whom we owe the first real, albeit confidential, edition of *The One Hundred and Twenty Days,* published in 1931 with a preface showing that he recognized in this "exceptional work" an "exemplary attempt to analyze the human person in the most ferocious terms" — even Maurice Heine rather minimizes the importance of *The One Hundred and Twenty Days* and its key position in the development of Sade's thought. Admittedly, Jean Paulhan, Georges Bataille and, more recently, Michel Tort and Philippe Roger have all considered this text in turn and from very different points of view; and unlike many others, they have seen therein "the basis of Sade's work." However, none of them really pauses to consider the implications of their weird recognition; no sooner is it expressed than it becomes a sort of trampoline, serving to catapult them hastily along some other avenue of thought.

No doubt about it, Paulhan does observe, in his famous preface to *The Misfortunes of Virtue:*

> For a long time it was thought that this gargantuan catalog of perversions, *The One Hundred and Twenty Days,* formed the culmination of his work. By no means. It is the cornerstone, and the first step. A step which the Encyclopedia might well have been proud to own.

But that's as far as it goes: with reference to the Encyclopedia, the Sadian exception is simply swept off on a literary tide wherein the names of Diderot, Rousseau and Voltaire soon bob about at Paulhan's will. On the other hand, Georges Bataille is possibly alone in having tried to describe the work's intolerable excessiveness:

> Sade aims at each of us individually: inasmuch as it has human qualities at all, this book strikes home like blasphemy, like a disease of the skin, marking all we hold most sacred and most dear *(Literature and Evil).*

But Bataille does not venture to explore the nature of this blasphemy; rather, he tries to pin it onto his reflections about sacrifice. As for Philippe Roger, he rapidly resolves the whole enigma by stating, in his *La Philosophie dans le pressoir* (Paris: Grasset, 1976): "What is 'established' in *The One Hundred and Twenty Days* is a new relationship with knowledge, which passes through a new relationship with desire." From this he concludes, here and elsewhere, that "Sade does not attract anyone to crime, nor to turpitude; he attracts us to the text."

It would seem, then, that each time *The One Hundred and Twenty Days* is recognized as an exception of fundamental importance in Sade's work, the act of recognition is immediately befogged by a systematically superimposed reappearance of each author's own thematic bias: literature for Jean Paulhan, the "sacred" for Bataille, and for Philippe Roger, "writing" itself. The mere fact of drawing near the birthplace of the Sadian monstrosity seems inevitably to prompt the same emergency procedure in very different types of thought: a return to structures of the old familiar kind.

I admit that it took me some time to become aware — and to assess the full consequences — of this quasi-occultation of Sade's most powerful text. Something was working away inside me, as it did outside me, preventing me and anyone else from asking why Maurice Heine, for example, who had been the first to notice Sade's "constant rejection of pity, [which] links the human with the inhuman in his work and constitutes the main force of his singular genius" (preface to the 1931 edition of *The One Hundred and Twenty Days of Sodom*) — why Maurice Heine did not say what an incredible intellectual *coup* Sade had pulled off, beginning with *The One Hundred and Twenty Days,* which comes to represent the absolute of his own thought.

Yet Maurice Heine was the first to realize what a terrible blow it was for Sade when the manuscript of *The One Hundred and Twenty Days* disappeared after the storming of the Bastille. He even asserts that "the rest of his literary life will be governed by the need to repair the consequences of this irreparable mishap." This seems highly likely if one thinks of the splendid letter to Gaufridy of May 1790 in which Sade, recently set free but long since disenchanted, ponders his life and works and is thus driven to mention Madame de Sade's unforgivably cavalier behavior after his transfer from the Bastille to Charenton:

> Why did she not hasten to remove my personal effects? . . . My manuscripts? . . . My manuscripts, for whose loss I've shed tears of blood! . . . One can replace beds, tables and commodes, but ideas — never! . . . No, my friend, no, I could never succeed in expressing the despair I feel at this loss, which is beyond repair.

In all probability, Sade is thinking of the manuscript of *The One Hundred and Twenty Days* which he'd spent thirty-seven days recopying. He did this between the hours of seven and ten, from October 22 to November 28, 1785, all in a "microscopic hand," on a roll of paper "formed by leaves about four-and-a-half inches wide, stuck together to form a strip of more than twelve yards long," according to Guillaume Apollinaire in his 1909 introduction to selected works by Sade. Isn't it therefore rather alarming that, except for Maurice Heine and Gilbert Lely, critics seem scarcely more impressed by the appearance than by the disappearance of this manuscript, to which Sade was so attached? Perhaps now is the time to wonder if the general habit of pinning *The One Hundred and Twenty Days* to the whole body of Sade's work doesn't simply serve to mask the differences between this *School for Debauchery* and all the other texts, together with its influence on them.

It is astounding, all the same, that neither Jean Paulhan, Georges Bataille, Maurice Blanchot, Pierre Klossowski nor even Gilbert Lely has paused to contemplate the earthquake caused by *The One Hundred and Twenty Days,* both in the histories of thought and sensibility. Instead, they have hastily dug over the abyss opened by this book, being content to see Sade as a genius prefiguring Krafft-Ebing, Freud or Havelock-Ellis; for its part, academic criticism is content to view this dodecameron of horrors as the daring continuation of Boccaccio or Marguerite de Navarre. For once, Jacques Lacan shows clearer sight in the cunning parallel he draws, between Kant and Sade:

> That Sade's work anticipates Freud, even as concerns the catalogue of perversions, is a piece of absurdity reiterated in the literary world, and for which the specialists, as always, must be held responsible.
>
> On the other hand, we maintain that the Sadian boudoir equals place-names taken by the schools of classical philosophy: Academy, Lyceum, Stoa. In both cases, the way for science is made ready by reforming the position of ethics. Here, yes, a clearing-up takes place which will then have to swim for the next one hundred years across the depths of taste before the path of Freud can be practicable. Then count in another sixty years for everyone to realize why. *(Kant avec Sade,* in *Critique,* no.191, April 1963)

Regrettably, Lacan forms this reflection with respect to *Philosophy in the Bedroom.* He does not even mention *The One Hundred and Twenty Days,* which could be read precisely as a diary kept during the development of the mental site in question here.

Is it not equally regrettable that Maurice Blanchot's fine beginning in *La Raison de Sade* treats only of *Justine* and *Juliette?* In fact, it is surprising to find Blanchot expertly stating, with respect to *Justine* and *Juliette,* something which should first have been said about *The One Hundred and Twenty Days.* At least, this is what I can't help thinking as I read Blanchot, who tries to determine exactly why Sade is "unexceedable," but without really taking into consideration that work which Sade himself considered most essential. In discuss-

ing *The New Justine followed by the Story of Juliette, her Sister,*
Blanchot writes:

> If there is a forbidden room in libraries, it exists for
> books like this. One can safely say that never in the
> literature of any period has there been so scandalous a
> work, that no other book has ever inflicted such deep
> wounds on human thoughts and feelings. What writer of
> today dares rival Sade in his licentiousness? Yes, indeed,
> we have here the most scandalous work ever to be written.
> Shouldn't it concern us more? We are lucky enough to
> gain acquaintance with a work no other writer has ventured
> to surpass — which means that in our relative world of
> literature we have seized upon an absolute — and yet we
> ask it nothing? We do not ask, what makes it so excessive,
> unexceedable and so perennially unpalatable? It is a strange
> omission. But then, perhaps this very omission is what
> makes the scandal pure?

But once Blanchot has posed the Sadian enigma in these terms, his
own questions can be turned against him, for his own neglect of
The One Hundred and Twenty Days immediately becomes a matter
of concern. Perhaps Blanchot, too, has unconsciously become the
plaything of this "strange omission."

It is a very strange omission, since it conceals the essential fact
that *The One Hundred and Twenty Days* completely eludes this
"relative world of literature," a world Blanchot seems to find all
the more credible, in that it can include and enclose — and thereby
make more relative — that absolute he finds in the stories of *Juliette*
and *Justine.* Does this mean it remains a strange omission, or is it
simply an elegant way of putting everything back into order —
literary order, of course? In any case, it is a dangerous omission, a
veritable powder keg, one that contains those fatal inconsistencies
which Sade first made manifest. An omission which disturbs, from
having become the major omission of our terminal modernity:
namely, the criminal frivolity of thinking that words can exist independently of things, and that people can exist independently of
words. Sade's whole life and thoughts are there to demonstrate the
contrary, even supposing we were unable to imagine the effects this
apparently intellectual problem might have upon our actual lives.

For even if our way of "saying" always proceeds metaphorically
from our way of living, there is no separate, no relative world of

literature. There is simply the world, with its infinite possibilities of representation. All these means of representation, true or false, help modify the world, help make the life we choose, true or false — less blindly than is often thought — in the symbolic darkness we advance in, across that shadowy forest of signs which eventually absorbs all literary works, both nourishing and venomous.

That is still how matters stand, with our daily reality coming into focus just short of the imaginary, and our lives unfolding just short of the unreal. This is hard to accept, when the action takes place against a backdrop of murder; that is, above the abyss of the human heart, where blood is always the obligatory color. It is hard to admit, too, that literature is not a citadel of words and images from which we can survey this horror safely, at a distance. On the contrary, it is an all-too visible, open-air stage, where everything is shamelessly enacted under masks. It would be far more convenient to believe in a literary game, where masks were only masks and words were only words. It would hardly matter, then, if the stage were suddenly to crumple up within its own illusion, or if literature abruptly closed its door across the lie of its autonomy, thereby making everything a little more opaque. Isn't that exactly what we want, careful as we always are *not* to know our destination? This is what is threatened here: we want literature to go on being a world apart, and that way, life can't stop it from rotating. In other words, prevent it from erecting barriers that separate us from ourselves, instead of opening up a path inside our monstrous strangeness.

That is what is threatened in the apprehension we feel with respect to *The One Hundred and Twenty Days*. Especially since the illusion of literary autonomy could prove most useful in protecting us from whatever literary thing is likely to devastate us internally. The fact that customary critical approaches are extremely ineffectual here probably explains why critics unanimously agree to term the work a catalog — a curious one, doubtless, but nothing more than that.

In our own defense, we can admit that circumstances have contributed, still do contribute, to a good deal of tricky maneuvering around *The One Hundred and Twenty Days*. Lost, then found again, then kept from public view until its relatively recent publication, this text has acquired the curious power of seeming like the culmination of works which it in fact preceded. For a long time, I myself was inclined to place it at the chronological conclusion of his work — and I'm far from being alone in that. In *Le Philosophe scélérat* Pierre Klossowski who, describes the book as a general table of perversions, goes on to observe that, "The ensemble forms that genealogical tree of vices and crimes, already [sic] mentioned in *Aline et Valcour*" — when *Aline et Valcour* had not as yet been written. That sooner or later, we should all fall victim to this chronological confusion is probably no accident. But then, what obscure reasons can we have for wanting all that starts to end with *The One Hundred and Twenty Days?*

The ploy is nonetheless transparent. In speaking of this book as an index, a reference list, a catalog, we are starting to imply it has a *before.* The mere idea of a *before* would almost enable us to conceive and measure what it is that drives us off in panic. The mere idea of a *before* would block all backward wrigglings from this text. This, however, raises other questions. In trying so hard to find unfindable preliminaries to this monstrosity, aren't we being tempted — irresistibly, in spite of everything — to take our tickets for Sade's show, even if it proves intolerable? Wanting so desperately to believe in some incredible period of apprenticeship, of which *The One Hundred and Twenty Days* would be the result, we may unconsciously be wishing to experience it too, with the sole aim of slipping into Silling Castle, if only by the tradesman's door.

Quite possibly, the revulsion we feel both cancels out and reveals, in an inverted form, the strength of our attraction. But it reveals much more. Even as we think we're maintaining a safe distance from Sade's insane building, it is actually Sade who is holding us at bay from the ramparts of his solitude. Just as the quartet of libertines who organize these one hundred and twenty days prevent anyone alien to their experiment from entering the walls of Silling, so Sade begins by forestalling every kind of literary access to his solitary keep. We need only recall how deeply buried in an "uninhabitable forest," how in a "nook of that forest, accessible only to the birds, owing to precautions taken," Sade saw fit to place the fortress of his passions. The site is deliberately abnormal and requires an abnormal passport to get in. Like the infinitely corrupted libertine he is, the Duc de Blangis immediately grasps the underlying sense of these topographical arrangements, as Sade relates: "I do not know what is to happen there, but what I can divulge without detracting from the interest of my narrative is that, when all this was described to the duke, he discharged three times in succession." This exemplifies the extreme delicacy distinguishing the libertine from other men, just as Sade is quite distinct from other writers: in both cases, there is a withdrawal from the ordinary conditions of thought — a definitive withdrawal.

This, then, is the start of the inconceivable outrage of Sade. It is also the outrage of that inconceivable which claims us all, but which we all seek to exclude from our existence. It is the inconceivable outrage of Sade, who thereafter devotes himself entirely to excluding anything within himself and us that tries to deny the inconceivable.

And yet, shouldn't we know more about the Château de Silling, considering that in the last fifty years, an ever-increasing number of people out for a walk — strolling, loitering, or even doing research — have taken to wandering about the walls, some of them obstinately trying to define its shape, others sensing, in its mysterious presence, the course through which our main perspectives pass? So many expeditions, resulting in so few real explorations — it rather suggests that the majority of visitors come to seek refuge under Sade's immensity, as if hoping that his vast contradictions will serve to blunt and mask their own. This would explain a kind of devotion often felt for Sade that is particularly useful in disguising our incapacity and fear when having to define the instant, place or point at which his thought escapes us. In fact, his own manner of existing, so resolutely atheist, might not be utterly foreign to devotion of this sort. Through being impregnable, Silling quite possibly conceals the secret of the semi-sacrosanct intimidation still exercised by Sade.

That is why I find it hard to believe in scientific objectivity, when certain critics suddenly take it into their heads to compare the *interior castle* of Saint Teresa of Avila with the edifices built by Sade. Such comparisons owe more to coincidences of interpretation than of representation. "The castle of the soul has many points in common with the castle of the flesh erected by Sade," as Béatrice Didier is not afraid to write, even though her exposition of those common points is far from convincing (*Sade,* Paris: Denoël-Gonthier, 1976). For even though she discovers a similar concentric structure in both Sade and Saint Teresa, sheltering the same imperious interiority and yearning for the absolute, her discovery does not amount to much. But although this comparison is largely one of form, it does have the merit of concretizing — as opposed to representing figuratively — and of reinforcing the tradition of religious readings of Sade.

I am thinking here, of course, of Swinburne and his famous *Apologia for Sade:*

> Draw near and you will hear, beating in this muddy, blood-ied carrion, the pulsing of the universal soul, its veins swollen with divine blood. This cesspool is all tinged with the azure; something of God remains in these latrines.

Of course, I also have in mind Pierre Klossowski and the epigraph to his essay *Sade mon prochain:* "If some strong-minded person had thought to ask Saint Benoît Labre what he thought of his contemporary, the Marquis de Sade, the saint would not have hesitated to reply: 'He's my fellow-man.' " Then again, I have in mind Georges Bataille, playing — with that desperate conviction which was his special strength — with the idea of sin, a sort of religious trans-formation of dialectic that Bataille uses to transport back into the realms of the sacred precisely those for whom the sacred, ambivalent or not, does not exist; for whom "there is nothing sacred," as Sade deliberately puts it, around 1787, in the poem called *La Vérité.*

Last but not least, I have in mind Maurice Blanchot and the seductive analyses set forth in *L'Inconvenance majeure.* They prob-ably proved seductive because they allowed us to include Sade in our twentieth century ideas of what is sacred: I mean, that new sphere of the sacred generated by the concept of Revolution, even though Sade — without going into the troubling complicity of vice and virtue — desanctifies revolution by assimilating it into a natural phenomenon. For him, it is a "crisis" of the social body essentially no different from an erotic crisis, or one of those major expenditures of energy capable of enforcing "the silence of the law." When Blanchot discusses the political pamphlet *Frenchmen, another effort . . .* (from *Philosophy in the Bedroom),* he attempts to make "Sade's folly" coincide with Revolutionary "Reason." It would seem here that he is dressing up Sadian excessiveness to make it resemble the impossible "negative community" and "sacred conspiracy" which Blanchot and Bataille never cease aspiring to. But actually Sade's text is a masterly desanctification of the idea of any community, and practically demonstrates that such a notion is impossible.

The question of Bataille's intentions must remain unanswered until we have determined the nature of that devastating force of feelings and ideas which begins to be manifest in *The One Hundred and Twenty Days* and which prompts, among almost all Sade's commentators, a critical approach that is not just tinged with religiosity, but frequently is actually religious. This kind of skidding about often occurs as one draws near the lands of unbelief. They need stretch only as far as one can see for a religious nerve to twitch in most people, a nerve one would have thought definitively inert, but which revives like a last defense against the void. This curious bond of anguish is, I think, what joins those readings of Sade which have most influenced our apprehension of his thought. I make no judgement here; I simply state that if these interpretations have had so much importance in revealing Sade, it's that we needed them, being incapable of withstanding the intolerable storms of truth whipped up by his atheism. For everything begins physically, even if properly decorous criticism would have us all think otherwise.

The time has come to say it: no one has ever entered Silling Castle *normally*. No sooner does one think to go in than one seems to lose one's balance on a missing step, never to regain it. The price of entry is a dizzying fall through one's own personal darkness. Only at that price does one reach the inner stronghold, for this is the secret that protects it from outside attack; one must pass through the dungeons of the self to gain access into Silling. This essential condition negates the very idea of literature, excluding at the outset anyone who refuses to submit to the merciless arrangements Sade has imagined here.

I myself had long been obsessed by the castles of the Gothic novel, built into the leaden skies of thunderstorms, when finally I entered Silling without really knowing how. One day, however, I realized this was the scandalous construction I'd been searching for, the object of my blind and naïve quest through all those Gothic novels, and that never again would I stray far from this spot. Decidedly, I'd been won over by its paradoxes, truth, its lyrical expansiveness, its ineluctably organic burial. But having once recognized Silling, I did not get to know it better. Quite the contrary. I shall not say how often I stopped short, about to do a U-turn, before going on, driven by an indecent curiosity to see and know just when, in this evocation of the intolerable, I would finally collapse. Collapse is certainly the word, given the physical abuse this text inflicts on all its readers. I came back from Silling ill, like travelers returning from a foreign land they haven't really left, able only to communicate with other hapless tourists who've had the same misfortune. For after this particular trip, the world is never quite the same again. I don't believe those who claim to wander about freely, as if it were a windmill, in the fortress of human passions constructed by Sade. I know the book well. Each time I've read it has been different, as is the case with any book; but each time, I've been equally disturbed, disoriented, and shaken to the core.

But how can I describe the physical agitation caused by any real reading of this text? There was a time, at the beginning of my rediscovery of Sade, when I was more or less obsessed by it. I couldn't pull myself away. Perhaps I had been leaning too far over the abyss; in any case, I felt as if my life was sliding heavily towards it. What bothered me most was the coupling of this feeling with a growing wish to succumb to an imprecise desire — a desire that was harder to resist, for being vague. I was at the mercy of feelings which, apparently devoid of any object, stripped me even of my nudity. For the first time in my life, deprived of the reflecting mirrors of pleasure, I found myself being sucked into a seemingly limitless erotic quagmire. It got so bad that one evening in April, after one of those sudden storms that empty the embankments of the Seine, I found myself utterly alone, imprisoned in reflections from a sulfurous, metallic sky that caused the horizon to lurch wildly as I walked. No doubt this was the immediate visual response dictated by the system of erotic throbbings holding me in thrall. At the same time, I felt myself groped and tickled by ideas, by shimmering sensations and glimmerings of memory, by lingering perspectives, all obeying the unforeseeable, luminous imperatives of the organic which had made of me its stage.

I remained in this state — and expected to remain in it much longer — until several weeks later, when I was visiting the Bronx Zoo in New York. Once again, the backdrop was a thunderstorm, but this time gray as lead, while I stood opposite four birds of prey: two vultures, a condor, and an eagle. At first I could only see splashes of color emerging from the diagonal shadows cast by branches, and circular patterns of feathers, which the wet metal bars of a vast aviary kept all enclosed. Unexpectedly, and for the first time in ages, I felt myself at home, though actually visiting a foreign country. There was nothing unusual about my circumstances: a late Sunday afternoon, a thinning crowd, my absent-minded friends. I watched the crowd pass by, passing with that strangeness which is natural to a crowd whose subtle texture is as yet unknown: over here, the curve of someone's thigh, the corner of a smile, a straying curl; over there, some pretty eyelashes, a glimpse of neck, an arching wrist — these things seemed unintelligible. I felt at the center of a curious void, from which arose the aviary — or rather, its sovereign inhabitants, the sudden, absolute masters of a space which grew in all directions.

The birds of prey were what I'd recognized. Luxury, indifference, cruelty, magnificence: they had it all. It was that same fine animal elegance enjoyed by Sade's four libertines at Silling. After all, Sade had been demonstrating as never before the sumptuous and savage nature of desire. Had he not therefore endowed each of his four overlords with amorous tastes no less astounding than the white eyes of the King Vulture, ringed with colors of fire? Or as troubling as the condor's mossy ruff, its owner strutting with restrained indecency? Or as evident as the tawny vulture's wings, closing like a prison of the sky? There it was, parading up and down, that horrid gorgeousness whose prey I had become for having failed to recognize it. Wasn't my desire just like those leather claws, issuing from feathery sleeves whose plumes were more like knife blades? Didn't it resemble that grainy orange skin, screaming like the sun amid a swelling tuft of sea-green plumes? Couldn't it be confused with that earth-colored costume from some obscene parade, the nude neck of the vulture with its wrinkled head of skin?

Through seeing the potential forms of my disturbance spreading themselves with so imperturbable an innocence and ease, I gradually recovered — or so it seemed — the strength to rise from the abyss. What was previously inconceivable, I saw taking shape — excessive, intense, necessary shape, and it made me feel free. I did not entirely escape from the erotic tension which had troubled me so long. But the mere fact of seeing concrete equivalents of this disturbance — of knowing that they could be seen — gave me back some sense of outline and of shape. It did not matter that this shape was vague, mobile, changeable; it still helped me escape from the curse of the utterly indeterminate, just as that very instability which Sade was making me confront helped me to escape from the prison-cell of forms.

Here, due honor must be paid to Georges Bataille who, alone among the Sadians, actually mentions the physical effect this text can have on readers: "Short of being insensate, nobody finishes *The One Hundred and Twenty Days* without becoming ill: and the person who most suffers is the one who is sensually irritated by the reading." (*Literature and Evil*.) The truth is that if this book proves so unsettling, it's because, *in spite of everything,* in spite of the aberrant, unimaginable horrors it depicts, whoever reads it becomes "sensually irritated," and that is where things start to get intolerable. Bataille has certainly chosen the right word: it's more a matter of erotic irritation than excitement, but irritation in the sense of enervation — that is, almost a removal of nerves altogether, as might result from excessive and prolonged excitement. For the effect of this book is such that it disturbs even our manner of being. It would all be very simple if the prerogative of disturbance were limited to those few persons capable of recognizing their own peculiarities in Sade's vast experiment. But that is not what happens; one is perturbed by scenes quite contrary to those one always thought — at any rate, guessed — would correspond to one's proclivities.

Unfortunately, words oblige me to be too precise about something rather hard to define: a very strong impression of having lost, not one's identity, but one's *erotic identity*. This feeling of loss, I find, is what characterizes the perturbation invariably produced by a reading of this book. We are all the more stupefied by this disturbance in that, egged on by psychoanalysis, we had grown used to thinking — Bataille being the first to do so — that our more spectacular losses of identity originated in the discovery of a repressed erotic self. But in *The One Hundred and Twenty Days*, even this suppressed landmark disappears, taking with it all that diffused positivity generated around the notion of desire during the last thirty years. And so, not the least of the erotic riddles posed by *The One Hundred and Twenty Days* would involve a systematic confrontation with the prelude of desire: a sort of primordial trouble or anticipation, which would be like foothills to the mountain of desire itself. This is probably why we cannot get accustomed to the horrors here unveiled, if these horrors have the effect of making us stop short of ourselves. From Sade's point of view, this should be pointed out, because the general opinion would have us get used to everything, especially to horror. But reading *The One Hundred and Twenty Days* would seem to indicate this is impossible.

From the very outset, Sade leaves no doubt concerning his intentions. He addresses the reader in these terms:

> Now is the time, dear reader, when you must open heart and mind to the most foully tainted narrative ever recounted since the world came into being, for there is no comparable book among either the ancients or the moderns. Tell yourself that any actual pleasure, whether forbid-

den or allowed by the beast which you so endlessly and ignorantly discuss, and which you will call nature — and such pleasures, I tell you, shall be expressly excluded from this catalog; and should you happen upon them fortuitously, it shall occur only when they are accompanied by crime, or tinged with some vile infamy.

This much is clear: all "natural" pleasure being excluded, no less than six hundred passions, divided into "simple passions," "double passions," "criminal passions" and "murderous passions" must thus be conjured up and solemnly described. Everyone knows how this turned out: Sade apparently gave us the first natural history of sexual abnormalities, "a century before Krafft-Ebing and Freud." Agreed. But if Sade is indeed the man who first undertook to "methodically observe" and "systematically describe" the sexual perversions, as Maurice Heine tells us, then it is hard to understand why we still find *The One Hundred and Twenty Days* quite unbearable in this day and age, familiar as we are with numerous psychosexual observations pertaining to the most astounding and diverse of cases. Why does Sade upset us so, and not Havelock-Ellis?

Even if the specialists all recognize the semi-clinical exactness of Sade's table of passions, he himself is far from keeping to a strict scientific objectivity. Undeniably, his exceedingly heinous characters, a setting that subverts space to turn it into a pleasure machine, and his deliberately scandalous commentaries all cause the whole design to slide into fiction. But none of this explains why this book continues to have such an intimate effect on us — rather the reverse. Furthermore, we're a lot more familiar with depictions of horror than we care to admit. The twentieth century is not exactly miserly in that respect; wars, assassinations, extortions of every kind, as relayed by the media, more than satisfy our appetite for realistic images and living examples. We should admit, however, that the preceding centuries were scarcely better off. Then again, it is hard to tell how much we all owe to the latent or manifest violence contained in Christian imagery, whose depictions of torture, martyrdoms and crucifixions rival each other in intensity, inventiveness and realism. To say nothing of the numerous Biblical scenes which have inspired some most disturbing paintings, even if their aim is to edify. Considering, therefore, that we have seen so much, that we have memories so choked with blood, what is so appalling about Sade? Aren't we being ridiculously squeamish, given that for the last fifty years the words "final solution," "nuclear menace," and "extermination camp" have all carried meaning? Given that every year reports from Amnesty International tell of mutilated corpses and slashed lives? Condemned as we are to drag along this constantly renewable burden of horror, how can we still find it unbearable to read *The One Hundred and Twenty Days of Sodom?* What nerve is it Sade touches, to upset us in this manner? What is the secret of this text, whose form is as enigmatic as its content?

Here we have a text which begins like a historical novel, moves into a theatrical structure, is transformed into a philosophical dialogue, thins out into a catalog, and finishes as a balance sheet of those who are massacred and those who survive. Here we have a book which begins with all the pomp of a historical novel, and which ends with the laconic formulas of simple subtraction. Until now, this incongruity of form has never given problems. One rather wonders why. Isn't it odd, not to say astonishing, that all we have done with this stupefying work is to emphasize the unfinished condition of its manuscript? Is that really enough?

I'm not at all sure it is, especially since our curious propensity for soliciting historical data has led us rather to minimize the fact that in the Bastille, Sade had all the time in the world — from autumn 1785 to July 1789, before his transfer to Charenton — to give another form, had he so wished, to this text which he so valued. One may reasonably assume that if Sade did not see fit to rework it during those four years in which he wrote *The Misfortunes of Virtue, Eugénie de Franval* and *Aline et Valcour,* it was because he thought the project was complete. I think we must therefore consider *The One Hundred and Twenty Days* as being finished, and take the existing version as the definitive one, assuming that the internal economy of Sade's design engendered this particular form, which imposed itself in such a way it could not then be modified. Otherwise, why would Sade — whose intellectual tenacity was only equaled by his boldness — why would Sade stop working on this *School of Debauchery,* knowing fully how important it would be?

The text is driven by too forceful an internal motion to be thought unfinished. From the shadows cast all round it, there gradually emerges a structure like a petrified tornado. The astonishing account of these days passed in sexual pedagogy is marked by a vertigo of which Sade is the victim; but a mercilessly lucid victim, one who is firmly resolved not to yield an inch to the forces which would sweep him off and alienate him from himself. A vertiginous sculpture depicting vertigo itself — Sade seems to have wanted to erect a final milestone, implacable and frenzied in its form, against the far horizon of his solitude. I say his solitude; but I'm aware that everybody else prefers to say his madness. I'm also aware that this has been the subject of some fine literary inspirations — rather short ones, on reflection — whereas Sade's insanity lay more in his refusal to go mad, when everyone and everything condemned him to go mad. His vertigo is the enormous yardstick of his struggle, one of the most formidable struggles to keep sane ever undergone by anyone.

This vertigo, a product of imprisonment, has not escaped unnoticed. It is redundant to analyze it further, however, after one has read what Sade himself wrote to his wife about it:

> Today is Thursday, December 14, 1780, the *fourteen hundredth day,* the *two hundredth week,* and the *occasion* of the *forty-sixth month* that we've been separated. At this time I have received from you some sixty-eight lots of fortnightly provisions and one hundred letters, while the present letter is the one hundred and fourteenth that I have written you.

This vertigo is echoed both in mind and body, so that deviation soon becomes their only means of functioning. For when incarcerated thus, deviation is the only mode of behavior which does not deceive or give rise to deception. The vertigo is brought about by the enforced isolation of mind and body, which, being isolated, tend to draw farther and farther apart from each other, causing serious deviations.

All the same, I shall carefully refrain from imagining what was passing through Sade's mind in those years which precede the sudden apparition of *The One Hundred and Twenty Days.* I shall imitate the discreet indiscretions of Mallarmé as he sets about describing Rimbaud in *Medallions and Portraits:*

> I know at the very least how gratuitous it is to substitute oneself for someone else's consciousness: and one which was obliged, on occasion, to speak out loud, on its own behalf, in periods of solitude. To arrange other people's lives into fragments that are both intelligible and probable, the better to translate them, is simply impertinent: all that is left is for me to carry this species of misdeed to the limit. But I'm collecting information.

Happily, we too can collect information, since we now have access to Sade's correspondence in which are woven and unwoven, for almost thirty years, his sole ties with the world. Reading them, it is impossible not to see that, between 1782 and 1785, his letters bear witness to an extraordinary intellectual effervescence. It is much like the physical effervescence which the prisoner of the Bastille describes to Madame de Sade at the end of 1784 in that letter known as "Vanilla and Manilla," on account of its opening lines: "I am quite aware that *vanilla* causes over-heating and that one must use *manilla* in moderation. But what do you expect when that is all one has — when that is all one can resort to!"[1] The document in question relates the "terrible crisis" with which Sade's sexual activity becomes increasingly identified. Sade is worried enough to tell his wife:

> If you know a trustworthy doctor, I would like you to discuss with him everything I describe here, for I'm convinced that no one in the world experiences what I experience in these attacks. It is my most certain intention to consult such a man, upon my release, and demonstrate the problem. . . .

Sade then goes into a detailed description of his affliction:

> It is a veritable epileptic fit — and if I did not take some tedious precautions, I'm sure they would suspect as much in the Faubourg Saint-Antoine, from my convulsions, spasms and pain — you saw a sample at La Coste — and if anything, it's twice as bad, so judge accordingly. . . . I've tried to analyze the cause of this fit and I think I found it in the *extreme thickness* — as if one was endeavoring to squeeze cream through a most narrow-necked flask. This *thickness* causes the vessels to swell up and so tears them. At which people say: the arrow must leave the bow more frequently. Indeed, I know it well — but the arrow will

---

1   Translator's etymological note: vanilla, French *vanille* 1664, often vanailla from Latin *vaina,* diminutive of *vagina,* "a sheath"; 1664, also an aromatic substance derived from the vanilla bean. *Manilla:* French *manille,* a handcuff or ring, 1680, formerly the ring to which the chain of a convict was attached.

not leave, and to constrain it to leave brings on mortal faintness.

Judging by information garnered some two centuries later, it would seem from the symptoms of the "crisis" that Sade was suffering from an infection of the prostato-urinary tract. This would thicken his secretion (the sperm becomes quite granular) and render all ejaculations very painful and unpleasant. Once again, it would seem that the clinical description furnished by Sade is remarkably precise. At the same time, this letter, which is almost entirely concerned with these difficult ejaculations, provides Sade with an opportunity of reaffirming something he will never tire of stating, all through his work: "Pray do not object it is the mental state which thus affects the physical — I shall reply to the contrary, I have conducted hereupon all possible experiments. . . ." He even adds:

It is most untrue that an excited mind can cause this; quite the opposite: the more it is excited, the less the arrow flies — as you have seen, and as you must recall. The less it flies, the more the mind is heated — thereby provoking incommodities of every kind.

This all tends to prove that, if these attacks are not caused by the mind — and Sade insists that they are not (rightly, we now know) — the mind can at least affect their prolongation or their resolution. Either, as Sade puts it, an overheated mind prevents the "arrow" from flying; or else an overheated mind perpetually rekindles the excitement of the senses. Both interpretations rely on a disunity of mind and body which Sade's infection may certainly have aggravated, but does not entirely explain. Sade's physical distress is marked by his conviction that such mind-body splits cause maladies of mind and body alike. Occurring in the close, limiting quarters of a prison, this dramatic schism not only becomes intolerable, but produces a situation that is literally explosive. Suddenly, one sees the fear of madness leaving dangerous ripples in the calm humor which otherwise succeeds in containing the distress of this letter. Thus, when Sade attempts to explain to his wife the chain of "appalling episodes and violent attempts" which increasingly characterize his sex life, he writes:

Imagine an artillery piece that fires balls, loaded with a ball whose particular nature is to swell in proportion to the time it lingers in the barrel; if you fire the piece after two days, the explosion is a small one; but if you leave the ball to grow, it will eventually burst the cannon when it fires.

He could just as well apply the same metaphor to the effect of prison on his mind. It is also remarkable that the image of explosion occurs, to express the malady afflicting him. For the passage from the reality of his inflammation to the metaphor of explosion typifies those depictions of tumescence which obsess him at the time. This swelling of the impulse of desire, as Fourier would say, occurring in all Sade's statements from those years, grippingly illustrates the misery brought on by such a total blockage of his amatory system.

Here we should all take note of the letter dated July 1783, by the Marquis de Sade:

> . . . you all think you have accomplished a miracle, I would bet on it, in reducing me to an appalling state of abstinence with respect to *carnal sinning*. Well, you are mistaken: you have merely fired my imagination, causing me some fantasies it is imperative I carry out. It was beginning to wear off, but now it will return all the more strongly. When one overheats the pot, you know quite well it must boil over.

Even if Sade's sexuality is not a direct result of his incarceration, prison seems nonetheless to increase his sexual functioning — originally solitary and excessive — by reproducing it through artifice and symbol. Besides, Sade goes even further, suggesting a means of curing the deviations of the body, even when he is thought to be concerned only with those of the mind:

> If I had had to cure *the gentleman in number 6,* I would have gone about it very differently; instead of shutting him up with cannibals, I would have shut him up with girls, and in such quantity that Damme! if, during the seven years he's been there, the oil in his wick did not all get consumed! When one has too spirited a horse, one doesn't shut him in the stable, one takes him galloping across ploughed fields.

Here, once again, Sade reasserts the supremacy of the physical. He does so after following a detour that allows him to speak of the body rather than the mind; but he is never so naïve as to confuse the workings of the two:

In acting thus, you would have set him on the *right path*, on what is called the *honorable path*. No more of these *philosophical stratagems,* these quests so odious to nature (as if nature had anything to do with it); no more of these alarming indiscretions, the product of too ardent an imagination which, always chasing happiness without finding it in anything, ends up putting fantasies in place of reality and *vile deviations* in place of honest pleasure . . . set inside a harem, Number 6 would have become *a friend to women.*

What is more, if Sade does not subordinate body to mind, neither does he subordinate mind to body, as one might be inclined rather quickly to assume. And just as there seems to be no trace of sublimation in his work — as Gilbert Lely has accurately remarked — so would it be useless to look for a psychological ploy capable of reducing the workings of the mind to those of the body. In other words, there is neither sublimation or somatization in Sade.

How, then, should we explain this continual shuttling from body to mind and back again? It appears more as a mark of Sade's sexuality than of his genius. In fact, the inner structures of his work will be modeled on this erotic particularity, on this erotic literalness — equally discernible in beings, things, and also ideas. Critics have often wondered why the most theoretical disquisitions follow the most debauched scenes in Sade's novels; perhaps they wonder to avoid noticing that this juxtaposition constitutes a double refusal to give preferential treatment to either mind or body, and that it evinces an *irrepressible need for objectivity,* capable of upsetting, purely and simply, even the conditions of thought.

I say this because I want it to be realized that during those years, Sade is playing a game of literally capital importance. The game involves his mind, his body and the world; the wager is his own thought, and *The One Hundred and Twenty Days of Sodom* could well be the report of it, barely disguised. There is only one way of knowing what really took place, and that is to undertake the journey with Sade and his experimental crew.

The journey must be undertaken from the very beginning, and will be profitable only if one can decide, quite quickly, where the opening sentence is transporting — or deporting — us:

The extensive wars which Louis XIV was obliged to wage in the course of his reign, while they exhausted the state

> Treasury and the resources of the Nation, nonetheless af-
> forded a secret means for the enrichment of huge numbers
> of those leeches always on the watch for public calamities
> which they inspirit rather than appease, in order to profit
> from them with the greatest possible advantage.

One cannot avoid this incredible opening sentence, in which an entire era crumbles, eaten away by those very forces that were supposed to sustain it; in which a century lies dying, devoured by those beings who were supposed to nourish it. With this sentence, the universal tottering begins; at one blow, a kingdom is bereft of its substance; warlike pageantry appears and disappears in a disturbing glow of light, fading like weapons and gold helmets in the darkness of time. In this pitiless attack, everything that begins as a particular world comes to an end; the sentence supplies both the theme and the essential rhythm of the Sadian undertaking. In the next sentence, this passage from external brilliance to inner gloom is accelerated in a rapid oscillation between the brilliant surface and the gloomy depths:

> The end of this reign, so sublime in other respects, is
> possibly one of those periods of French history to witness
> the greatest number of these hidden fortunes, which only
> become manifest through a magnificence and a debauchery
> as secretive as they are.

In describing the decline of pomp into secrecy, and the concentration of splendor in the heart of silence, Sade first suggests the potential explosiveness of this worthy historical tableau. At the same time — and this is the first of his assaults — he takes us beyond the appearance of order, beyond the shadow of this world, right into the lair of individual savageness.

Such is the first step in an educational program which immediately disorients us by turning us away from the appearance of established order, and despite our protests. This results in a growing tension, and accounts for much of the difficulty we have reading this text. Right from the start, Sade systematically contrives to lead us into places where we do not want to go, where we no longer know how to look at things, where we would probably prefer to be blind. So much for his method, defined at the outset: no one can be surprised, after this, to hear Sade frequently declare his unique wish to withdraw and deviate from any "natural" or "honest" pleasure. It is also quite to be expected that he should choose the word "deviation" as a generic term for any passions he finds interesting:

> Once provision had been made for everything of a lubricious nature that best could satisfy the other senses, it remained to arrange for the narration — in the minutest detail, and in order — of all the different deviations of debauchery, its branches and abutments; in short, of everything which libertines refer to as their passions.

This notion of deviation is also what determines the agenda of these one hundred and twenty days, together with the instructions given the four women who are in charge of operations, the four female "historians." All four must be able to narrate, in the context of their past adventures,

> . . . the most extraordinary deviations occurring in debauchery, arranged in such an order that the first woman, for example, would include in her narrative the hundred and fifty simplest passions and the most ordinary or least elaborate perversions; the second, in the same context, an equal number of the more unusual passions, involving one or several men and several women; the third, too, should introduce into her story one hundred and fifty of the most criminal obsessions, such as do most offend the laws, nature and religion; and as all such excesses lead to murder, and as murders committed from debauchery are of infinite variety, proportionate to the torments formed in the libertine's inflamed imagination, so should the fourth woman add to her life's events the detailed account of one hundred and fifty such tortures.

But why would anyone rely on the accounts of these four historians, to give form and substance to the world's first encyclopedia of deviations? Is it just because ". . . it is admitted, among true libertines, that the sensations conveyed through the organ of hearing are more agreeable and most acute"? That is certainly the foremost reason, and we shall soon see that the term "historian" rapidly becomes ridiculous, since memory serves only to make present things that are immediately, continually submerged in waves of sensation. But the sensation has been drawn from the remotest corners of the depraved chronicle, from the most inaccessible and intemporal regions of perversion, and that is what the four historians must strive to depict. It is an in-depth study, which drags things from the depths, and it is connected with Sade's attack on historical representation, apparent in his opening sentence; above all, with its dissemination in the real world. As soon as he has swerved away from the historical order, Sade takes advantage of this momentum to diverge from the social order, too. And so, having quoted the Duc de Blangis and his brother the bishop, Durcet and Judge Curval as examples of these "hidden fortunes," Sade hastens to announce:

> For six years these four libertines, united by their con-
> formity of wealth and tastes, had planned to strengthen
> their ties by forming alliances in which debauchery counted
> far more than any of those reasons which normally do
> justify such bonds.

There follows a precise description of the arrangements made by the four libertines in their plan to marry each other's daughters, since marriage seems the best way of legalizing incest. It also seems the best way of confounding the taboo enforced by sacraments and institutions, since their incestuous project strikes at the very heart of matrimony. Here again, derision suddenly appears, as if rebound-ing from the Sadian perversion: instead of showing us the improve-ments marriage is supposed, normally, to bring about in people's lives, Sade continues to describe in minute detail the customary orgies of his libertines, thereby demonstrating that wedlock has in no way modified their five weekly sessions. With this, we are swept beyond the normal social order, into a region where marriage is left drifting like an empty hulk across an ocean of perversions. Thus matrimony is supremely mocked, an empty form whose sole purpose is to cause amusement in so hardened a debauchee as the Duc de Blangis: ". . . no bond is sacred in the eyes of people like ourselves; the more it seems so to you, the more it tickles our perversity to shatter it."

But Sade does not stop there; he proceeds to unite the four debauchees and their wives in a gallery of portraits. And here he succeeds in surpassing psychology and indeed, all laws of individual depiction. Portraits of character, portraits of physique — he forgets none of the psychological conventions, but uses them as a grid, the better to uncover precisely what portraiture never normally reveals. He casts the Duc de Blangis and his brother the bishop in exactly the same mold, and does not hesitate to say so, displaying scorn for the habitual toil of novelists: "By conserving exactly the same moral and physical characteristics and adapting them to a physical existence infinitely inferior to the one just described, we obtained the portrait of the Bishop of . . . , brother to the Duc de Blangis." For Sade only resorts to the portrait grid when he wants to shift it downwards — deviation, once again — and reveal, in all their violent physicality, sexual organs instead of feelings. He shows sex organs and bodies, which immediately become more telling than the subtlest psychological analysis, as is readily apparent in the incomparable portrait of the libertine Durcet:

> Durcet is fifty-three years old, small, short, fat, extremely thickset, with a pleasant, fresh sort of face and very white skin; his whole body, especially the hips and buttocks, is exactly like a woman's; his bum is fresh, fatty, firm and plump, the hole unusually enlarged owing to his sodomistic wont; his prick is quite extraordinarily small, scarcely two inches in circumference and four inches long; he never has erections now; his discharges, which are rare and very painful, are rather small in quantity and always preceded by spasms; these send him into furious states which drive him towards crime; he has a woman's throat, a soft, agree-able voice, and sounds very honest in society, although his features are at least as depraved as his colleagues'; he and the duke were at school together, and still besport them-selves daily; in fact, one of the Durcet's favorite pleasures is to have his anus tickled by the Duke's enormous member.

We should also notice how Sade borrows from the art of min-iature, in order to convey "an idea of the four wives of these honest husbands." First of all, he tells us they are all "fit to be painted" — precisely to avoid depicting them. Then, hastily, he glosses over their skins, "whiter than the lily," their eyes, "solemn, black and smoldering," their "blond hair, the finest one could hope to see," and their "delightful curls," using the most hackneyed clichés as short cuts, so as to proceed with all haste to their erotic charms, which form his true medallions. Thus, in the case of Adelade, as soon as the habitual banalities are out of the way, we find him lingering over her "satiny-smooth belly," before setting, like a pre-cious stone,

> . . . a little blond mound, sparsely furnished, [which] served as a peristyle to the temple where Venus apparently

received the honors due to her. This temple was so narrow that not even a finger could be put inside, without her crying out. Nevertheless, thanks to the judge, the poor child was no longer virginal, either there or in the delightful other places I still have to describe.

In all these portraits, Sade can be seen cleverly playing on the banality of clichés, using them as one might a neutralizing agent to blur the social aspects of each character, the better to bring out his or her intimate particularities. He seems always to begin by trying out his brushes on, for example, Constance's "most delightful form," on her "extraordinarily noble features," on the "alabaster firmness of her bosom," and so on, until his imagination reaches those attributes which are definitely unique:

> . . . her flanks, with their extraordinary curve, led with a delightful suddenness to the most finely and artistically sculpted bum that nature had produced for some time. It was of a perfect roundness, not especially fat, but firm, white, plump, barely revealing the sweetest, neatest and most delicate of little holes; a touch of tender rose tinged this bum, a charming refuge for the sweetest pleasures of lubricity.

It may well be that having to conform to the conventions of portraiture assisted Sade like a fine-tuning device, or some other preliminary mechanism necessary in focusing exactly on what it is that defines a character, in an entirely physical way, without reference to social modes of being.

There is nothing in common between these portraits and the sort of professional card-index description Sade uses to present each of the four women chosen as historians:

> . . . four women already past middle-age (most necessary, experience being of paramount importance here), I say four women who, having spent their lives indulging in the worst excesses of debauchery, were well equipped to give an accurate account of their research.

Naturally, Sade tells us that Madame Champville "had a rather prominent mound and her clitoris protruded by more than three inches when aroused." But this is more a professional idiosyncrasy than an individual detail. And it is significant that this particular clitoris — just like the "withered, worn, marked and ravaged backside" of Madame Desgranges, resembling "mottled paper more than human skin" — in no way affects the disposition of the portrait, whereas the slightest emphasis placed on any sexual attribute belonging to the wives completely unbalances their image. The historians' function is not to reveal an intimate detail which decency keeps hidden. On the contrary, as hardened prostitutes and superannuated bawds, their social function is to show what the wives must conceal. Accordingly, they have nothing to "show" but everything to "tell," in the general scheme of Sade's project to "tell all."

As to their physical peculiarities indicated here, these constitute the most rapid and effective means for referring to the precise professional aptitudes behind their local authority, at the expense of all the rest. If, indeed, the "missing breast," the "three amputated fingers," the six teeth and an eye lost by Madame Desgranges are to be taken as irrefutable proofs of service, the only physical peculiarities Sade keeps of the historians are registered first as weals, scars, and imprints. These peculiarities justify the choice made of these four persons, because at this point their bodies are no more than memories, mere spaces to be marked by other people's memories, because their bodies will soon fade as their voices take on more importance. Into this curious absence, at the very center of his narrative, Sade fixes and installs each of these interesting creatures, since the emergence of their voices seems to parallel the disappearance of their bodies. Once again, he succeeds in so doing after distancing them — even doubly distancing them — by demanding that each one of them should " . . . give an account of all excesses, analyze, enlarge, detail and classify the same, establishing thereby the interest of the narrative." Beneath an apparently objective exposition, Sade resurrects the special features of biography, as if only the most extreme subjectivity could guarantee objective rigor. At the same time, this will to objectivity strips each of the four historians of all her subjectivity. For as women whose bodies have become entirely public, existing only in memory, they need only publicize these memories to disappear completely behind their own voices. Their speaking voices, neither objective nor subjective, but rather, unobjective, rank among Sade's great inventions. By virtue of this double distancing, from both subjective and objective modes, Sade passes definitively beyond appearances, causing both the introspective illusion and the encyclopedic illusion to seem equally superficial.

Since we are still in the preliminaries, I shall refrain from describing the effects of this voice, which rids the world of sham and decides where — now that it belongs to no one in particular — would be a good place from which to address everyone. Except that, in order to be perfectly clear, Sade leaves no room for illusions, especially human ones. Thus, nothing could be more pertinent than those final preparations which precede the departure for Silling:

> Once these women had been found, and proven satisfactory in all respects, it was time to see to the accessories. At first, they had wanted to include large numbers of lewd objects of both sexes . . . but finally only thirty-two such subjects were selected, including the historians.

This functional equivalence between accessories, subjects and objects, apparent from these few lines, indicates that Sade has already passed beyond the human order, into a region where the inhuman starts splitting off from the human silhouette; a region where the object can slough off the hide of subject, where what we are collides with what we think we are. From now on, Sade will constantly anticipate our inhumanity, the inhumanity we bury deep inside ourselves, and which we are so petrified to discover. A stone of scandal where the heart should be, a stone which cannot be avoided, that unshatterable touchstone from which Sade constructed Silling.

We still have to decide why Sade seems concerned only now with the staging of this unbearable ordeal. We still have to think why the castle chosen as his citadel still towers above everything that's said today. Towers very far above.

CHAPTER TWO

THE IMPACT OF THE SENSUAL ATOMS AND ITS EFFECTS

In 1782, Sade wrote the *Dialogue between a Priest and a Dying Man,* a work which any of his atheist contemporaries need not have disavowed. In 1787, Sade wrote the poem called *La Vérité,* a work of equally materialistic inspiration which not one of his atheist contemporaries could possibly avow. For in 1782, in the *Dialogue between a Priest and a Dying Man,* we read that "all human morality is contained in this sole precept: *make others as happy as we would like to be ourselves,* and never do them more harm than we would like them to do us." But in 1787 we learn, in *La Vérité,* that:

All things please nature: she has need of our misdeeds.
We serve her as we sin: the bloodier our opus,
The greater her domain — and her esteem for us.

Between these two dates there is, of course, the advent of *The One Hundred and Twenty Days of Sodom,* which represents Sade's rupture with the world — both his contemporary world, and our world of today. It would be far too easy, however, and certainly inaccurate, to see a simple relationship of cause and effect between the incomparable violence of 1785 and the radical departure of 1787: the castle at Silling is firmly implanted in the atheistic landscape. It would be impossible to conceive of Silling's secret, if one took it into one's head to abstract it from that landscape. Only after scanning atheism's full horizon did Sade conjure up this alarming edifice, investing it with all his blasphematory powers. The very originality of Sade's peregrinations in the realm of atheism is probably what gives us access to the castle's foundations.

First, this much is obvious: the theoretical aspect of Sade's revolt originated in an atheism that was coherent, rigorous, and founded on a logical refutation of God's existence. Sade was not content simply to adopt notions circulating at the time — whether those of La Mettrie, Diderot or d'Holbach — all of which found grounds for support in recent biological discoveries. On the contrary, he behaves as if he wished to acquire the persuasive power of the first atheism of all: he starts all over from the beginning, doing all the demonstrations for his own satisfaction. Admittedly, he does borrow certain formulations on the way, but only to create added pretexts for repeating his own convictions, on every possible occasion, without ever being at a loss for words. Sade's atheism is first and foremost linked to a logical revolt. It is thus inseparable from the very basis of his thinking — whose functioning it also guarantees.

Here Sade rejoins the mainstream of the materialist tradition, rediscovering the logical rigor of, for example, Nicolas Fréret. As Antoine Adam has recalled (Preface to the *Opuscules, Oeuvres complètes du Marquis de Sade,* t. XIV, Paris: Cercle de Livre Précieux, 1968), Fréret succeeds, between 1722 and 1739, in his *Lettre de Thrasybule à Leucippe,* in establishing that one "cannot even suppose the existence of a Divinity or a universal cause as distinct from the universe itself." In his turn, Sade goes back along the causal chain in order to demolish, through simple reasoning, the idea of a primordial, transcendental cause. By virtue of its logical origin, Sade's atheism is as unshakable in its foundations as that of Molière's Don Juan: for both of them, God's inexistence is as certain as two and two make four. What is more, Sade never misses an opportunity to demonstrate as much. This is one of the constants of his thought, determining the deeper structure of the *Dialogue between a Priest and a Dying Man,* even if La Mettrie's influence is large; we find it again in *La Vérité* and in all his subsequent major novels. It's almost as if Sade endowed this demonstration with hygienic value, like an exercise that should be regularly performed to develop mental muscle. But it would seem — after seeing him take up this demonstration at least once in each of his books, putting it into the mouths of very diverse characters, causing it to be reiterated in all manner of circumstances — it would seem that he accords it a more important value. Founded exclusively on pure analysis, quite independent of the state of scientific thinking at the time, doesn't this demonstration testify to a sovereignty of thought which could hardly fail to charm Sade? For when it abolishes the notion of primordial cause, man's thought opens up the universe and flows into infinity. The invention of logical freedom — authorizing the thinker to deny the idea of limitation in discursive thinking — would seem to possess all that is needed to arouse a mind like Sade's. Developing henceforth as a means of access to infinity, doesn't logical freedom give man an idea of his own grandeur essentially no different — contrary to what one might expect — from the idea of greatness that Pascal bestows upon his thinking man? For Pascal declares:

> It is not from space that I must seek my dignity, but from the ordering of my thought. I could not then be richer, had I great estates. Through space, the universe can understand and engulf me like a speck; through thought, I understand the universe. (*Pensées,* no. 256, Paris: Gallimard, éd. de la Pléiade, 1954)

Paradoxically, it is by a similar assertion as to the power of thought that Sade establishes his atheism:

> "O Juliette!" said Madame Delbène, "let us have no doubt: it is to the limits of our intellect, and that alone, that we owe the chimeric notion of a God. Not knowing how to account for what we see, in the extreme impossibility of explaining the incomprehensible mysteries of nature, we have gratuitously placed above her a being endowed with the power to produce all those effects whose causes are unknown to us.

Whatever Sade may say of metaphysics, God's inexistence casts him down between infinity and nothingness, and leads him to confront most of those questions generally thought to be answered by the concept of God. Sade's intellectual honesty is such that he will never dodge them. It is even rather distressing, when reading the *Etrennes philosophiques*[2] addressed to Mademoiselle de Rousset, to see just how much he has made them his own. Breaking mentally free of his confined reality, like a wild beast bursting from a trap, the prisoner of the "Vincennes chicken-run" conducts a splendid reversal of his thought and wonders: What is movement? What is matter? Is it inert, or not?

> . . . and, if matter moves, if it is the sure and lawful cause of generations and perpetual alternation, tell me what life is, and prove to me the nature of death; tell me what is air, analyze its different effects, teach me why I find sea-shells on the tops of mountains and ruins at the bottom of the sea.

Yes, like a wild beast, since Sade's savage logic is what emboldens him to hurtle through the void, the void where atheist thinking supposedly travails. As a general rule, such thinking carefully skirts round the void, eager from the outset to plant railings for the concept of Nature, a concept which limits and delimits, even today, its field of activity. After this first stratagem, atheist thought then tries to stem the inevitable flow of questions about how the world works and is arranged. It is an understandable stratagem, given the immensity of the task, to say nothing of the powerful attraction deism continues to hold for the good minds of the moment, even the encyclopedists. It is also an ideological wile to avoid confronting nothingness. On this point Sade is very clear since, as early as 1782, he makes his dying philosopher declare: "Besides, it's neither horrible nor absolute, this nothingness." Sade never partakes of that devoted reliance, criticized by Grimm, which the more important atheists such as d'Holbach and La Mettrie place in the idea of Nature; yet he does use Nature to justify a morality of pleasure and voluptuousness he seems to have adopted in both the *Dialogue between . . .* and the *Etrennes philosophiques.* We have even got into the habit of considering this recognition of nature as one of

---

2   This really refers to the letter written by Sade to Mademoiselle de Rousset on January 21, 1782. Gilbert Lely has extracted this from the rest of Sade's correspondance and presented it under the title of *Etrennes philosophiques* (*Season's Gifts of a Philosopher*), which is his own. To avoid confusion I shall use this title even though it seems a bit misleading. (Author's note)

the downbeats of Sade's thought, destined to be countered as that thought grows more assertive.

But here we should return to the actual texts, and not allow ourselves to be sidetracked by so seductive a hypothesis as that advanced by Maurice Blanchot in *La Raison de Sade,* in which he declares:

> Men, God, nature — each of these notions seems endowed with a certain value at the point where it encounters negation; but if one considers the entire experience, these moments no longer have the slightest reality, for it is the particular characteristic of that experience to spoil and annul them, one after the other.

But this is not absolutely certain, at least as far as the *Dialogue between . . .* and the *Etrennes philosophiques* are concerned. In both these texts, the theory that mankind should count on virtue appears only at the work's conclusion, appended like an afterthought. At no time is this virtue actually negated; however, it always appears side-by-side with seemingly incompatible propositions. There is, for example, the reflection that rises rebelliously from the *Etrennes philosophiques.* Emanating from man's insignificance compared to nature, it poses the fundamental question of morality, and in these terms:

> You expect the universe to be virtuous, and yet you do not see that everything would perish in a trice if only virtues existed here on earth; you will not accept that, since vices must exist, it is as unjust to punish them as it is to mock a one-eyed man. . . .

How can we believe that a reflection of such portent can fit inside this final proposition:

> Remember, it is to make your fellow-beings happy, to succour, love, attend to them, that nature has placed you in their midst, and not to judge and punish them, especially not to keep them locked away.

When he refers in this way to the idea of nature — so typical of the average atheist's thought — Sade does not grant it any value whatsoever, not even the "certain value" Blanchot thinks negation must confer. Here, the idea of nature is already neutralized before it has even been formulated, by the vigor of the motion which precedes and exceeds it. Such lulls are customary in Sade: a brusque suspension of the deviation of his thought, a chilly pause to readjust, just long enough to keep up appearances before attacking with fresh strength. This frequent shuttling between the surface and the depths could well illumine the succession of contradictory perspectives, with their odd polarization, constantly occurring in Sade's work. Especially since he soon becomes so proficient in this practice of deviation that, no matter how ensconced he may be in the labyrinthine regions of the self, he always allows a portion of his thinking to freshen in the breezes of contemporary thought. In fact, all of Sade's theories develop at the cost of his dynamics of successive dives, more or less connected, from the common sense of the surface to the drunkenness found in the depths. The best example probably occurs in *Frenchmen, another effort . . .* where these dynamic plunges take place in the still mobile mass of revolutionary activity. Here a troubled surface layer provides Sade with an excuse to show us the tempests brewing in the depths, and which are, in reality, the storms of his desires.

Seen from this perspective, the power of his negation becomes a secondary effect, and not the prime mover of his thinking, as Blanchot affirms: "Having discovered that in man, negation equals strength, Sade tried to found man's future on negation carried to the limit." It could be objected that I am imprudently venturing to contest Blanchot's thesis — echoed by so many others — on the basis of Sade's early writings, which do not fully bear his mark. No doubt this is true. But it is striking to find, in these first texts concerning atheism, a question so essential for Sade, a rough version of that effort to maintain an inner contradiction which so strongly typifies his later thought and generates his reputation for insanity — the best-disposed minds being the first to think him insane.

Indeed, once Blanchot has convinced himself that "writing is Sade's proper madness," he precludes all possibility of following him, being content to stand and observe him from the shores of non-madness. Having neither the naïveté nor the impudence to think it possible, or even desirable, to suppress the distance Sade puts between his thought and ours, I shall do no more than contest the notion of "Sade's madness," because it necessarily presumes a perspective of non-madness which the person speaking is supposed to maintain. And this perspective of non-madness differs so radically from the one adopted by Sade that one begins to wonder if, from such a viewpoint, one can still perceive what really troubles Sade.

Blanchot's description of Sade's dynamic motions is certainly quite admirable. But he describes them from a distance, on the evidence of those surprising ripples they stir up on the surface of Sade's discourse. Paradoxically, nothing in these rather abstract descriptions permits one to answer the most pertinent questions raised by Blanchot himself at the beginning of *La Raison de Sade:*

> . . . What is the substance of Sade's thought? What exactly did he say? Where does one find order in this system, where does it begin and end? Is there anything more than the mere hint of a system in the motions of a thought so obsessed with reasons? And why do so many well co-ordinated principles not add up to the perfectly solid whole which they should form, which they even do appear to form?

And how can these questions find an answer, when the perspective of non-madness selected by Blanchot implies a stationary point that in turn encourages a gap between himself and "Sade's madness" — especially since "Sade's madness" consists in this shuttling back and forth between the surface and the depths, thereby shaking us to *our* own depths. It follows that Blanchot's fixed point of view leads him intently to observe the manner in which Sade's oscillations leave traces through his own line of vision — but he does so at the expense of the movements themselves. Although Blanchot deserves credit for deciphering, in these traces, the workings of "supremacy, across the spirit of negation pushed to its utmost point," he is only speaking of the traces left by Sade's deviations. But each deviation constitutes a plunge into the depths of self, a self that develops perpendicularly in relation to the order of things, to open like a trapdoor onto that universal instability which so occupies our thoughts and our desires.

Blanchot also remarks that, in Sade:

> . . . his theoretical thoughts are constantly liberating the irrational powers to which they are related. These powers both animate and disturb them by exerting pressure such that thoughts resist and yield to them, seeking to control it — indeed, do control it, but only by freeing other latent forces, which in turn bear them off, deflect them and pervert them. In consequence all that is said is clear, but seems at the mercy of something which has not been said; later on, what has not been said shows itself, and is repos-

sessed by logic, but obeys in turn the impetus of a still latent force; in the end everything is brought to light, everything becomes expressed; but everything is immediately plunged back into the darkness of unconsidered thoughts and moments which cannot be formulated.

It is obvious from this that the principle of negation alone cannot account for this intermittency of light and darkness. Otherwise, why does Blanchot seem to see such a threat in the reappearance of darkness? And doesn't the darkness he evokes serve to cover over precisely that space which each of Sade's deviations has uncovered? Furthermore, these "irrational powers" look as if they're holding Sade's reason as a hostage, reducing it to a most uncharacteristic passiveness, quite unlike his normal vigor. For Sade is always he who speaks and never — as is good form today — he who is "spoken."

I have searched vainly in Sade's work for these "unconsidered thoughts." Such weaknesses would never suit his savage logic. As for these "moments which cannot be formulated," do they really exist for Sade, who proposes to "tell all"? For Sade, who announces, "As for me, I destroy and simplify," equipping his dying man with the weapon of denial, but never thinking this should be a principle: "You're heaping error upon error," says the latter to the priest; "I strive against them all." If one should ever come to doubt the firmness of Sade's speech or his clarity of argument, it's a good idea to reread the *Dialogue between a Priest and a Dying Man.* Here again the conclusion, which conforms to natural morality — "All that is needed is a generous heart" — may surprise the reader, whom Sade was introducing, on the previous page, to different and more disturbing considerations:

> We are swept along by irresistible force, and never for an instant are we able to determine anything beyond our inclinations. There is not one single virtue which nature does not need; and conversely, not one single crime she finds unnecessary. All her science consists in maintaining us between the virtuous and the criminal, in perfect equilibrium. But then, can we be held guilty for the inclination that she gives us?

Once again, the problems raised here cannot all be solved by the appeal to a "generous heart." Nonetheless, Sade's curious progression from one page to the next does not seem to be dictated either by negation or insanity. It's simply that, having indulged in a deviation which takes him far from the atheistic thinking of his time, having ventured into the depths of atheist materialism, having already exceeded the bounds of atheism's most audacious specula-tions, Sade suddenly swims back to the surface. To do so, he quickly discharges ballast — too quickly, perhaps, for anyone still unaccus-tomed to his dives.

Proceeding from these distant regions, from what he sees in these far depths, proceeding from that nothingness which he considers with more calm than any of his contemporaries — "It has never frightened me, and in it I find only consolation and simplicity" — Sade now travels back through different philosophies of nature, both radical and conformist, taking them one after the other, until he has scanned the length and breadth of the subject which absorbs his attention in those years: the question of moral judgment. First, he takes the drama out of nothingness by means of a proposition reminiscent of the English thinker Toland: "Nothing perishes, my friend, nothing is destroyed in the whole world." This leads him to stress nature's indifference, almost as if echoing a remark made by Grimm in 1759: "Blind, without affection or predilection for any particular form, nature is content to maintain the general fermen-tation. That is her one and everlasting law." From here, he can easily pick up the theories of La Mettrie, through a criticism of remorse which the transition to a "generous heart" seems to neu-tralize entirely, turning into a virtuous sort of hedonism.

I say "seems," because Sade does not stop there, either in this dialogue or in the *Etrennes philosophiques*. In both texts, he has no sooner reached a point of reconciliation with the world than he immediately draws away, each withdrawal being effected with a violence inconceivable in terms of philosophy. Thus, just when he has practically convinced us that the overall progression of the *Etrennes philosophiques* is leading to this exhortation to make our fellow-beings happy — "to succour, love, attend to them" — he continues: "and not to judge and punish them, especially not to keep them locked away." Here, brutally, he presents the facts which bump into ideas and send their pieces flying, one by one, on nature's handsome chessboard. The word "judge" knocks down "succour," "punish" sends "love" flying, and "keep them locked away" cancels out "attend to them." It is like a pitiless game in which the philosophical proprieties are massacred. It responds, like a mirror image, to that game of massacre found early in the *Etrennes philosophiques,* when Sade describes his judges and, through them, his immense distrust of humanity: "Wretched creatures, cast down for an instant on this petty ball of mud, has it been decreed that half the flock shall persecute the other half?"

And so, the *Etrennes philosophiques* are cast like a sounding rod into the darkness of a substance culled from somewhere between the social order and the order of philosophy. This sounding serves as much to comfort Sade as to harden him in his revolt, as we can see from this troubling postscriptum: "In the Vincennes chicken roost, this 26th day of January, after fifty-nine and a half months of *being squeezed like a grape* — without success, in truth." The postscriptum itself inversely reflects another such remark: "If my situation has its thorns, it must be admitted that it often inspires philosophical reflections of a most amusing species."

This may well provide a key to Sade's particular humor, which tries to catch reality between two of its appearances, so that the parallel similarities cancel each other out and expose their mutual deceptions. This also accounts for the all-important, steadily augmenting repetition in Sade's work. Similarly, his frequent transitions into literalness provide a good way of emphasizing this double gap between an object and its various depictions. For there is certainly a gap, in that Sade's humor always springs out from some sudden swerve of his rebellious thinking. And so, at the close of the *Dialogue between a Priest and a Dying Man,* just as one is certain of the virtues of the generous heart, and certain that the "Dying Man" will die happy, our hero suddenly announces: ". . . my end is drawing near, six dazzlingly beautiful women await in the adjoining room; I've been reserving them precisely for this moment" — obviously convinced that happiness will come to him through pleasure. We have here the same type of reversal, the same mocking of philosophical decency as in the letter to Mademoiselle de Rousset, culminating in a sentence which is every bit as startling as the troubling P.S.: "The dying man rang, the six women entered and the preacher became, in their embrace, a man depraved by nature, for not having been able to explain what a depraved nature was."

I would like to stress the savage beauty of this final scene, which seems to me to anticipate Jarry's *Le Sumâle* and the sexual prowess of the Indian. Not because these two texts demonstrate a wish to put oneself in the hands of a few charming and highly skilled young women. But because, in both cases, these splendid creatures will contribute — in the devastating armor of their bodies and their charm — to the dismembering of false ideas on nature and on love. Thanks to them, indeed, there will be nothing left to say afterwards, because philosophy has said it all. Particularly eloquent in this respect is the profoundly frivolous conclusion to the *Dialogue between* . . . , in which the man who dies is not the one who was supposed to die; in other words, the preacherly function dies, and a man is reborn to pleasure. Actually, a man is born from the mirrorings of pleasure, since his image now returns as an inverted reflection of the gloomy remonstrations his priestly functions initially required of him:

> Having reached this fatal moment, when the veil of illusion is rent asunder and the wayward man is shown the cruel picture of his errors and his vices, do you not repent, my son, of the numerous delinquencies which human weakness and fragility have caused you to commit?

Sade's entire work will take as its paradigm this scandalous rebirth, this outrageous transformation from a deathbed to a boudoir — every bit as subversive as Rimbaud's *salon* at the bottom of the lake. His work will be like a prolonged staging of what might well be termed his *existential humor.*

Sade's sense of humor derives from the spectacle of life reasserting its rights over the illusion of ideas and feelings. It is an essentially atheist humor, opening up a subversive region between life and its deceitful representations. Indeed, from a strictly spectacular point of view, Sade's humor corresponds to a theatrical depiction of the utter collapse of any form of representation. Nothing could be more opposed in principle from Brechtian distancing, which aims only at replacing one system of representation by another. Sade's humor, however, theatricalizes the emergence of nothingness on every possible occasion, determines, for the first time, the arena to be occupied by atheism, and proposes the formidable perspectives of that space, both as a way of thinking and a way of being. If atheism consists in drawing all possible consequences from God's inexistence, then Sade is certainly the only writer to have actually embodied this metaphysical disrespect, as Maurice Heine has so ably shown:

> We should not lose sight of the fact that Sade is an *absolute* and that he goes straight ahead to the very limit of his thought, to the utmost limit of its logical consequences. He couldn't care less if that upsets prejudice,

stereotyped ideas, social conventions and moral laws. He doesn't just write, whenever he can, that God does not exist; he thinks and acts it constantly, he tests it out and dies in consequence. This unshakable arrogance is certainly what people have forgiven him for least. (Foreword to the *Dialogue between a Priest and a Dying Man,* 1926)

This is what people still do not forgive him for, since the theory of "Sade's madness" — even allowing it could be a "madness of writing" — has proved to be the most recent means of rejecting his furiously coherent atheism. How can we not understand Sade's fury, when his very being is contested, even today, by all those who would like to rectify his way of thinking? In this respect, critical and textual evaluations of Sade are scarcely better than the worst condemnations. Roland Barthes, for example, probably means to blast these condemnations when he declares, in *L'Arbre du crime:*

> . . . when, no longer invoking the monotony of Sadian eroticism but, far more freely, the "monstrous turpitudes" of an "abominable writer," we start to imitate the law and reach the point of banning Sade on moral grounds, it's simply because we refuse to enter into the Sadian universe, which is the universe of discourse.

But it soon becomes clear that this type of interpretation gains credence at the cost of a tragic misconstruction. How can one base one's entire analysis of Sade on the "entirely *literary* constitution of the Sadian work," when this work is only the manifestation of his "way of thinking"? For Sade himself has said quite enough about his way of thinking in a letter of 1783 to Madame de Sade, about a year after the *Dialogue between . . .* and the *Etrennes philosophiques* — enough, one would think, to discourage anyone from frivolous talk of "literature" in his regard:

> My way of thinking, you say, can never meet with approval. What do I care? Certainly the man is mad, who adapts his way of thinking to suit others! My way of thinking is the fruit of my reflections; it derives from my existence, my way of organizing things. I am in no position to alter it; and even if I were, I would not. This way of thinking, which you so admonish, is my life's one consolation; it alleviates the sufferings of prison, it constitutes my pleasure in the world and I am more attached to it than to my life.

My way of thinking is not responsible for my misfortune; the thought of others has caused that. If, then, as you say, my liberty is priced at the sacrifice of all my principles and tastes, we can bid each other an eternal farewell, for I should rather sacrifice one thousand lives and liberties, were I to possess them. I am a fanatic of principles and tastes, and fanaticism is the handiwork of the tyrants who do persecute me. The more they continue their vexations, the further they implant my principles within my heart; and I do openly declare there is no further need to speak to me of freedom, if it is offered only at the cost of their destruction. . . .

This way of thinking is, indeed, absolutely atheist. Having refused, in the idea of God, everything which limits man, it naturally comes to resist any idea of limitation at all. From this point of view, there can be no attempt to comprehend and include Sade within a system, even that of literature, which does not end up by parodying his thought. It does not so much caricature as immobilize it — and that is quite enough, when "Sade's way of thinking" illustrates and proves his atheism through being, above all, *the* analysis of nature seen as "always in action, always in motion," and matter which "moves by its own energy, as a necessary consequence of its own heterogeneity." It is a way of thinking which, henceforth, must brook no obstacle if it needs analyze the constant motion of the universe. Sade's vehement blasphemies may well be linked to that state of mental insurrection from which he never, in his whole life, swerves, continuing to think out this perpetually moving universe whose qualities he knows he shares:

> Nothing is born, nothing essentially perishes, everything is but an action or reaction of matter; there are the waves of the sea which rise and fall within the mass of waters; there is perpetual motion, which has been and always will be, and whose principal agents we become, without ever suspecting it, by reason of our virtues and our vices. It is an infinite variety; thousands upon thousands of different bits of substances, appearing in all kinds of forms, annihilating themselves before becoming manifest in other forms, subsequently to dissolve and form again.

This is what the Pope explains to Juliette. Without being so naïve as to think that each of Sade's characters speaks with Sade's voice, the fact remains that Juliette, of whom Sade is especially fond, expects a great deal from the Pope's opinions. She addresses him like the high-class, professional atheist he is. She even insists that his answers to her questions about life, death and crime shall be the sole price of her favors. This is just to show that as far as atheism goes, we shall take the Pope's opinions every bit as seriously as Juliette.

Indisputably, atheism was still at that time perceived as a danger. There was, therefore, a real risk attached to professing oneself an atheist. Apart from this, one can easily understand, from Sade's blasphemous insistence, that he was constantly concerned with preventing a resurgence of the idea of limitation which, reappearing with the notion of God, would prevent a thinking through of this "diversity of movements of ways of acting, which alone constitutes the diversity of substances."

Such a God inhibits thinking, since he causes thought to revolve around the notion of primordial cause; like a conjuror he also whisks away infinity, the better to squash man into the prisons of finitude. If Sade never forfeits an occasion to deny him, it's because the vigor of his own thought is at stake, this new type of thought which he is busy training to confront that absolute uncovered by God's absence. So convinced of this is Sade that he is even aware that far more is at stake: that thought in general is at stake, its very basis and its functioning. The following extract from *The New Justine* attests to this. Here, Sade takes up certain theories of the Baron d' Holbach, but exaggerates them, so as to extract those elements essential to a trial of thought:

> But nature, you will tell me, is inconceivable without a God. Ah! I understand; this means that, in order to explain to me something of which you comprehend very little, you need a cause, of which you comprehend nothing at all: you claim to cast light on something obscure by giving it curtains that are twice as thick; you think you're rupturing a fetter, while all the time you're adding further chains. Credulous and enthusiastic physicists, why not copy some botanical treaties, to prove that God exists; draw up a detailed description of man's every part, like Fénelon; hurl yourself into the atmosphere, the better to admire the paths of stars; go into raptures at the sight of butterflies and insects, polyps and well-organized atoms, wherein you think to find the greatness of your God: in vain, for all these

things will never demonstrate the existence of this absurd and imaginary Being; they will simply prove that you do not have the ideas you should as to the vast variety of substances, and the effects to be produced by infinitely varied combinations, all of which assemble to constitute the universe.

After this splendid indictment, it is impossible to dissociate Sade's atheistic fury from the breadth of his observation. But where does all this violence originate? This haughtiness of vision? Is Sade alone in this? In any case, one cannot separate him from that tradition of atheism which runs from Fréret to Diderot, the Curé Meslier to Grimm, from Toland to d'Holbach — unfettered intellects of such great breadth and vigor that they upset western thinking in the space of a few decades. And so, apart from the obvious divergences, how does Sade's atheism differ from that of his contemporaries? Once again, it's necessary to return to the text to see, quite suddenly, that Sade is the only one of them to have what I shall term a *physical awareness of infinity.* For if his language differs from the legislative discourse of the Baron d'Holbach or the mechanistic speech of La Mettrie — as from everybody else whose ideas he refers to and adopts — it's through a force of conviction manifest only when the speaker is entirely committed to what is being said. This leads to a constant concretization of the violence of Sade's thought, of which the final scene in the *Dialogue between . . .* provides a striking example. But that is true of all the ideas tossed about inside this dialogue; all of them, no matter how abstract, become so plastic and so malleable they almost seem familiar. The same can be said of Sade's later works, even where the most scandalous propositions are concerned. In *Philosophy in the Bedroom,* for example, Madame de Saint-Ange will suddenly declare, as if confiding a particular delight: "Look, my love, look at all the things I'm committing all at once: there's scandal, seduction, bad example, incest, adultery and sodomy!" In fact, all the stage directions given here or elsewhere as to the motions of the bodies as they intertwine, separate, embrace again — "one gets into position, one prepares, the act is carried out, the group breaks up, the posture is relaxed" — all these directions are as valid for ideas, and the way that they prepare and meet, combine and separate. Indeed, this is what Sade wishes us to see.

In the domain of philosophical dialogue, therefore, Sade is quite unlike Diderot, who with virtuosity exploits the genre's full resources. Sade, for his part, exhausts them, until the intellectual "posture" of each speaker falls apart, as do the groups of bodies. This permits the frivolous exchange of ideas to harden into attitudes. In *Philosophy in the Bedroom* Sade brings us directly into contact with this theatricalization of thought. But that is a process which occurs in all his novels — the progressive hardening of opinions into convictions, taking shape the way one builds a theatrical set. This hardening explains the incredible pressure exerted by Sade in keeping hold of his reader. Whatever one does, Sade is there, and he stays there for the very simple reason that whatever his mind proves, his body rediscovers; then again, whatever his body proves, his mind will rediscover. In the same way, the idea that God does not exist is what makes the universe more concrete and more present to him. It almost seems that Sade's reason causes the demise of deceptive ideas so that his sensibility can engender worlds in motion:

> . . . in a world built like ours, there necessarily were crea-
> tures like those we see in it; just as there must doubtless
> be some very different ones on some other sphere, in this
> swarm of spheres which fill up space. But these creatures
> are not good, nor beautiful, nor precious, nor created; they
> are simply froth, the consequence of nature's own blind
> laws. . . . *(The Story of Juliette)*

I would be willing to bet that this constant presence of the universe in Sade's thought has also impressed us deeply, as we imagine the lyricism of its movements, the tragic aspect of its transformations. Before or after Sade, Pascal is the only writer I can see who is able to evoke, so strongly that we feel it physically, this truth of man without God:

> For what is man in nature? He is nothing with respect
> to infinity; he is everything, with respect to the void: a
> middle point, between nothingness and everything. Infinity
> far from understanding these extremes, the reason and the
> principle of things are insuperably hidden from him in
> impenetrable secret, incapable as he is of perceiving both
> the void from which he came, and the infinity engulfing
> him.

Given the similarity of these two views on man's place in the world, who could be surprised if Sade, like Pascal, seemed to bet on God's existence — but bet the other way? Pascal stakes God's infinity against human limitations; Sade seems to bet on the infinity of the universe to demolish human finitude. If Pascal wagers in and for a fixed, immobile world, once finity has been reserved for man, Sade, inversely, could well wager in and for a universe in motion, once the idea of man has tipped into infinity.

Nonetheless, Sade does not bet. In fact, he is probably the only eighteenth-century philosopher not to place a bet, whereas all the rest are wagering, some on nature, some on man, and none as honest as Pascal, explaining with the terms of his bet that "reason counts for nothing here." Where reason does count, however, is in the rigor of Sade's thinking, physically experiencing the absence of its limits in a world perpetually transformed. Of course, Sade is not the only person in the eighteenth century to think the universe is always moving; but he is the only one actually to experience it within himself, and to say so, with such stunning physical acuteness that each sentence of the *Etrennes philosophiques* is etched in sensitivity:

> You seek to analyze the laws of nature, and yet your own heart, in which those laws are graven, remains an enigma which you cannot possibly resolve! You seek to define them, these laws, and yet you cannot explain to me how it is that some swollen little vessels can instantly send someone out of his wits, and in the space of a single day transform the worthiest of men into a wicked scoundrel.

Sade is avidly delving into the philosophical biology of his time at this point. He turns to it first as to a pool of images, which help him visualize the motions that obsess him. More than that, however, these images offer an enormous advantage: they command respect as an objective, physical justification of his atheism.

Thus, it is not surprising to find Sade describing life either as an "assemblage of motions," or sometimes as an "electric fluid," seeming equally content to refer to chemical, mechanical or else electrical images. For what matters to him most is to grasp the essence of the "general agent" capable of provoking the "impact of the sensual atoms." The effects of this strange vital energy, which was on everybody's mind, were known to Sade through his own sexuality. This energy gave him the physical awareness of infinity and hence, the wild audacity to seek love's secret within human viscera.

No one else will ever dare observe, from such close quarters, the volcanoes of our sexual night. But although Sade's sexuality inwardly connects him with the universe, teaching him everything he knows of lightning, currents, tides, fire and electricity, it also separates him from the rest of mankind. By the same token, this awareness of infinity is what encloses him in solitude, just as his perception of nature isolates him from all the other natural philosophies. And *isolates* seems certainly to be the proper word, considering that at that very moment atheism is rallying to the password of *gravitation round the self,* a notion defined by d'Holbach in his *The System of Nature,* as:

> . . . [a] necessary disposition in man and in all beings which, by various means, tend to persevere in the life they have received, as long as nothing disturbs their mechanism or its primary inclinations.

D'Holbach further specifies that this *gravitation round the self,* the equivalent to what Newton calls the *Force of inertia,* and the moralists, *self-love:*

> . . . is only the tendency to self-preservation, the desire for happiness, the love of pleasure and well-being, the readiness to do everything which seems advantageous to one's life, and the marked aversion for everything which threatens or disturbs it: these are primary feelings, common to the whole human race, and which all their faculties strive to satisfy, which all their passions, will and actions have as their continual goal.

No one could provide a better definition of that conformity which Sade is trying, in his thinking, to avoid; not just in order to review his sexual deviations, but also to establish the deviation which any passion signifies. Nothing could better illustrate how Sade's reflections differ from those of his contemporaries, precisely at the point where something of the atheist revolt gets lost in trying to re-establish a meaning, or even a transcendence, when evidence suggests that no such affirmation can be made. Especially as this "gravitation round the self" tends more and more to provide theoretical grounds for a reconciliation between interests and passions — which happens to have been the principal concern of economists, philosophers and moralists for almost a century. There is but a short step from this "gravitation round the self" to a morality of interest, and that step is taken at the expense of passions, of which "those that are harmful" are sacrificed to "those that are useful to society." Since most eighteenth-century atheists have no difficulty believing, with d'Holbach, that "good is what is useful, evil is what is harmful to others and mankind," it is obvious that the antinomies of physical materialism and utilitarian morality will keep cropping up whenever the question of good and evil is discussed. Now that there is no more God, how shall one distinguish between them? Who shall decide what is harmful and what is not? The individual, or society? And how is one to choose among the passions, when no one knows what causes them?

So many questions, to which materialism cannot find a reply but which the current philosophy claims to answer through the idea of usefulness. As d'Holbach would have it: "Usefulness is nothing other than true happiness; to be useful is to be virtuous; to be virtuous is to make people happy." So many answers which are not answers, and which Sade alone does not find adequate — especially the Baron d'Holbach's conclusion, which closes all those doors onto infinity just opened up by materialist philosophy: "in a word, the spirit of philosophy is the spirit of utility; it is on the scales of usefulness that a philosopher must needs weigh men, together with their works and claims." There is only one way to resist this ideological show of force, and that is to recover atheism's original impetus, at the point where it was interrupted — especially with respect to the passions. It becomes particularly important to consider them quite independently of good and evil. In *The One Hundred and Twenty Days of Sodom,* Sade proposes, and for the first time, to do just that. And so, take a good look: rising from the spot where historical atheism turns faint, founding its own solidity on the weakness of its contemporaries, the castle at Silling — conceived to represent the passions in all their range and oddness — Silling is the first, if not the only, absolutely atheistic monument.

CHAPTER THREE

A SUMPTUOUS BANQUET AND ITS CONSEQUENCES

Snow had fallen in alarming quantities, filling the surrounding valley and seeming to put the lair of our four scoundrels beyond even the approach of beasts; as for human beings, surely none could still exist who were bold enough to venture so far.

On the morning of the fourteenth day, nature sets a white and silent void around the Château de Silling. This further emphasizes the besieged situation of the individual passions which Sade has deliberately transformed into a fortified and deviant position — a position of conscious, desired, even exalted deviation. But we are doomed simply to record this deviation, as long as we refuse to think how it materialized and fail to examine the stupefying chain of closures which detach the castle utterly from ordinary life, and thereby put us at an even greater distance.

First, the numerous geographical obstacles. There is the "tortuous and difficult road, absolutely impassable without a guide," then the "charcoal burners' nasty hamlet," leading towards a "mountain almost as high as Mount Saint Bernard, and infinitely harder of access," surrounded on all sides by precipices, including the "fissure of more than thirty fathoms at the summit of the mountain, between its northern and its southern walls," which leads into this "small plain of about four acres, surrounded by vertiginous rocks whose summits touch the clouds," a "small plain so well surrounded, so well defended," in the middle of which stands Silling. The castle itself is surrounded by a "wall some thirty feet in height," reinforced by a "very deep moat filled with water," defending a "last enclosure in the form of a circular gallery." And yet, having shown how each of these obstacles creates an impasse, uncrossable in either direction, Sade still finds it necessary to add that, on the evening of October 29, "Durcet . . . had the bridge from the mountain cut down as soon as they had crossed," and that, in order to "prevent attacks from the outside, which were not greatly feared, and escapes from the inside, which were feared rather more," they had walled up "all the doors to the inside," so as to be "enclosed absolutely, as in a citadel besieged, leaving no possible way open, whether for deserters or for hostile forces," until it becomes "impossible even to recognize where the entrances had been." Is this not extraordinary?

So great a determination to be isolated at all costs is not entirely explained by the grim necessity of secrecy, which Sade had been the first to recognize as an essential condition of debauchery:

> A solitary and remote retreat had been chosen, as if silence, isolation and tranquillity were potent agents for debauchery; and as if anything abetted by those qualities to inspire a holy terror of the senses must necessarily lend further appeal to licentiousness.

Such isolation is essential in encouraging the full range of perversions; however, it does not need such numerous reinforcements in order to work. Throughout the growing tension which accompanies the journey to Silling and the ensuing walling-in, it is actually the move towards deviation — apparent on the opening page — which receives concrete and theatrical expression here. There is a correspondence between the chain of deviations found in the work's novel-like beginning, and the principal stages of the ascent towards Silling. Thus, in leaving Basle, we take farewell of historical reality; moving on from the charcoal burners' hamlet, we say goodbye to the last vestiges of social reality. Departing from the mountain peak — "a new barrier so utterly impassable that only birds could cross it" — we leave behind all human reality; and finally, in moving from the "path of the bridge," which has been destroyed so that "no earthly inhabitant of any imaginable species could find it possible to reach this little plain" where the château is situated —

finally, we leave reality itself, to topple off into the unreality of Silling. This site will now become the world — or rather, the world's buried heart, a stone heart and an empty heart.

Even if everything is arranged theatrically, with a series of concentric circles forming the most incredible stage-set ever imagined — in other words, even if a thought takes shape across a décor — that is absolutely no reason to believe in some literary or aesthetic whim on Sade's part. This progressive concretization of his thought has something so anguished and fatal about it that it deserves attention. We should also remember that *The One Hundred and Twenty Days* appears just as Sade is swerving from the current trends of atheism, just as he finds himself obliged to invent his own trajectory. This is, in fact, what the book narrates: the approach to Silling corresponds to the distance Sade puts between himself and atheism on the question of socialized passions. And there is something dramatic in this divergence, for even while checking and experiencing the gap, Sade remains in deep agreement with the basic tenets of atheistic thought. At no time does he challenge atheism's main ideas. Like his characters, he is familiar with, and quotes from, d'Holbach, La Mettrie, Montesquieu, Voltaire, Fréret and Buffon, even borrowing from them on occasion, as Pierre Naville first noticed in his study, *D'Holbach et la philosophie scientifique au XVIIIe siècle.* Jean Deprun will subsequently analyze these borrowings in detail and show that, very often, Sade dramatizes and exaggerates the texts he uses, making them lighter, more condensed and shorter. Jean Deprun also remarks that in many cases Sade "radicalizes his sources in two ways, through the addition of a supplement of cruelty and a supplement of sarcasm," recalling that lack of respect for philosophical propriety exemplified in both the *Dialogue between a Priest and a Dying Man* and the *Etrennes philosophiques.*

At the same time, it would be hard not to stop and take notice of Pierre Naville's forceful analysis in "Sade et la philosophie" (*Oeuvres Complètes du Marquis de Sade,* t. XI):

> That Sade pushed this deduction beyond every limit one might wish to impose on him does not modify the credit he accords the initial *System* when he uses it, although the *System* leads d'Holbach to quite different conclusions. The atheism and materialism of *The System of Nature* did not leave room, in their principles, for any reserve, and Sade has never added to it. What he has done, on the other

hand, is to use it quite differently from the way it was used by d'Holbach, Diderot and their friends.

And that is most important, because Sade's divergence from atheist thinking occurs not so much in respect to some particular point, as in the way in which he uses the acquisitions of atheist materialism, as Pierre Naville points out again:

> . . . what d'Holbach and the confirmed atheists taught him, and to which he subsequently held, was to postulate a few simple principles from which one can reason, imagine and deduce in an unlimited way about morals and comportment.

This leads Naville to contest the interpretation of Maurice Heine, and especially that of Maurice Blanchot who declares, in *La Raison de Sade:* ". . . to the extent that he has been able to overtake naturalist ideology, in which he has not been fooled by external analogies, he proves to us that his own logic has gone to its very limit, and has not shied away from the obscure forms supporting it."

Without a doubt, Sade's savage logic leads him to continue where everyone else comes to a halt, overcome with dizziness at this new freedom of thought, which was in theory limitless. Everyone else comes to a standstill — like the Baron d'Holbach, for example, who so ably deduces the necessity of direction from the idea of motion: "Without direction, we cannot have the concept of motion." What starts out as a physical direction then becomes a moral one, by means of an illogical recourse to the ambiguity inherent in the notion of direction, the better retrospectively to justify a choice which is ideological, rather than logical. For we know that through this notion of direction, to be "regulated through the properties of each being," d'Holbach rapidly gets back to the idea of *gravitation around the self* and with it, the structuring value of limitation.

One could not hope to find a better example of what Sade himself does not do, since he never indulges in this sort of posterior rationalization, so indicative of reason's own incapacity to find grounds for itself and also, of other atheists' refusal to recognize this helplessness. But it is precisely because nothing grounds logical thinking — and therefore, nothing limits it — that logical thinking constitutes in Sade's eyes the one mode of functioning which can account for nature's endless fermentation. Not even death can limit it, since death undoes the literal forms, but without affecting matter in its endless motion. Nothing could be simpler; but again, nothing could be more scandalous, for even the concept of ethics is pulverized by this unstoppable form of thought — a thought which by its very principle cannot be stopped by anything at all. After that, it is easy to imagine the divergence which will soon occur between Sade and atheistic thinking. And yet, his characters — all acting in the name of reason — never fail to justify, abundantly and with ever more logical theoretical elaborations, the most contradictory positions.

His characters, yes; but not Sade, who provokes and plays with their contradictions, as if seeking to establish the absence of any grounds for reason, and so implicitly denounce its pretentions to universality. I do not remotely think that Sade confronts these "obscure forces" which supposedly prop up his reason, as Maurice Blanchot argues; on the contrary, he demonstrates how extremely fragile reason can become when it aspires to universality and grounds itself on an order that does not exist. What does exist, on the other hand — and Sade is once again the first and only writer to cast light on this — what does exist is this passion for order which reason comes to serve. It is mankind's equivalent to nature's invention of forms. This passion for order is something Sade reveals as being common to both intellectual and erotic activity. A most desperate quest for order is found even in the most frenetic orgies: "Let's put some order in our pleasure, one only enjoys them by deciding what they are," says Madame Delbène, all "flushed with excitement." Order is a human need which Sade is alone in showing as precarious and monstrous. This need explains the stagings and orderings, erotic and theoretical, which saturate the Sadian universe; all of them derive from *a* reason, which is never *the* reason. That, indeed, is their monstrosity, since their sole reason for becoming organized is to get disorganized again. And yet there is not one which does not seek, mentally or erotically, to occupy the entire intellectual or erotic stage. They are monstrous productions, which nonetheless illustrate, in their normative pretention, the tragic and absurd law of desire: "All men would be tyrants when their penises are hard." So says Sade in *Philosophy in the Bedroom,* and so will he say and demonstrate repeatedly in the stories of Justine and Juliette. Such is the incontrovertible law of desire to which reason must continually submit, since desire always finds every reason to justify its very thought, in its own fraudulent will to generality.

That is Sade's incredible outrageousness — at the very outset he erodes the cornerstone of reason on which everybody else is staking all. I'm not sure that we can measure, even today, the full extent of this outrage. Our own thinking turns out to have been fashioned by that extreme naïveté, or that decorous swindle, which constitutes the notion of objectivity. Today we have to turn to Wittgenstein if we want to hear any sort of critique of reason by itself; his claim that logic does not act, but justifies, echoes from afar this essential revolt of mind against reason that runs through Sade's whole work like a trail of gunpowder. Except that Wittgenstein is careful not to say what lies behind reason's deceit, while Sade shows us an imposture organically related to the fierceness of desire. It is probably because Sade, not content just to suggest this, actually shows it to us — even making us experience it physically — that the journey to the Château de Silling upsets us so. The way the castle is constructed, separate and aloof from all philosophies of nature, sends us back to the same rational impotence experienced by all such philosophies when grounding their principles. More seriously still, its daring rehabilitation of the passions heralds a definitive revolution in perspective, showing them to be the only true foundation of our thought: "People rail against the passions without realizing that in the blaze of passion's torch, the torch of philosophy is lit" *(The Story of Juliette)*.

But in this essential respect, does Sade really differ from his various contemporaries? From Diderot, for example, who affirms as early as 1749 in his *Lettre sur les aveugles (Letter on the Blind):*

> I have never doubted that the state of our organs and senses greatly affects our metaphysics and our moral state, and that our most purely intellectual ideas, if I may thus express myself, correspond very closely to the structure of our bodies.

On first inspection, they seem very close. It must be admitted, though, that Diderot implicitly recognizes a deficiency, or at the very least a weakness, in the human mind. But Sade, without for one second being deceived by the precariousness of our judgments (his arguments in this respect are worthy of the least complacent seventeenth- or eighteenth-century moralists) turns this precariousness — this aberrant tendency to aspire after universality on the basis of the most irreducible particularity — into a strength, the strength of his own thought and, indeed, of all thought. We have already seen the letter of November 1783 in which Sade needs only three lines to demolish the customary connections between reason and particularity, determinism and liberty: "My way of thinking is the fruit of my reflections: it derives from my existence, from my way of organizing things. I am not in a position to alter it; and even if I were, I would not." Quite clearly, Sade presents his "way of thinking" as the "fruit of his reflections," — that is, as the result of a labor of reason. This being postulated, he specifies its foundation: "it derives from my way of organizing things." This foundation is as arbitrary as it is absolute, since Sade continues: "I am not in a position to alter it," seeing in the singularity of this determinism the distinguishing mark of his freedom: "and even if I were, I would not." Considering how deeply in the human heart Sade establishes an organic connection between freedom and singularity, we can perhaps better understand the inexhaustibly scandalous force of his thought. Sade brings about an identical inversion of the traditional link between laws and passions through Monsignor Chigi, a friend of Juliette and the Princess Borghese. The prelate quotes Helvetius in order to arrive at conclusions which could not fail to embarrass the latter:

> People dare to rail against the passions, people dare to chain them up by means of laws; but just compare the two, laws and passions, and you will soon see which have done mankind the most good. Who can doubt, as Helvetius says, that passions are to the moral part of man what movement is to the physical? Individuals who are not driven by strong passions are merely mediocre. Only great passions can create great men; one becomes stupid, as soon as one ceases to be passionate. This being so, I wonder what dangers may result from those laws which hinder passion? Compare the centuries of anarchy with those most subject to the law, with whatever government one wishes; it will soon appear that the greatest deeds were performed in those moments when the laws fell quiet.

One could give many such examples, so often does the link between Sade and the philosophy of his time pass through this strange operation of deflection, consisting in a logical and theoretical re-endowment of the particular with the omnipotence accorded to the general. After this, it can easily be seen that thinking in terms of a simple reversal, or even dialectic negation, does not really allow us to elucidate what is taking place in *The One Hundred and Twenty Days of Sodom*.

Thus, the fundamental divergence between Sade and d'Holbach is based on their conceptions of society. The author of *The System of Nature* sees a natural construction resting on a balance between the individual and the collectivity, excluding all the individual passions and retaining only those which are socially useful. In the opening pages of *The One Hundred and Twenty Days,* Sade takes up this distinction on his own account, choosing, as one may imagine, to exalt all the passions which are socially destructive. But above all, he makes quite remarkable use of this exclusion of the harmful passions from the general list of mores: he uses it to build a world from those same elements which normally are banished. This social rejection provides him with his method: he retrieves his possessions from the moral night, and then examines them in a light which will henceforth be absolute. Thus, for the first time, desire can be considered as free from all previous fetters and deflections. Now, at last, the libertine enclosure, suddenly desocialized, provides the best setting in which to hasten the advent of the rule of passions:

> You cannot imagine how greatly pleasure is enhanced by these precautions, nor what can be performed when one can tell oneself: "I'm alone here, at the ends of the earth, far from all observing eyes, with no possibility of any living thing being able to reach me; no more restraints, no more barricades." From then on, desires spring forward with an impetuousness which brooks no further limit, and that impunity which favors them increases most deliciously the ecstasy they cause. The only witnesses are God and one's conscience; now, of what consequence can God be, to a confirmed atheist? What sway can conscience hold, over someone who is so accustomed to overcoming his remorse that remorse is practically a pleasure?

Instead of denouncing the idea of natural socialization found in d'Holbach's thesis — so far from being natural it must exclude all the unusual passions — Sade actually recapitulates it for himself, thereby effecting the most artificial but definitive desocialization of the human passions.

It would certainly be tempting to see Sade's artificial desocialization as an exact negative of that natural desocialization in which

Rousseau, for example, seeks the secret of man's happiness. For, unlike the Encyclopedists, philosophically close to d'Holbach's point of view, Jean-Jacques Rousseau rather resembles Sade in claiming that society — and therefore, civilization — runs contrary to human happiness. These claims are found in both the *Discours sur les sciences et les arts* of 1750, and the *Discours sur l'origine et les fondements de l'inégalité parmi les hommes* of 1754 *(Discourse on the Sciences and Arts; Discourse on the Origins and Foundation of Inequality)*. The two writers differ in that Rousseau sees happiness residing in respect for natural virtue, and Sade thinks it derives from the exaltation of an equally natural vice. But in the middle of this eminently social century, it is astounding to see Sade, with his theory of "solitarism" converging with Rousseau in his defense of the solitary savage who loses both happiness and independence once he consents to live in society. Sade even entrusts one of his most wicked libertines, Noirceuil, with the task of explaining this to Juliette:

> All creatures are born solitary and with no need of each other: therefore, leave men in their natural state, do not attempt to civilize them and each will find his food and sustenance without having need of his fellows.

As for the stratagems and prejudices with which social life burdens its participants, and which "stifle the instinct for original freedom for which they seem to have been born, causing them to love slavery, and turning them into what we call policed peoples," which of the two writers really denounces them? Which of the two exclaims: "Mad fools always complaining about nature, why can't you learn that all your troubles come from yourselves!" Is it Sade or Rousseau? And which of them asserts: "No country has ever been known to return to virtuous ways once it has been corrupted"? Isn't this a sentence out of *Frenchmen, another effort . . . ?* Actually, no; it's Rousseau, sounding like Sade. To be brief, couldn't one just substitute the word virtue for vice, and thereby make Sade recognize the accuracy of this speech:

> O virtue, sublime science of simple souls, do we really need to go to so much trouble and contrivance in order to know you? Isn't it enough, to learn your laws, simply to withdraw into oneself and listen to the voice of conscience when the passions silence theirs? That is true philosophy . . .

What should one conclude from these alarming coincidences of expression and, indeed, of thought? Comparing Rousseau with Sade has, of course, the merit of revealing unexpected propinquity, just where one expected a divergence. Maurice Blanchot undertook such a comparison in *L'Inconvenance majeure,* when he related certain texts of Saint-Just and Sade. The true interest of such a comparison lies in its allowing us to think that similar coincidences can be found between Sade and any of his contemporaries currently engaged in the intellectual debate resulting from atheism, even if its actors are not atheists, as is the case with Rousseau. So what does this add up to? How does Sade stand with respect to the philosophy he claims, and the one he does not claim? Doesn't his resemblance to Rousseau — something like a photographic negative — provide the missing clue? The closed, completely artificial world of *The One Hundred and Twenty Days* is frantically unlike the rustic cottage or the cabin in the woods which Rousseau so nostalgically promotes; each of the four totally corrupted libertines within its world of fortified lewdness represents the absolute antithesis of that "good savage" who is Rousseau's human ideal. Again, the rules of its licentious constraint, as arbitrary as they are depraved, establish in domains both intimate and futile that very inequality which Rousseau uses all his strength to censure and resist. Could not this conclave of evil ultimately be seen as the anti-Utopia of Rousseau's world, the world Rousseau dreams of in *The Social Contract* in terms of this pact: "Each one of us joins in putting his person and his whole strength under the supreme direction of the general will: and we still admit each member as an indivisible unit of the whole"?

This total abdication of individual free will in favor of the community provides a most curious reflection of what happens within Silling, and further justifies our questions about the negative value and function of Sade's edifice.

In actual fact, Sade does not deny the world he lives in any more than he denies the worlds dreamed up by his contemporaries. If one looks carefully, *The One Hundred and Twenty Days* does not propose another historical period; at the most, it opens up an historical parenthesis. In cutting itself off socially, it does not propose another type of society, for the quartet of libertines forms an enclave capable of functioning in any kind of society. In diverging radically from mankind's habitual notion of itself, *The One Hundred and Twenty Days* does not propose another notion of mankind: man appears in it as an object of study and "this results from our work on the human heart, and its history." Finally, in diverging from the conventional forms of the novel and the play, of the philosophical dialogue and the catalogue, *The One Hundred and Twenty Days* does not propose another kind of literature, as has been claimed these last few years. At whatever level these various divergences take place, they still require the existence of a reality from which to diverge. Thus, they contribute in establishing a *method,* the only method that allows us to consider these passions on whose account philosophy is both so helpless and indebted. This is probably the true meaning of this school for debauchery, whose pedagogical aspects — apart from the course in masturbation for inexperienced young people — would seem to be extremely limited. In this school there are neither students nor professors, but only erotomaniacs of quality, historians and libertines of equal competence, meeting for a conference. But what sort of an exchange of views do they envisage, and to what end?

Once again, Sade is most explicit as he addresses his reader:

> Doubtless, many of the perversions you will soon see depicted will displease you, as we realize. But there will be others that excite you to the point of costing you some sperm, and that is all we need. If we had not said and analyzed it all, how do you suppose we could have guessed what suits you? It's up to you to take it and to leave all the rest, someone else will do the same; and bit by bit, everything will find its place.

I shall not try to determine, as others have, if this project is encyclopedic, dialectical or textual — surely a ridiculous exercise — when Sade need only these few lines in which to destroy the very idea of pedagogy, and with it our habitual means of access to knowledge.

About to embark upon this course in debauchery, what does Sade say? Immediately, he tells us not to expect to approve of everything that we will read: "Many of the perversions . . . will displease you." This frees us from the customary pedagogical relationship based on intimidation through knowledge. Then he reminds us that approval and comprehension are indissociable from desire: " . . . there will be others that excite you to the point of costing you some sperm, and that is all we need." Here Sade denies any possibility of pedagogical authority, since only desire can be authoritative here. However, at the same time he asserts the need for some global view — though not a normative one — opposed by principle to any form of evaluation or censorship. This view alone can guarantee the freedom and authority of desire: "If we had not said and analyzed it all, how do you suppose we could have guessed what suits you?" At this point, Sade transforms the pedagogical pretention to totality into an infinite possibility of choice available to desire. Finally, he sees our power of discrimination in desire itself: "It's up to you to take it, and to leave all the rest; someone else will do the same," which presumes a denial of pedagogical objectivity or, indeed, of any objectivity. As for order, it will impose itself naturally: "and bit by bit everything will find its place." Here Sade is counting on the structuring power of individual passion against pedagogical seduction, which is simply a disguised authority relationship. For Sade intends to free us from all relationships of power exercised through knowledge, and so establishes both a new relationship with erotic knowledge (in complete contradiction with the usual libertine pedagogy) and a new erotic relationship with knowledge itself. Consequently, the authority of knowledge is now questioned in the most radical fashion, since pleasure both leads to and is increased by cognition.

Once again, accustomed as we are to the traditional alliance of authority and knowledge, I'm not sure we can visualize the sort of mental revolution Sade proposes here, rebellious and consistent as he is to the point of rejecting any ideas whose accuracy he has not physically verified. Previously, we have watched him trying to return the energy of philosophical freedom into the individual sphere; now we can see him giving us the means to do so on our own account. This is a most luxurious gift, which unfortunately none of us has yet assessed at its true worth. A hint as to its value is nonetheless provided in the sumptuous feast to which Sade summons his reader:

> This is the story of a magnificent banquet, where six hundred different dishes are offered to your taste. Will you devour them all? Of course not; but the prodigious quantity extends the limits of your choice and so, delighted by these incremented options, you don't think to scold the amphitryon who is offering you the feast. Do likewise here: choose, and leave the rest, without railing against it merely because it was not fortunate enough to please you. Remember it is likely to please others, and so be philosophical.

Apparently, many of Sade's critics have not been philosophical enough, otherwise they would have noticed what choice morsels Sade reserved for them. Right in the center of these morsels [Sade reserved for them] is the question of the general versus the particular, served in an unprecedented way. Assisted by this image of the banquet, Sade clearly shows that, for him, the particular is what determines the general. Not only that, but the general has no value, except that it comprises the sum of the particulars; more precisely, it represents the particular as exalted by large numbers. In other words, your favorite dish will taste all the better for having been selected from among six hundred others, since this plurality of choice permits a most accurate response to the singularity of your desire. Such is the luxurious order of passions, with this corollary: if your favorite dish is missing from among the six hundred, then the whole magnificent meal will seem dull. Similarly, if some particular being is not present, then the entire category of the general will immediately disappear. But has this been adequately noticed? Proceeding from this gastronomic metaphor, Sade simply topples over the conditions of our thoughts. For it is here that he substitutes a *logic of the passions* for that formal logic we still struggle to fit into, like an old dress uniform we try to wriggle into with most desperate contortions. Before or since, no one has dared to avail himself so authoritatively of this logic of the passions. Of course, there is Fourier, who takes the diversity of human passions as a starting point for his project of an Amorous New World *(Nouveau monde amoureux).* But this physical, psychological and social revolution does not attack the roots of individual being: Fourier is too sure of the socializing power of passions — no matter how unusual they may be — and of their essential harmony, disturbed by civilization. Fourier seeks to reveal an order which Sade constantly denies, once he has discovered an insuperable solitude present at the source of both desire and thought; once this solitude, which all men have in common, becomes in his view the only truth of both desire and thought.

Yet surely most of us have learned to live by cultivating a healthy respect for this tyrannical domination of the particular by the general, even though our slightest whims would seem to aim at toppling such a hierarchy. If not, why do we continually exercise our thought by always recognizing what is numerous, and not what is unique; what is abstract, and not what is concrete; the rule of law, instead of life itself? It is at this point that Sade's revolt really poses a threat to the order of things. If, as Sade thinks, the general is only to be seen as the sum total of particulars, and nothing more, it follows that what is particular, unusual and unique becomes the only stable element in any relationship between particulars and generals that we are destined to live out. And this is very serious: for, as the perpetually variable summum of all its particulars, the general immediately becomes a synonym for instability. However, all the representations which we habitually deem to have a structuring value in our contact with the world are founded on the notion that the general will be stable, even providing a guarantee against the possible mishaps of particularity. And so Sade undermines our most reliable modes of thinking and the bases of our society, indeed, of any society; for the instability which he ascribes to the general utterly discredits the very idea of law.

At this point, everything changes: do our passions suddenly become like the glass orbs children play with, imprisoning the snows of time; or is it that the world turns into a miniature globe, spinning inside the enormous orbit of desire? Whatever the case, this revolution in thought is enacted in the buried theatre of *The One Hundred and Twenty Days,* whose own action is played out inside an incarcerated mind; subsequently, it will be rolled up on a paper scroll and hurled forth like a bottle in the sea. We should never forget that this ravelling and unravelling of *The One Hundred and Twenty Days* constitutes the one, aberrant path Sade finds from his own bottomless despair. Constrained to think with reference to a sexual eccentricity which earned him the treatment we all know, Sade decides to stick with that reality and stops trying to escape from it on any pretext whatsoever, social, literary or philosophical. But this eccentricity which sets him apart from other men also inspires him with a means for drawing close to them again: he proposes to snatch each of them from the deception of their generality, the better to study them in the truth of their particularity. In the introduction to *The One Hundred and Twenty Days,* therefore, having just defined the passions in term of deviation, Sade hastily adds:

> It cannot be imagined how men vary them, once their imaginations are on fire. The distinctions between them, already vast in all their other manias and tastes, are even more excessive in the case of passions, and whoever could assess and give details of these perversions might well

produce one of the finest imaginable works on human mores, and perhaps one of the most interesting.

This finest imaginable work is what Sade proposes to write. He firmly intends, however, to avoid at all costs the deception of a supposedly exhaustive classification, based on a generality which would ultimately blur these distinctions. That is why the female historians are so important in elaborating this "story of the human heart," so radically new in concept. Sade himself emphasizes as much:

> Besides, we have incorporated these six hundred passions into the historians' narration: this is another matter of which the reader should be advised. It would have been too monotonous to enumerate them any other way, one by one, without placing them within the body of a story.

Simply by resorting to this "body of a story" — actually, the story of a body — Sade finds a way of expounding the six hundred passions, using an order which does not clarify itself at the expense of the particular; on the contrary, it exalts it. Presented by a singular voice in all their singularity, these passions thus escape from any sort of order which could otherwise take precedence. Sade is even careful to distinguish their classification from the story of the historian's body, which serves to support it:

> But as some readers, unaccustomed to this sort of subject, could perhaps confuse the designated passions with some adventure or simple event in the life of the storyteller, we have carefully distinguished each of these passions by a short mark in the margin, above which is the term we can apply to it. This mark is placed exactly where the story of this passion starts, and there is always an indention where it ends. But since there are many characters involved in this type of drama, despite the care taken in this introduction to depict and designate each one, we shall include a list, containing the name and age of every actor, together with a brief description of his portrait. Thus, whenever one encounters a confusing name, one can refer back to this list, or the lengthier portraits, if this slight sketch does not suffice to remind one of what has been said.

In terms of subject matter, therefore, Sade extends his magnificence to the point of offering us diverse modes of classification, comparable to the six hundred "dishes" set before our tastes. Not only does the body of each historian serve as a reference chart, on which is inscribed the enunciated passion in the course of its gradation from the single to the compound; but at the same time Sade plays with the bodies of all the characters in action, like so many theatre scenes with multiple entrances and exits. That, too, appears as a complete novelty in this sudden gaze brought to bear on human affairs, for Sade offers each reader the possibility of extracting directly, in its most plastic form, the passion which excites him. That passion is presented both as an eccentricity occurring in the referential tissue of each historian's tale, and as a deviation through the bodies that it activates. On the very first day Madame Duclos is scolded by Curval, precisely because she has omitted certain bodily details, necessary in order for the passion in question to arouse the listeners' minds:

> "Duclos," interrupted the Judge, "Didn't we inform you that your accounts must include every detail? That we cannot judge how the passion you describe relates to the mores and character of man, unless you set forth every circumstance? That we rely on the slightest particulars in your narrative, in order to inflame our senses?" "Yes, my lord," replied Madame Duclos, "I was advised not to omit any detail and to enter into the most extreme minutiae each time it could cast light on someone's character or type of perversion. Have I committed some omission of that sort?" "Yes," said the Judge, "I have no idea what your second friar's prick was like, no idea at all of his discharge. Furthermore, did he rub your cunt, and did he touch it with his prick? You see what details you omit!"

Indeed, what details she omits, since it is those very details which permit differentiation of the passions, and above all, a measurement of whatever deviation they may represent.

But deviation from what? From normalcy? From law? Let's not be absurd. No one has managed to describe the relativity of customs better than Sade, or has better demonstrated the arbitrary nature of all laws and the insanity of morals. But what then is a deviation? Where is it found? What are its effects? Isn't it with the intention of answering such questions that the four libertines decide to meet in secret? These libertines, who have seen, done and imagined absolutely everything, and whose one remaining wish is to acquire more knowledge of their pleasure, in order to increase the pleasure of their knowledge? The direction taken by this conference seems to conform to such a project, as does the strict arrangement of the chamber where debauchees, historians and subjects assemble every evening to study, through the six hundred examples, the notion of deviation which is posed like an enigma there — which Durcet unhesitatingly proposes as *enigma itself*:

> . . . is it possible to commit crimes as one conceives them and as you describe? For my part, I admit that my imagination has always been beyond my means in that respect; I have always imagined a thousandfold more than I have done, and have always complained of nature who, while endowing me with the desire to outrage her, continually deprived me of the means to do so.

In attempting to resolve this enigma, we must consult the program of study planned for Silling:

> At six o'clock exactly, the historian will begin her narration, which the four friends can interrupt whenever they wish. This narration will last until ten o'clock at night, and during that time, since the intention is to arouse their imaginations, every kind of lewdness will be allowed, except for that which might disturb the planned order of the deflorations, which will always be most scrupulously observed. Apart from that, anyone may do exactly as he pleases with his fucker, his wife, the quatrain or the old woman assigned to the quatrain, even with the historians if the fancy takes him, either in his alcove or the adjoining cabinet. The narrative will be suspended for the duration of the pleasure of the persons whose needs have interrupted it, and will resume as soon as he has finished.

No better definition could be found of the deviant space between word and enjoyment. It remains to be seen how this space will take shape.

To figure in the historians' narration, each passion must first have been extracted from the habitual triviality of human comportment. It owes this extraction to its concrete peculiarity. The historians' memories, therefore, act as a filter through which each peculiarity must pass. However, the historians need only to present this concrete example in its extreme, exalted peculiarity to create, in their debauched auditors, an image which succeeds in utterly disturbing their fancy. This representation functions as a second filter, through which an image turns into an imaginary object, as unreal as that image is strong. This very unreality inflames the libertines' minds, henceforth uniquely concerned with causing this unreality to become concrete. This need for concretization acts in turn as a third filter, turning the body into a site where a boundless desire for objectification is in fact objectified. Similar to the installation of an optical system, deviation thus becomes this curious detour from body to body via the imaginary, measurable only in terms of the size of that detour.

What is most extraordinary is that Sade has subordinated the inner architecture of Silling to the optimal functioning of this optical system. I shall return to this, but for the moment we can simply observe that this system is organized like an enormous mental eye, with its successive transparent humors, behind which the sensitive surface of the imagination behaves like a retina, inverting both perspectives and virtual images. One of the obvious merits of this optical system, which controls all that is depicted in the heart of Silling, is to show how each deviation must be utterly purged of ideology if it is to appear in its own pure path. Without a doubt, the successive filters of memory, imagination and objectification contribute greatly to the intolerable sharpness of Sade's discourse. Just as the historians' presentation tends completely to erase the social reality of the conduct they describe, so does the image in the libertines' minds tend to efface the psychological reality behind the passion they find interesting. Similarly, the objectification practiced on the neutral bodies of the subjects tends to efface all physiological reality. A raw passion, whetted by the imagination, without any frills — that is what Sade's optical machine shows us, and what we find so unbearable.

For no matter how horrible and unjustifiable are the massacres, torturings and murders which history and present reality never cease to offer us, aren't they always accompanied by a panoply of justifications which we, in spite of everything, are so unforgivably weak as to take into consideration? Whether it's a question of race, religion or one's country — invoked, classically, as masks to horror — we reject these excesses with the deepest conviction, and at the same time retain them in some hidden region of ourselves, returning to them later as to an ideological cache. This is because it is always more convenient to consider crime as the result of an aberrant ideological choice, rather than an expression of human nature. It is a comfort most of our modes of thinking have come to depend on; but it is a comfort Sade does without and makes his readers do without. In laying bare the most unjustifiable passions in the heart of Silling, Sade foils that questionable play of justifications which can be made to serve *any* feelings, especially the loftier ones, from motherly love to heroism. The fact that these justifications are all equally inadmissable alters nothing. They all dress up human savageness in ideological uniforms. Fascism, which draws on all the gaudy stereotypes of race, family, fatherland and countryside, constitutes one of the most spectacular examples of this ideological masking, so utterly opposed to the disrobing found in Sade. And so, any attempt to absorb Sade into a totalitarian ideology of any kind — and such ventures are not lacking — only ends up passing judgment on the person who attempts it. The judgment is a serious one, for it seems as if the person making the attempt has been simultaneously terrified and fascinated by the feelings Sade's text awakens in him, and has hastily repressed these criminal urges by dumping them into that area still known as absolute historical evil. This is a crafty but dangerous maneuver, because in thinking to confine these criminal tendencies elsewhere, one thus loses the power to prevent their apparition close at hand. Unfortunately, all this is quite familiar, since every powerful ideology functions by this process. But then again, every good conscience has given rise to this process, too.

This, then, is where Sade concerns and worries each of us in turn, since his thought denies us, by its very principle, those disguises our ferocity has hit upon to cloak itself. Since all our cast-off ideologies, private as well as social — and all of them equally repulsive — help obfuscate what Sade is determined to expose. And our disgust on reading certain of his pages is as much a sign of emotion at the revelation of our criminal tendencies as a sign of our hatred for Sade, who prevents us from attempting to justify the unjustifiable. Of all the reproaches humanity addresses Sade, this is perhaps the most serious, and the most irrational. Even when one thinks one is used to his work, one suddenly finds oneself rejecting it, with an unsuspected violence which nothing can repress. There is always a moment when the mind cannot bear to be confronted with its latent criminality.

How, indeed, can we bear it, when Sade not only parades intolerable images before us, but simultaneously attacks our modes of thinking? I say modes of thinking, but subterfuge would be a better word. We should remember that the slightest ideological justification available to crime always has the advantage of transferring responsibility onto some more or less vague psychosocial entity. In consequence, resorting to this imprecise responsibility helps lessen the horror of the crime that has been perpetrated — precisely because that responsibility remains so abstract. Far from deceiving himself in this manner, as we always tend to do, the Sadian libertine assumes full responsibility for his delinquency and thereby exposes the deception in this vague responsibility, so favorable to ideological justifications. But this should not be confused with the idea of reappropriating evil, as some people have thought, a bit too hastily:

> In a word, murderers are to nature as wars, plagues, and famine; they are one of nature's means, like all the scourges she inflicts on us. Thus, when someone says a murderer outrages nature, he is pronouncing an absurdity as great as if he said that plagues, wars or famine annoy nature or commit great crimes; it is utterly the same. But we cannot burn alive plagues or famine, nor break them on the wheel, whereas both are things that we can do to man; and that is why man is wrong. Almost always, you shall see wrongs measured, not according to the size of the offense, but rather by the weakness of the one who offends; and that is why influence and wealth must always prevail over indigence.

Such is the instruction that Juliette receives from the Pope, engaging here in a vast attack on ideology, since murder, war and famine are all judged the same way as natural phenomena. Not for one second does this deprive the libertine of his free will; he can still choose whether or not to challenge nature by asserting his own singularity, just as Sade asserted that he found his freedom in his singularity, in the letter of November 1783. Once again, I don't know if we can really assess the size of the chasm opened up by Sade in depriving us of all our ideological framework; the remark "we cannot burn alive plagues or famine, nor break them on the wheel" withdraws the foundations from under law itself. It also launches a radical criticism of the notion of legality, thus striking at the very basis of society:

> With respect to that cruelty which leads to murder, let us be so bold as to say that this is one of man's more

natural emotions; . . . it influences him in all his actions, in all his discourse, as in everything he undertakes; education can sometimes disguise it, but it swiftly reappears, then to manifest itself in every sort of form.

A divestiture of ideology, yes; but also an effort to desocialize passions that runs absolutely counter to the current philosophy, full of a social optimism that tries to ideologize all forms of behavior, the better to socialize them after. Even if most philosophers, moralists or economists then agree to recognize self-interest as the motive for all human actions, it is society, and society alone, which is supposed in their eyes to put this passion to good use and deflect it from possible harmful or criminal development. One can even see the most diverse philosophical trends organizing themselves in a huge effort to eject evil from the individual sphere, thereby heralding the advent of collective responsibility.

With all the passion of his lucidity, Sade will never tire of combating this recourse to collective responsibility, together with the individual irresponsibility that it engenders. Above all, he does not want the idea of criminality to vanish, something that the collective way of thinking tends to encourage. This is apparent in the startling interpretation of western evolution given by the good king Zamé, ruler of the kingdom of Tamoé, in *Aline et Valcour:*

> In completing your civilization, the causes changed, but you maintained the custom: no longer did you sacrifice victims to gods athirst for human blood, but to laws, which you deem sage because you found in them a specious reason to indulge your former habits, together with the semblance of a justice which was, at bottom, nothing other than the desire to preserve those horrid practices which you could not abjure.

One could hardly be more explicit. A fundamental part of Sade's criticism of law develops via his opposition to the disappearance of criminality, through its being reabsorbed into law. It is here that Sade's revolt takes root most strongly: it is here that he grafts his radical opposition to capital punishment, a direct consequence of his refusal to accept any sort of predominance of the general over the particular. From now on, he fights that exorbitant deception with which, through an illusory exoneration, the new, collective man must pay for an even more illusory freedom. Concerning criminality itself, Sade will never stop postulating the equivalence of laws and crime:

> Not only will the law be useless, dangerous, abusive and a nuisance, as has just been shown; it will also be absurd and shocking, and as long as it punishes by means of affliction, can only pass for another kind of villainy, with no further grounds for authority than custom, exercise and force, reasons which are neither natural nor legitimate; in short, no better than the reasons of Cartouche.

These reflections of King Zamé on the subject of capital punishment, which he deems "doubtless the most appalling" of all laws, totally reflect the opinions of Sade. Law will always benefit from the surplus of criminality conferred upon it by the authority of the general. As Chigi will explain several years later to Juliette's lovely friend Olympia:

> Nothing contradicts the general interest more strongly than the interest of the particular; at the same time, nothing is more just than the interest of the particular. Therefore, nothing is more unjust than the law which sacrifices all particular interests to the interest of the general. . . . Ah! Let us be convinced then, once and for all, that laws are but useless and dangerous; their one object being to multiply crimes, or to cause them to be committed in safe wise, on account of the secrecy which they compel.

On this point, Sade will never change his mind. He remains as unshakable as on the matter of atheism, because this definitive criticism of the law is in fact the mark of an atheism carried to its ultimate conclusions.

Even if Sade is utterly alone in entertaining this reflection, it is far from inconsequential that he does. A few short years later, history gives violent and concrete reality to the problems it raises and casts it, with the events of the Revolution, like a fearful shadow over the horizon of the Enlightenment. In this respect, it would seem at first that Pierre Klossowski is right in seeing Sade's theoretical advance — for no one has yet caught up with him — as one of the major reasons for his having been so vilified:

> The more successful an individual is, the more he concentrates within himself the diffuse energies of his era, and the more dangerous he is for his era; but the more he

concentrates within himself these vague forces, causing them to weigh more heavily upon his own destiny, the more he liberates his era from them. Sade forged his own destiny out of the latent criminality of his contemporaries, and tried to expiate it alone in proportion to the collective guilt his conscience had invested.

Saint-Just and Bonaparte, on the other hand, managed to discharge onto their contemporaries everything which the era had caused to accumulate within them. From the point of view of the masses, these men were perfectly sane; and they themselves were aware that the best proof of sanity a man could give to the masses would be his willingness to sacrifice them. From the viewpoint of the masses, Sade is an eminently insane man. . . .

There can be no doubt that this interpretation of the link Sade tries to forge between his own and other people's criminality is most enticing. Nonetheless, it becomes difficult to follow Klossowski as soon as one examines his theory closely: the masses do not necessarily trust a strong man because he shows a willingness to sacrifice them, and Sade did not attempt to sacrifice himself, nor did he make himself the expiatory victim of anyone or anything at all. Here we have a perfect example of the critic who projects his own problematics onto Sade: with considerable skill, Klossowski reveals one of the mainsprings of Sade's thought, but only to remask its novelty, immediately and more effectively. Klossowski, who is influenced by Joseph de Maistre's theories on the resuscitation of original sin via revolutionary criminality, here contemplates within a Christian perspective Sade's novel turn of atheism. In so doing, he considerably diminishes the implications of Sade's view of criminality. He turns it into a simple question of conscience, whereas it is in fact one of the basic elements of Sade's revolt. Klossowski's perspective is so inappropriate to his purpose that it ends up giving us a rather distorted image of Sade's thought.

As for the masses, why should they rush towards the man most willing to sacrifice them? Instead of seeing this vague instinct for collective death, wouldn't it be better to admit that every man feels attracted to any solution, be it religious or ideological, that allows him to ignore his own criminal tendencies, his and those of his peers? Furthermore, one never finds a trace, in Sade, of this conscious or unconscious determination to "expiate alone . . . the latent criminality of his contemporaries," as Klossowski would have it. First of all this is because Sade, like all his characters, clearly speaks only of himself and is interested only in himself. This being said — and it is quite important — he only admits to any guilt when taking prejudices into consideration, but never, never with respect to men, still less where nature is concerned. He knows himself to be different, "other," and has not the slightest difficulty in admitting it. But even if he goes so far as to concede that "the person blessed with unusual tastes is infirm," he never ceases to grow angry that "the norm is the war horse of all imbeciles," just as he never stops complaining, in both his novels and his correspondence:

> Fools that you are, when will you learn that as great a difference exists between the characters of men as does between their countenances? As does between their moral and their physical dispositions? That what agrees with one may not suit another one at all? Or even, that medicine for one is poison to another . . . (Letter of March 22, 1779).

All the same, the fact that he recognizes, even asserts a right to, deviation, does not preclude his feeling scandalized, like the aristocrat he is and always will be, at having been arrested on the evidence given by some prostitutes. In January 1780 he writes to his valet, one La Jeunesse, known as Martin Quiros:

> For you are aware, Monsieur Quiros, that in France strumpets are respected. One may speak ill of the government, the king, religion; all that is no matter. But a strumpet, Monsieur Quiros, Zounds! man, a strumpet, one must be careful not to offend her. . . .

In the same letter he suggests: "If you have a sister, a niece, a daughter, Monsieur Quiros, advise her to become a harlot; I defy her to find a finer occupation." To which one might perhaps retort that these protestations of innocence are not inconsistent with a will to assume the evil of his time. Perhaps; but has an expiatory victim ever been seen to revolt like this for years on end? For Sade is continually in revolt, in his books, in his letters, even physically, in his prison; and always with the same degree of violence and acuteness. Has anyone ever caught a benevolent expiatory victim tranquilly admitting, as in this letter of October 4, 1779, to La Jeunesse: "It is true that I behave as bulldogs do, and when I see this pack of curs and bitches baying at my heels, I raise a leg and piss upon their noses." Or has a benevolent expiatory victim ever been found to declare: "Should I be disembowelled alive, I shall never change a word of my maxim: *gentle and honest, when people are thus with me; sharp and severe when people fail me.*" This was on September 17, 1780. And surely no benevolent expiatory victim ever evinced the kind of pitiless humor Sade bestows upon his wife in the letter of April 20, 1783:

> Good evening, then, go off and take a good bite out of your nice God, and murder your parents. As for me, I'm off to waggle my cock and I shall certainly believe, afterwards, that I have done much less harm than you.

This type of humor cannot be dissociated from the responsibility Sade totally assumes, but which he assumes as violently as he revolts. It cannot be detached from the awareness of his own criminality, nor from the potential criminality hidden inside all of us. This criminality is not to be expiated, but *seen,* and discerned beneath the sentimental trappings with which men adorn themselves. It must be recognized within those institutions where they seek shelter; and also in their dreams, which criminality directs. In his determination to *see,* so as not to deceive, Sade goes right to the limit, and that is his greatest crime: "I have the misfortune to have been endowed by heaven with a sturdy soul which has never been able to submit, and which will never submit. I am not afraid of antagonizing anyone at all . . . , " he admits on February 20, 1781, at the beginning of what he terms his "long letter." In the course of this "disdainful confession" to his wife, he will assert, in the name of this same incorruptible lucidity:

> I am therefore guilty of debauchery pure and simple, as it is practiced by all men, more or less in proportion to the greater or lesser degree of temperament or inclination for it, which they were given by nature. Each man has his faults; let us not make comparisons, for my executioners may not prove the winners in such a parallel.
>
> Yes, I admit, I am a libertine; I have imagined all that can be imagined in that domaine; but I have certainly not *done* all I have imagined, and certainly shall never do it all. I am a libertine, but I am neither a *criminal* nor a *murderer.*

That his pride and strength are both drawn from this lucidity is apparent as early as 1777: "I shall always be greater, by virtue of my innocence and frankness, than my enemies, by virtue of their baseness and the secret rancour which impels them."

In this sense only, from Klossowski's "viewpoint of the masses," could Sade definitely be considered an "insane man," for trying to expose what all societies prefer to conceal; even more so, for striving to uncover that attempted burial of criminality with which the fundamental aims of any social group soon become confused. But once again, there is nothing at all expiatory in this, when by the same token Sade asserts himself as mankind's enemy, subverting that basic lie which enables men to live together by constantly denying their own innate ferocity.

How, therefore, can one fail to see Klossowski's interpretation as a supreme effort to stop Sade from forcibly removing the last of our ideological masks? *"Beneath the mask of atheism,"* writes Klossowski, as if to show us how deluded was the man who strove to rid himself and us of all illusions. And Klossowski succeeds, taking advantage of the deliberate absence of perspective in the Sadian world in order to impose a Christian perspective upon the bare horizon which Sade is desperately attempting to show us. In my opinion, this is doing Sade a considerable injustice. One must either not have read, or not have wanted to read, *The One Hundred and Twenty Days* to dare to claim that Sade could ever engage in the bartering of energy implicit in the notion of collective or individual redemption. Has anyone even noticed to what extent Silling is a place that *empties?*

As the optical machine sets about showing us the intolerable scoreboards of criminality, characters and accessories start to disappear. With them, our last possibilities of refuge are swallowed up inside the shadows Sade has dragged us into. Even the four libertines who instigated the experiment begin to fade, disappearing behind movements which already scarcely seem like human deeds. Thus on February 24, in the account of Augustine's final torture, the obsessive, impersonal use of the pronoun "they" echoes like a litany inside the void created by each movement:

> . . . they leave the scalpel, they plunge in a hand, they search inside her bowels and force her to shit through the cunt; then, through the same opening, they set about splitting the wall of the stomach. Then they turn back to her face: they cut off her ears, burn the inside of her nostrils and extinguish her eyes by pouring molten Spanish

wax in them, they cut a circle round the skull and hang her up by the hair while attaching stones to her feet, so that her body is weighed down and the cranium torn off.[3]

There is no way of knowing who is doing what, no longer any way of telling who is who or who is what: the bodily mechanics are undone by a mechanism which displays its fatal coherence against a total void. In consequence, there is no longer either subject or object: the account of what is being done is no longer differentiated from what is being said.

Do we detect any difference between the account of passion number 99, dated February 19, of a brute who:

... puts the woman on a stake having a diamond-shaped head inserted in the rump, her four members maintained in the the air by nothing more than strings; the effects of this torture cause laughter, and the agony is extreme ...

and the "vexations" inflicted on Marie:

... They plunge a red-hot iron into the bum and cunt, they burn her in six places on the thighs with hot metal, on the clitoris, the tongue, on her remaining tit, and they pull out all her teeth that are left ...

There is no difference at all, and that is what is terrifying. This haunting coincidence between what is real and imaginary ensues from a kind of illusory osmosis in which the imaginary not only turns into reality, but reality also tends to become imaginary. Our horror at reading *The One Hundred and Twenty Days of Sodom* further derives from a dizzying derealization accomplished at the cost of an implacable objectification, this objectification in turn being accomplished at the cost of an absolute derealization. Suddenly, we have nothing left to hold onto, not even the uncertain parameters of self-awareness, which has disappeared unnoticed. Sade hurls us into the abyss we naïvely thought existed between the real and the imaginary, but which turns out to be the unbearable infinity of freedom.

---

3   Sade's text uses the impersonal pronoun "on" (one) throughout this passage, lending considerable force to Annie Le Brun's remarks. Since repeated use of the word "one" is unconscionably awkward in English, I have replaced it with the slightly less impersonal "they." (Translator's note)

This abyss is a space which fills all space, and from which we cannot ever emerge, since it consists of all that is real being negated by the imaginary, and all that is imaginary, negated by the real. It is an infinite space from which we can never withdraw, since we are perpetually present at its perpetually mobile center. It is a space infinitely enclosed, or it is an infinity consisting of closed spaces. Either way, it is a space into which Sade will never now stop dragging us.

"On March 1, seeing that the snow had not yet melted, it was decided to dispose in detail of all that was left." Of this world conceived apart from all conventions, only a subtraction remains:

Total Count:	
Massacred before March 1 in the early orgies	10
Since March 1	20
Those returning	16 persons
Total	46

This subtraction propels us directly into something we could never conceive. We are faced with the horror of a perpetually murderous desire, which never finds its object, and therefore becomes infinitely impatient in searching for its form. A desire without object, a naked desire, unacceptably naked, unmasked in its original ferocity by Sade's utter solitude. As if the absolute of solitude demanded the infinity of desire to turn freedom into a desperate quest for form.

Part Two

CHAPTER FOUR

THE SCENE CHANGES, AND IT REPRESENTS

A fixed set, representing a drawing room. On the floor at the back of the stage is a canvas fully mounted on its stretching rods, depicting the far side of a public square. A small settee, on which were draped all those parts of the set having to do with the aforementioned square, and all those parts of the set having to do with the prison. At the back of the theatre, against the door, are four large wooden stretchers necessary for the changes described here. In the embrasure of one of the windows is a stone painted for different rooms. The wings are equipped with sixty-five tin-plate sockets for candles, and all the rods, flats, ropes and pulleys needed for scene changing. In the back of the theatre are eight large counterweights and two small ones for the aforementioned changes. In the same area there are also two large boards for night scenes. In the recess of the second stage there are twenty-four lanterns having to do with the said stage. Two primed gas lighters are to be found in the rear wings.

Strangely, this "state of furnishings and effects" of the stage and theatre room, drawn up at the Château de La Coste on April 12, 1769, could well represent the state of Sade's dramatic writings, abandoned but not yet in disrepair, waiting to be re-animated by a vainly sought-for presence. Even stranger is the fact that Sadian criticism has generally made it a point of honor to seal off this portion of his work, under the curious, spoken or unspoken pretext that so traditional a theatre could only tarnish the image of a Sade who normally presages much darker forces. It is odd how conformity can sometimes turn into a disquieting strangeness. Without Jean-Jacques Pauvert, we would have had to wait even longer before getting acquainted with this troubling aspect of Sade's work. Pauvert has a disarming passion for publishing — sometimes against the will of the whole world, in this case, against the will of the Sadian true believers — texts which people obstinately refuse to read. To him we owe the original edition of Sade's plays, which were not published until 1970.

Nonetheless, what great hopes Sade had of his theatrical activities, from early youth until the last years of his life! This is immediately apparent from a letter dated April 1784, as from others of a similar tenor, addressed to his old tutor, the Abbé Amblet:

> I find it utterly impossible to resist my genius, who involves me in this career in spite of myself; and whatever anyone does, I shall not be discouraged from it. In my portfolio there are more plays than many reputed authors of our time have ever written, and outlines for more than twice as many as I've already penned. If I had been left in peace, I would have fifteen comedies ready by the time I finally emerge from prison. They found it more diverting to annoy me; time will tell my tormentors if they were right or wrong.

On this same topic, Gilbert Lely states:

> According to the present state of our documentation, the Marquis de Sade is the author of seventeen plays, and it seems unlikely he has written more: indeed, the conventional nature of his theatrical writings has preserved his manuscripts from both domestic and administrative bonfires.

Sade's dramatic work has such a disastrous reputation among his unconditional admirers that its existence has scarcely been recognized. In any case, people prefer either to ignore, or at the very least, forget it, as Gilbert Lely points out in his biography of Sade:

> We have already given warning that . . . a study of Sade's theatre would certainly not add to his literary renown. After our own lukewarm comments, there is little left to say in conclusion, save that M. de Sade's true comedy is never to be found on his stage, but only in the aberrant notion he has formed of his own dramatic genius.

This may well be true; but it does not solve the very real enigma of these dramas. Why did Sade devote so much energy to the composition of his plays? After all, wasn't he at work on them precisely in those years when his whole enterprise assumes an irreducible air, when his thought grows ever darker? And yet, in the midst of these diverting plays, which doubtlessly conformed to every cliché of the time, there suddenly appears the grim dissecting table of *The One Hundred and Twenty Days of Sodom.*

Such is the real question raised by Sade's theatre, which is actually much better than is generally made out, especially where the comedies are concerned. The question becomes even more disturbing when one knows how important theatre was to Sade, in terms of his life and sensibility. After directing a society theatre at his wife's uncle's house at Evry in 1764, Sade restores the theatre room in his own castle, at enormous cost, and as soon as he is able. In 1765 he produces several shows at La Coste and even invites actors; in 1772 he has one of his own compositions staged there. He retains this passion for the theatre until the final years of his imprisonment. Shortly before his death, he will still have the responsibility of being in charge of entertainment at Charenton. He even chooses most of his mistresses in theatre, beginning with Mademoiselle Colet and ending with Constance Quesnet, the companion of his final days; in 1765, he has a scandalous affair at La Coste with La Beauvoisin. When numerous critics have all pointed to the stunning mastery of dialogue evinced in his novels, to say nothing of the truly theatrical dispostion of many of the scenes — erotic or otherwise — this would seem to be linked to the theatrical obsession that persisted so disturbingly throughout his tempestuous existence. Shouldn't we therefore look more closely at this theatre, looming as it does directly over our abyss?

Of all Sade's critics, Jean-Jacques Brochier has the honor of having recognized this problem and tried to resolve it, by propounding the idea that:

Even if it was written during or after the novels, and whatever Sade's goal may have been in writing it and them, everything takes place as if Sade's theatre was the only plausible, presentable and honorable aspect of a more personal kind of literature.

That is why it is impossible, even with a minute stylistic analysis, to fit his theatre into the system his novels seem more accurately to fit inside: that is, a pre-Hegelian system of dialectic in which the negation of evil would be the basis of any possibility of being. But perhaps, through an abnormal reversal, we could see his theatre — which is positive as regards conventional morality — as a humorous inversion of the scandalous negativity represented by *The New Justine* and *The Story of Juliette*. (Preface to Sade's theatre, in the *Oeuvres Complètes,* Paris: Pauvert, 1970.)

Brochier then concludes:

The theatre is perhaps that form of chatter which allowed Sade his anti-literature, or a-literature; like the works of Raymond Roussel, it allows the author to loop the loop and return to silence through the intermediary noise of words.

Personally, I rather doubt that Sade's theatre could have functioned as a sort of literary jamming device, especially as Sade begins writing his first plays before anything else. I would be more inclined to take it literally, as what it is: the unambiguous expression of a mode of representation still endowed, in the eighteenth century, with normative value. At this historical juncture, that is important. While all else starts to totter with the progress of philosophy, the stage remains, quite oddly, the last refuge of order: a closed space in which traditional figures, stereotyped gestures, and social codes continue to produce meaning, just at a time when men's minds are haunted by an absence of meaning. In this respect, Brochier is correct in insisting that:

It would be childish to reproach Sade for the traditional nature of his theatre and, at the same time, for the scandalous nature of everything else. It would be equally childish to blame Diderot for the impossible dialogue between *Le Rêve d'Alembert* and *Le Père de famille,* or Voltaire for the impossible dialogue between *Candide* and *Zaïre. . . .*

Perhaps the stationary nature of late-eighteenth-century theatre should be attributed to the visual dimension of theatrical representation. Don't paintings of the time betray a similar tardiness concerning the latest philosophical trends, so new in other domains? It seems the aesthetics of imitating nature continued to dominate the visual world, whereas new concepts of nature itself are already undermining the idea of imitation. Even so, most of these concepts can scarcely be confused with the one expounded by the Pope, to Juliette:

> Far from thanking this inconsistent nature for the small amount of liberty she vouchsafes us to pursue those very inclinations she inspires, we should blaspheme against her from the bottom of our hearts, for having given us so limited an access to the course of her designs . . . "You!" we should tell her, "You blind and imbecilic force of which I am the involuntary result. . . . I am willing to carry out your laws, since they demand heinous crimes, and since I have an unquenchable thirst for the same: but in that case, furnish me with laws that differ greatly from the ones which your debility presents."

The gap between Sade's novels and his theatre only becomes more troublesome, and cannot be measured by the same yardstick as the gap between *Jacques le fataliste* and *Fils naturel.* First of all, and despite the difference between his theatre and his novels, Diderot intends to modify the order of theatrical representation — and succeeds, as does Marivaux in his separate way. Sade, on the other hand, changes nothing; if anything, he scrupulously respects its reassuring mechanisms. But is that really so strange?

The fact is that in his youth, Sade tries to respect the techniques of social representation, without really believing in them. He believes in them about as much as any other young aristocrat, but seems to make it a point of honor to play the game, to be a good son, husband, son-in-law, nephew and lover. When, later on, in letters to his wife or Mademoiselle de Rousset, he evokes the life he could have led, and which he still dreams of leading with them, we rediscover the calm and peaceful atmosphere which predominates in his theatre, with its clear order and mechanism of naïve intrigues leading to a frivolous, spectacular *dénouement.* This is hardly surprising, for Sade started out his life in an exact replica of the world of his theatre. His growing astonishment at the importance his first lawsuits will assume is indissociable from this native frivolousness. We should never forget that Sade is the scion of a great family, raised in the acute awareness of those privileges due to rank. He is the child of a fixed world, immutable by principle, and the orthodoxy of his theatre owes much to a certain way of life typical of the ancíen régime; more so, in any case, than do the plays of Diderot, Voltaire or Marivaux. Sade will never rid himself of that divine right to nonchalance which brightens the beginning of *Aline et Valcour,* for example, however dark may be the forces appearing in the book later on.

An arbitrarily privileged world, then, and therefore quite protected from the habitual wretchednesses of the human condition, it is highly probable that this aristocratic representation of a harmony existing between people and things paradoxically fostered all those dreams of a golden age which were to haunt the European mind for a long time, just when the illusion of social harmony was beginning to dissolve.

With his customary honesty, Sade does not hesitate, in *Aline et Valcour,* to call attention to the origins of this abusive situation. He does so through the self-portrait of Valcour, which everyone agrees is autobiographical:

> Related, through my mother, to the greatest families in the realm; attached, on my father's side, to everyone of distinction in the province of Languedoc; born in Paris in the lap of luxury and plenty, I thought, as soon as I could think, that nature and fortune had combined to heap their gifts on me; I thought so, because people were silly enough to tell me so, and this ridiculous prejudice made me haughty, despotic and irascible; it seemed that everyone should yield to me, that the entire universe should flatter my whims, and that I alone possessed the right to conceive and satisfy such whims.

This does not prevent Sade from reminding his wife, in February 1779, when still a prisoner at Vincennes: "I was born to be served, and I would have it so." But can one give much credit to this impudence when, a few lines before, in the same letter, Sade asks for a knife and says, "I would like to be allowed to have three walks each week again"?

Too naïve and sensual to be insensitive to those daily pleasures which social incarceration transforms into acquired privileges, Sade is also too lucid and imperious not to realize how deceitful are those conventional paintings which enable a society to stay blind to its true self. I doubt one can proceed very far in understanding Sade unless one grasps to what extent he both refuses and accepts this privileged world, before, during and after the Revolution. Sade will always attribute to this world both a very real unreality and a no less unreal reality; one must also realize that his theatre has the requisite qualities to figure in such a world. Later on, the festivities occurring in his books are all illuminated by these artificial colors that beribboned his bright youth in a tangle of privilege and convention. Maurice Heine has most appropriately pointed out Sade's persistent sense of impunity, when asking, as concerns the matter at Arcueil: "Why so much ado about a spanking?" (In "Le Marquis de Sade et Rose Keller," *Annales de Médecine Légale,* no. 5, June 1933.) Sade asks the same question, and it constitutes his main defense; for in the conventional universe he inhabits, it is indeed a matter of a spanking and no more. The trouble is, believing himself infinitely free both to believe and not believe in convention, Sade has been too confident; he has forgotten that if one wishes to benefit from the impunity which respect for the conventions can confer, one must at least pretend to respect them all. Omit even one, and the integrity of the whole picture is affected; its composition is definitively disturbed. And after that, public opinion changes. You whip someone on Easter Sunday — in other words, you deride the holiday — and a minor moment of debauchery suddenly becomes a sacrilege.

This brusque change of opinion is what so upsets Madame de Saint-Germain, Sade's good friend, in her letter of April 18 to the Abbé de Sade:

> Public hatred is aroused against him beyond all description. Judge of it yourself: people think he indulged in this insane flagellation in order to mock the Passion. . . . He is a victim of the public's ferocity; the case of M. de Fronsac and many others only add to this: without any doubt, the horrors committed by members of the Court within the last ten years are quite inconceivable.

Although she does not realize it, Madame de Saint-Germain has just discovered another implacable law of social representation: once the opinion changes, the public changes too, as Maurice Heine again realizes in his commentary on this affair:

Doesn't the libertine appear to have deliberately chosen to commit his debauched deed on one of Christianity's most sacred holidays? Didn't he want to whip his victim in order to deride Christ's flagellation, just as he offered to confess her, the better to pour scorn on the sacrament of repentance?

As it happens, Sade is never quite convinced of the upheavals taking place in social representation, even if he does write to the Abbé Amblet in 1782:

> Society has certainly changed greatly since I left it. It seems to me that formerly it offered a relative degree of conso-lation on account of misfortune; and in supposing this, I felt I had a right to much consolation. Without suspecting it, you have offered me a sure consolation, for if men are as you portray them to me, one cannot much regret having infringed the laws of their society. My soul is filled with calm again, for which I thank you since I owe this calm to you.

Throughout his life, Sade maintains this nostalgic hankering after a world whose apparent frivolity serves mainly to efface all trace of culpability. Not that he allows himself to be taken in by this illusory vision; but he will always retain a certain preference for it. It may even be that this affection for the world of illusions is what makes him all the more intent on showing everything that negates it. His savageness seems inversely proportional to the naïveté of this worldy representation, a naïveté he maintains even though it is continually ripped to pieces by his terrible lucidity. I am inclined to wonder if his much-commented, intermittent adherence to the French Rev-olution does not owe something to a recognition of that spectacular naïveté found at the heart of revolutionary representation. Isn't it remarkable that Sade's most famous political texts, written while he belonged to the Section of Pikes, evince an ancient theatricality to which the writings of Robespierre and Saint-Just, for example, never do attain? This is as true of his *Discours prononcé á la fête décernée par la Section des Piques aux mânes de Marat et de Le Pelletier (Discourse Pronounced at the Feast Decreed by the Section of Pikes to the Shades of Marat and Le Pelletier)*, dated September 29, 1793, as of the *Pétition de la Section des Piques aux représentants du peuple français (Petition of the Section of Pikes to the Represen-tatives of the French People)* of November 15, 1793. One would have to be extremely hypocritical not to see the *peplum* aspect of Sade's revolutionary enthusiasm, visible even in so vigorous a text as *Frenchmen, another effort* . . .

Be it a naïve theatricality or theatrical naïveté, it smacks of that precarious order which Sade sees as a grid for human conduct. Depending on one's point of view, we have here the naïve or fierce theatricality of an order that invites disorder, or a disorder that invites order, as much at the peak of a solitary desire as in collective obscurity. It is as if theatricalization is the only mode of being Sade finds valid for both the individual and the collectivity; as if the idea of theatricality induces something which is never induced in Sade: the impossible encounter of the individual and the mass. It lasts as long as the performance: just long enough to set up an order and undo it, long enough for a scene to develop and disintegrate, long enough for desire to assume a form and then escape from it. In other words, it lasts as long as desire, which establishes the rhythms of Sade's thought and creates, like a vital necessity, the pattern of scene changes.

In this connection, there is a very curious play by Sade, to which nobody has paid the slightest attention. This neglect has occurred although Sade specifically states in his *Catalogue raisonné* or descriptive catalogue of "around October 1st, 1788" that the idea of his play, *La Ruse d'amour ou les six spectacles, (The Stratagem of Love, or the Six Spectacles)* an "episodic comedy of some six thousand lines, a mixture of prose and verse of varied meter, and lasting five hours in performance," is "utterly unique in its way." In actual fact this spectacle, originally consisting of five plays and ending in "a magnificent ballet-pantomime having to do with theatrical enchantment as much as with the basic plot," is entirely conceived around the principle of play within a play. This in itself would not be very interesting, were it not for the fact that each of the five one-act plays relates the same story, but from a different point of view. The story, which concerns a young girl whose greedy father wants to marry her off against her will, is therefore tragic in *Euphémie de Melun ou le Siège d' Alger,* psychological in *Le Suborneur,* dramatic in *La Fille malheureuse,* comical in *Azélis ou la coquette punie,* and lyrical in *La Tour enchantée,* as predicted in the *Catalogue raisonné.* It is odd, to say the least, that no one has ever called attention to the essentially "optical" composition of this piece, even if two plays — *La Tour enchantée* and *La Fille malheureuse* — are no longer to be found in the manuscript we have, still bearing its 1810 title of *L'Union des arts ou les ruses de l'amour.* Its composition is so optical that the true dramatic interest resides less in the untangling of the plots than in the general perspective of the entire plot, presented from these different points of view. Sade seems quite aware of the originality of his proceeding, since he further states in the *Catalog* that:

> What is particular about this play is that it has no moments of rest and the action is continuous, because after each episode the company is supposed to go back into the dressing-rooms to change costumes and rehearse the next episode; but these dressing-rooms are actually the stage, . . . the action thus follows continuously, seeming to be interrupted for the different episodes, but actually continuing with subtlety, and starting again in a more exposed fashion in the dressing-rooms, so one can say it's constantly in progress, without ever slowing down. . . .

The multiplicity of points of view leads to a multiplication of the planes on which the action will unfold, as if theatre's only function is to split reality into fragments of unreality, which then reorganize according to the whims of theatrical illusion. If it were otherwise, why would Sade return to the manner "in which this must be effected," explaining in his *Réflexions préliminaires* to the manuscript of 1810 that, "This is why, at the beginning of each episode, one reads *the scene changes and it represents,* and not *the curtain rises to reveal.*" Yes, the "scene changes and it represents," for with the *Union des arts* this very question of representation is what threatens to disturb the calmest place in Sade's imagination.

It is far from insignificant that this deep turmoil occurs in Sade's theatre at approximately the same time he is writing *The One Hundred and Twenty Days.* Unfortunately, we must be content with this chronological approximation, for as yet it has not been possible to establish the date of composition of certain of his plays. We do, however, know that Sade wrote a major part of his dramatic work, including *La Ruse d'amour,* between 1781 and 1788; that is, at the time when his revolt was at its violent height, and when his thinking — so astoundingly self-confident — risks its own equilibrium on the stage of *The One Hundred and Twenty Days.* And so, one cannot over-emphasize that in *La Ruse d'amour* Sade shows himself the master of a theatrical illusion he can, with equal pleasure, either multiply or destroy. Even when subjected to this excessive regimen, his theatrical machine still works. This technical competence has its importance: for in knowing as he does all the rules and subtleties of theatrical representation, as well as the mechanisms and principles of social representation, Sade knows exactly how to unhinge us on the mental stage of Silling. Having thrown into confusion all our safest modes of thinking, Sade also overthrows our best-tried modes of representation, in order to initiate, with Silling, a most curious way of looking at the world.

As opposed to the traditional theatrical representation typified by the boring indication "the curtain rises to reveal" — or even by the creation of perspectives just discussed — *The One Hundred and Twenty Days* presents a process of *focalization* that directs the whole system of representation inside Silling. The aim of this is most precise: one after another, each of the six hundred passions listed by Sade will occupy the entire dramatic space. As we have seen, this involves an absolute occupation of physical and mental space, the one constantly infringing on the other. Formed as it is to oppose this passionate focalizing, our thought is rather at a loss to take account of it. Nonetheless, this new way of seeing is an optical equivalent of the subversion of the normative connection between the particular and the general, and also determines the scandalous aspects of Sadian representation.

The scandal lies less in what is shown than in the way it is shown, since any scene will be directed by what Sade terms the principle of *delicacy*. This principle enables us to see, for example, the "bum of mottled taffeta, with its wide, revolting hole gaping in the middle" belonging to Madame Desgranges. Another of its effects is to make us notice, in the middle of a highly conventional description, that one of the wives had "a thin, narrow tongue, like the finest tint of dawn." On the evening of the sixth day, when "all the little girls were dressed as sailors and all the little boys as flower girls," it also shows us that:

> . . . nothing is more conducive to lubricity than this voluptuous exchange: one likes to discover, in a little boy, characteristics which make him seem like a little girl; and the girl is far more interesting when she assumes, in order to be pleasing, the sex which everyone would far prefer her to have.

Finally, this principle explains that:

> . . . while objects of the greatest beauty and freshness are
> there before their eyes, ready to satisfy their slightest whim,
> our two blackguards, on the contrary, indulge in most
> delightful pleasures with something that has been withered
> and dishonored by nature and crime alike: with the most
> dirty and disgusting object. . . . How can one explain
> mankind, after that! Both seem to be quarreling over this
> eagerly awaited corpse, just as two bulldogs worrying at
> carrion will indulge in the most repugnant excesses, and
> ultimately discharge their sperm. . . .

I shall not give any further examples of this erotic preciosity,
which transforms acknowledged tastes into the most licentious and
revolting festivals of the senses. They abound in Sade's universe and
make its texture shimmer, like myriad rare pearls slipping through
the folds of night. The principle of delicacy, by which they are
secreted, could well provide a dazzling example of the paradox we
find so fascinating in Sade. It helps him reveal a sort of *erotic
dandyism* to which we are quite sensitive. For if only very few
persons have the means and the audacity to satisfy their more
unusual tastes, how many more still dream of carrying out these
extravagant whims? Sade's genius is that he transforms this paradox
into a principle of representation that puts certain erotic possibilities
within everybody's reach — not the sum total of sexual peculiarities,
for he knows that is impossible; but a mode of vision capable of
exalting each of these singularities by giving them sufficient space
to grow in. This certainly heralds a revolution in representation for,
not content with changing the rules of the game, Sade changes the
game itself, revealing a desire which cannot be separated, at its
root, from the quest for singularity.

Thus, nothing is less aristocratic, originally, than the Sadian rake's
aristocratic preoccupation with giving body to the oddest phantasms; and nothing could be less aristocratic than the resulting mode
of representation. Moreover, in staging the oddities of his libertines
as so many examples of delicacy, Sade helps free eroticism from
the blinkering idea of beauty, an idea as subject to caution in his
mind as the customs and morals it embodies. Having carefully
replaced virtue in that very modest place it occupies in human
conduct, he now provides grave opposition to the idea of beauty,
by establishing the irreducible and infinite number of possible

objects of desire. At the same time, he proves that the idea of beauty, seen as a general aesthetic choice, thoroughly contradicts the principle of delicacy which so exalts oddness. In other words, beauty is only the palliative of a function of erotic discernment which starts to fail as soon as the principle of delicacy allows itself to be deadened by the social game.

All the same, Alain Robbe-Grillet is right to emphasize that "Sade likes what is pretty" ("Sade et le joli," *Obliques Sade,* édition Borderie, 1977). He is even right in doubting "today's stereotypical idea," according to which Sade needs "trashy prettiness" in order to emphasize the "violence of his discourse:"

> It is so obvious that Sade is carnally moved by prettiness that one is tempted to say the exact opposite: the trickle of blood is only there to emphasize perfection in the most delicate of curves, pain serves only to make the tender hem of lips tremble with emotion, to cause the eyes to flash from greater depths, the loins to move more exquisitely. . . .

That is how Robbe-Grillet continues, and I almost agree with him. In the realm of the erotic, Sade is as sensitive to the fake naïveté of conventional beauty as he is to that of the social spectacle. Here again, Sade's discourse cannot be reduced to the simple negation of accepted values, any more than it corresponds to the theories of Georges Bataille when the latter sees Sadian eroticism as an "inverted world," the "upside-down world" that we "really want," and all this to the extent that "betrayal is the real truth of eroticism," and "Sade's system is the ruinous form of eroticism" *(Erotism: Death and Sensuality).*

I know it has become almost unthinkable to sever Sade from Bataille; or rather, it has become unthinkable not to contemplate with appropriate devotion the image that Bataille gives us of Sade, even when the author of *The Tears of Eros* unhesitatingly confuses his own erotic preoccupations with those ·of Sade. And yet, one only has to read Sade to see, for example, that the principle of delicacy — which determines his erotic vision as rigorously as a precision instrument measuring desire — corresponds to absolutely nothing in Bataille. If anything, it essentially contradicts Bataille's conception of eroticism, dominated as this is by a vague metaphysics of increase, in which:

. . . the being who is *open* — to death, torment or great joy — the being who is both open and dying, sorrowful and happy, already appears in his dim light: this light is divine. And the cry which issues from his twisted mouth, which he tries, vainly? (sic) to make heard — this cry is a vast alleluia, lost in the eternal silence (Preface to *Madame Edwarda*).

Of course, Sade and Bataille do coincide in the importance they attach to erotic exaltation when it is linked to excrement, to any form of decadence, or even to murder. Both seem to invest transgression with an equal power to arouse. All this is true as long as one obstinately refuses to see that the same effects do not always have the same causes and that, in the present case, Sade's essentially atheist erotic vision cannot possibly blend with Bataille's essentially mystical, not to say religious one.

But let us return to the famous formula which marks the starting point of Bataille's thought: "Of eroticism, it is possible to say it is the commendation of life even in death." (*Erotism,* op. cit.) Bataille immediately goes about making this proposition more explicit — indeed, grounding it — by quoting Sade:

Here lies so great a paradox that without delaying further, I shall try to give some semblance of reason to my observation with the following two quotations:
"This secret is unfortunately only too certain," Sade observes, *"and any libertine even slightly addicted to vice is aware of what sway murder holds over the senses. . . ."*
The same author pens this even stranger phrase:
"There is no better way of gaining an acquaintance with death than to attach it to some libertine idea."

It is already evident how Bataille imbricates his thought in that of Sade, even if he does point out the scarcely logical use he puts it to; even if he is more or less aware of clumsily grafting his opinions onto Sade's, while all the time hoping to find in them a suitable foundation for his own:

I spoke of some *semblance* of a reason. In fact, Sade's thought could be an aberration. In any case, even if it's true that the tendency it deals with is not so rare in human nature, the sensuality in question is abnormal. All the same, there is a connection between death and sexual excitement.

It is this connection between death and sexual arousal which has fostered, in Bataille and his followers, such rampant confusion with respect to Sade. One only has to look closely at the opening pages of *Erotism* to see that this connection relates to very different realities in Sade and Bataille, contrary to what the latter claims. Consequently, when Bataille remarks, hoping to point out his proximity to Sade, that "In the transition from a normal attitude to desire there is a fundamental fascination with death," it's obvious that he is speaking of himself, and that he here describes an attitude which does not correspond to anything in Sade. One looks vainly in Sade for anything resembling this "fundamental fascination with death." As for the quotation Bataille uses to support his argument: "There is no better way of gaining an acquaintance with death than to attach it to a libertine idea," it certainly does not describe a fascination with death; on the contrary, it proposes a technique for escaping from that type of fascination, by forestalling all its traps. In the same way, if Sade notes that "any libertine even slightly addicted to vice knows what sway murder holds over the senses," he brings murder into voluptuous perspective as one of the strongest possible sensations, not at all as a "negation taking us to the limits of all that is possible," as Bataille would have it.

Therein lies the difference, insurmountable, despite the endless interpretative slippage Bataille perpetrates on Sadian thought. How can Bataille write, in the preface to *Madame Edwarda,* that "Nothing leads me to think that sensual pleasure is the essence of this life," or even, in his introduction to *Erotism,* that "eroticism opens onto death," without realizing that such assertions contradict fundamental aspects of Sade's thought? When Sade was the first to remark that pleasure is indeed quintessential and that eroticism does not open onto death, but is the expression of life itself, even if crime can be perceived as one of pleasure's modes?

Anyone inclined to doubt this would do well to take another look at the scene in which Saint-Fond initiates Juliette, handing her the theoretical keys to her future and her happiness:

> Give in, Juliette, give in fearlessly to your impetuous tastes, to your irregular and learned whims, to the burning impulse of desire; warm me with its excess, thrill me with your pleasures; have only this for law and guide; let your voluptuous imagination vary our disorders, for it is only by multiplying them that we shall find happiness.
> . . . All that causes you delight, is good; all that arouses

you, is natural. Don't you see that star which gives us light, alternately scorching us and giving life? Imitate it in your excesses, just as you reflect it in you own lovely eyes.

There is also this corollary:

Defile at leisure every part of your fine body; remember, there is no part of it which cannot be a temple to lubricity, and that the most divine such temples will always be those which you think anger nature. . . . Remember that nature belongs to you, that everything she lets us do is permitted, and that she has been clever enough, in forming us, to deprive us of the means to cause her trouble.

"Singularly flattered by this discourse," Juliette will have no difficulty following these precepts and discovers, little by little, the basis of her own sensual enjoyment in the erotic domain whose gates Saint-Fond so sumptuously throws open. For Sadian voluptuousness is inconceivable without this luxurious parade, whose meaning is to affirm life by catching it in the exuberance and iridescence of its minutest details. If this is so, what could be more different from the sort of stupefication that accompanies Bataille's eroticism, aiming as it does at unveiling "the continuity of people and death which are both equally fascinating" (*Erotism*), thereby leading to the no less fascinating, undifferentiated state of death? Finally, what connection is there between the luxuriousness of Sadian eroticism and this "negative experience" traced from the model of "negative theology" (*Erotism*), which Bataille ends up draping over his erotic concepts?

In this connection, I can't refrain from drawing attention to the way in which Blanchot, Bataille and their followers have inflected Sade's thinking to make it conform to their views, and to their metaphysics of negativity in motion. Thus, in a chapter of *Erotism* devoted to Sade ("De Sade's Sovereign Man") Bataille argues that "There is a movement of transgression which does not stop before it has reached the summit of transgression," and that "Sade has endowed one of his most perfect characters with this supreme momentum." The character is young Amélie, in *The Story of Juliette,* who makes one of her lovers promise that he will kill her the day after he betrays her: "I do not wish to die any other way: to cause a crime while dying is an idea that makes me dizzy." This is enough for Bataille and Blanchot to perceive her as Sade's most successful heroine, for the simple reason that she best corresponds to their idea of what a Sadian hero is. Amélie would seem to be the exception which confirms the rule: an extremely episodic character, she is, above all, the only one who embodies the spirit of negativity to the point of wanting to die of it. For, apart from Amélie — and this deserves emphasis — no Sadian hero actually seeks death. If anything, they all possess a remarkable ability for avoiding it, perhaps because their own deaths do not pose them any real metaphysical problems, even if Saint-Fond and Clairwil are both sufficiently coquettish to endeavor to invent a crime which will survive them. Evidence suggests that none of them really fears death, their materialism being in direct proportion to their definitive atheism.

It is hard to imagine a point of view more different from Bataille's. By means of eroticism, Bataille attempts only to "meet death face to face" in order to "at last perceive in it the opening to an unintelligible, unknowable continuity." It is also hard to imagine a more divergent procedure. Assisted by his principle of delicacy, Sade thinks only of specifying the singularity and infinite number of possible erotic actions. But Bataille pays attention to these actions not on account of their singularity, but because they are excessive, and being excessive encourage a "dissolution of the constituted forms" leading to the indefiniteness of death. This cruel absence of representation is found both in Bataille and those whom he has influenced. Concerning eroticism, this absence grows more serious in that it immediately opens on the yawning chasm of death. Perhaps this casts further light on the strange connection between Bataille and Sade: for want of the ability and will to represent, Bataille's thinking is obliged to feed parasitically from Sade's, in order to avoid being totally engulfed in mysticism. This lengthy operation has constantly focused on the life obtaining in Sade's thought: I refer to its materiality. Focused in vain, since Sade's choice of delicacy as a principle of representation enables him to conjure up each being in the full luxury of its presence.

I would like this comparison to show the poetic force of Sadian representation, seeing that it establishes a link between singularity and eroticism, which Bataille continually attempts to erase. It is as if poetry, fed by that strange subtlety found at the source of all unusual passions, embodies as the materiality of the unique:

> . . . so true it is that, for those things, everything depends utterly upon caprice; that age, beauty, virtue have absolutely nothing to do with it. Everything depends on a certain kind of tact, more often understood by an autumnal beauty

than by one without experience, though still endowed with all the gifts of spring. (*The One Hundred and Twenty Days of Sodom*)

So true it is, too, that: "Each has his idiosyncrasy; we must never either blame or be astonished at anyone's peculiarity" (*The One Hundred and Twenty Days of Sodom*).

This is why it is difficult to follow Pierre Klossowski when he argues, in *Le philosophe scélérat,* that:

> . . . conforming to the principle of normative generality in humankind, Sade wishes to establish a countergenerality, valid in this case for the specifics of perversions, permitting an exchange between particular cases of perversion, which, according to existing normative generality, are defined by an absence of logical structure. In this way the integral Sadian monstrosity is planned.

What can we do with this analysis, when as far as Sade is concerned, the category of perversion does not exist at all; when he expressly tries to convince us that "each has his idiosyncrasy"? On what are we to base these notions of generality and countergenerality, which the Sadian manner of representation seems to delete from human memory?

To resolve the question properly, we must turn back to the obligatory daily assemblies at Silling where, if they exist at all in Sade's universe, the notions of generality and counter-generality should have some effect. What exactly is expected at these general assemblies, held every evening, "right after dinner"?

> There, everyone will meet again. . . . There, everybody will be naked: historians, wives, young girls, young boys, old women, fuckers, friends; everyone will be jumbled together, sprawling on the flagstones, sprawling on the ground, and, after the example of animals, everyone will change, will mingle, will commit incest, adultery or sodomy and, with the continuing exception of deflorations, will indulge in every excess and every form of debauchery which can best inflame the mind.

Where is generality? Where is countergenerality? This jumble adequately shows that those who are behind it have nothing in common, except a taste for singularity capable of causing great excitement in the mind. The number of performers and the multiplicity of postures serve only, in these daily orgies, to confirm and exalt each person's particularities. In other words, this routine sharing of tastes and bodies, which brings about every imaginable redistribution, helps revive the dynamics of deviation through the principle of delicacy.

Every evening, therefore, Sade jumbles the kaleidoscope of passions, systematically revising the arrangement of each day. The next day, we can therefore see more clearly that the process of focalization, which determines all representation within Silling, opposes a *principle of exclusion* to the "principle of identity or principle of non-contradiction by which logically structured language coincides with the general principle of comprehension" (the terms are Klossowski's). This principle of exclusion explodes both the notion of generality and that of countergenerality. For what does the theatrical organization of *The One Hundred and Twenty Days* actually show us, if not the implacable mechanism of this principle of exclusion? When neither actors nor spectators remain in this strange theatre; when, by means of cumulative exclusions, traditional representation is disabled in favor of the oddness of Sade's staging? Once the "other" is excluded, individuality loses all sense of those very differences on which it is based, and it withdraws, revealing then the passion which obsesses it.

Despite these reservations, one will be tempted to recognize this focalizing process in Klossowski's analysis of the attitude of perverts:

> The pervert strives to execute *a unique gesture;* this lasts *but a second.* The pervert spends his existence perpetually awaiting the *moment when the gesture can be executed . . .* to execute this gesture corresponds in his mind to the *total fact of existing.*

True, but for the fact that this attitude is not at all perverted, since it characterizes every one of us, as soon as we attempt to satisfy our desires. In the event, perversion and normality admit of no distinction. Once again, while seeming to make Sade's thinking more explicit, Klossowski ends up distorting it. If there is perversity, it occurs contingently in the unexpected forms desire may take; on the other hand, the way desire functions is always the same, from one person to another, or from one object to another. Klossowski inconveniently confuses the container (or the form of desire) and the contained (the mechanism of desire), a confusion which considerably reduces the effect of Sade's words.

By conceiving the "integral monstrosity" of the Sadian character as a critique of the ordinary pervert — in other words, in conceiving the true libertine as "a type of pervert who, on the basis of his singular gesture, speaks *on behalf of generality*" — Klossowski turns the Sadian hero into a polymorphic, intellectual deviant, an aesthete of sexual weirdness. This enables him to tone down the true scandal of Sade's method: the revelation, in each being, of a mode of thought where singularity in no way refers back to generality. For what type of desire, perverted or not, cannot ultimately be reduced to the "execution of a tragic gesture"? This is precisely what Sade shows us, when staging this absolute spectacle which could very well correspond to the actual functioning of thought in the bottomless, solitary pit of human desire. Nothing comes to temper the existential cruelty of that desire, asserting itself at the expense of everything outside itself: such is the terrible spectacle shown to us by Sade. His unpardonable crime is to have found a means of plunging us back inside the motions of this constitutionally murderous thought, while we expend vast quantities of energy in trying to avoid it, or even in setting up derivations, bifurcations and partitions that give us the illusion we control it.

What Sade attempts to put under the spotlight is less what we refuse to see, than a way of seeing we prefer to ignore entirely. This accounts for the interest of a play like *La Ruse d'amour,* in which each theatrical space serves to disclose another; whereas in the theatre of *The One Hundred and Twenty Days,* there is no subterfuge at all: everything that's there is absolutely there. Unlike the theatre of amusement, whose very essence is to take us outside ourselves, the theatre of passions shows us into our own prison and locks the door behind us. It is as if the aim of deviation were to confront one inexorably with the self.

The confrontation is most curious, however, since it frustrates all normal methods of conceiving time. An example occurs in the description of the thirty-first passion of the month of January:

> He fucks a goat from behind, like a dog, while being whipped. He fathers the goat's baby, and then fucks that in turn, although the child's a monster.

This startling acceleration is actually quite typical of the peculiar tempo of Sadian representation. Here again, Sade's persistent use of a traditional theatrical model helps us understand how this passionate time does not actually run counter to the linear development of conventional time; rather, it diverges from it. In consequence, Sadian time can and does develop vertically at any moment in the traditional representation in which it is embedded. It does not take the form of an indecisive flight towards some vague background which might conveniently be assimilated into the mental setting; on the contrary, it develops most precisely, for Sadian time corresponds exactly to the time it takes to propagate an image. The spectacular temporal ellipsis of passion 31 simply parallels the speed of the imagination.

In fact, it is possible to reckon this speed rather rigorously, for each of the passions Sade describes. Thus, on December 7, passion 37 is remarkable on account of the infinite number of planes crossed by its image during propagation. The speed of the imaginary is seen to be considerable:

> He has six couples masturbate at the same time, in a hall of mirrors. Each couple is composed of two girls masturbating in various lubricious attitudes. He stands in the middle of the hall, watching the couples and their multiple images reflected in the mirrors, and discharges in the midst of this, frigged by an old woman. He has kissed the buttocks of these pairs.

Of passion number 42 of December 9, it remains only to be said that the time it takes to propagate the image is clearly the sole measurement of the deviation involved:

> He passes thirty women during the day, and has each one shit into his mouth; he eats the turds of the three or four most pretty. He plays this game five times a week, which means he sees 7,800 girls per year. When Champville sees him, he is seventy years old, and has been at this task for fifty.

All this is simultaneously comical and frightening, for in escaping from all our habitual concepts of time, the tempo of Sadian representation initiates a frenzied mode of drifting. No longer subject to any kind of law but that of deviation, which is a law of motion, bodies, objects, gestures and postures acquire a formidable autonomy resulting in accelerated circulation. This, too, we learn from *The One Hundred and Twenty Days of Sodom.*

In the beginning, Sade and the four libertines take their time — or more exactly, they suspend time in order to direct each passion.

But as soon as the mechanism for propagating the image is perfected, everything accelerates. It is useless to linger; the mental machine has been activated, whisking us away from our conventions of time, and from the time of our conventions.

Such is the principal lesson of this school of debauchery which reveals, in the time of deviation, the time frame of our freedom. By this I mean, a time which constantly deserts the teleological value ascribed to it, in order to reinvest each movement with the "innocence of its own becoming." This explains the apparently repetitive structures of Sadian representation and the incredible violence this repetition causes in Sade's critics. Even the best-intentioned of them are unable to forgive him this desertion from social and ideological time. In vain do commentators try to find him textual or psychoanalytical excuses: Sade lays bare the actual functioning of thought in this respect. As soon as our desires are felt, don't we all tend mentally to flee the continually developing phenomenon of social representation, and transform the theatre of our own mental discontinuity into a scene for objectifying this desire? All Sade's novels are entirely governed by an urgent wish to give rise to and repeat this labor of dis-ideologizing; a labor which, as Sade remarks in his *Reflections on the Novel*, is also the literal task of desire itself, causing us to:

> . . . see man, not merely as he is, or as he shows himself, that is the duty of the historian; but such as he might be, such as the influence of vice might render him, and all the jolts occasioned by the passions.

This, indeed, is the pretext for all the adventures Sade is to involve us in. He will make us walk back along the countless side roads of desire, paths that are blocked off, forbidden and condemned to remain unknown beyond the necessarily self-enclosed idiom of social representation. In all probability the texts which comprise *Les Crimes de l'amour,* written in 1787-1788, although not collected under this title until 1790, may be considered as an immediate, even slightly systematic illustration of the discoveries made during *The One Hundred and Twenty Days;* for each story refers back to a deviation defined in relation to a given *milieu,* a precise historical frame, a specific circumstance. In each case, a social group is thrown into confusion by the eruption of a desire so violent it bursts from the confines of accepted behavior. In each case, social representation is dramatically interrupted by the fate of a desire which nothing can subdue. It is perhaps significant that the hero of *La Double Epreuve,* the seductive Ceilcour, wishes to choose between the "two women who currently engaged his attention," and decides to put them to a most *spectacular* test. Having once resolved to "make use of anything which might prove seductive and anything which, his victory once assured, could, by destroying the illusion to which he perhaps owed it, convince him of the real value of his conquest," Ceilcour falls back on the supreme illusion of the *fête galante* to distinguish truth from falsehood, supposing that the truth of passion will frustrate the snares of illusion. However, this is not at all how things turn out. Because he does not really distance himself from social representation, but commits himself to gambling on all his own tricks — rather in the manner of the young Sade — Ceilcour becomes the game's first victim. On the other hand, the death of the delightful Dolsé, who is also a victim but desperately in love, destroys all stratagems of artifice together with the world which feeds on them. It would be misleading to draw a moral interpretation from this story, since it is more a question of an optical illusion set problematically between the fallacy of social representation and the truth of individual passion. Thus Dolsé's death, appearing as the very impossibility of artifice in an artificial world, destroys all the loopholes of illusion, and paradoxically returns the violence of deviant passion to its position center stage.

This reversal of perspective in the literal sense helps us to understand Sade's deep need for theatre, and its essential function. Through theatre, Sade tirelessly portrays, to us and to himself, the state and laws of the ideological tableau to which he belonged, by virtue of his birth, at that moment in history. That particular scene will be one Sade never stops studying throughout his life, blocked as it is like all social scenes, but blocked by precise conventions which refer to a precise geographical place, at a precise geographical moment. As far as Sade and French eighteenth-century society were concerned, it seems his theatre possessed the ethnographical and historical interest which he accords to the customs and mores of distant lands or remote epochs. In this sense, Sade's theatre is *exotic,* exotic in a way that permits him to avoid the deceptive realism for which he reproaches Restif de la Bretonne, accusing him, in *Reflections on the Novel,* of only writing "what everybody knows." This realistic hoax led Restif, like many others, to take and pass off as natural things which were often the result of social custom.

Not that the eighteenth century was not concerned about the innumerable forms of confusion between nature and culture; this was one of its favorite themes. But here again, Sade radicalizes the thought of his contemporaries as soon as he feels it's about to escape them. Whereas other writers find it audacious, in philosophical tales, to introduce naïve strangers, who are either astonished or struck dumb by European customs, Sade needs no such subterfuge. He conceives all deviations from the very heart of social representation, just as he writes *The One Hundred and Twenty Days of Sodom* while working on his theatre. His perceptions never lose the disturbing objectivity of childhood, which men contrive so thoroughly to lose, and which they sometimes try to retrieve through artifice, as a means of thwarting habit.

Indeed, this deceitful habit of the world he lives in is something Sade will never quite acquire. Rather the reverse: he is more attentive than anyone before or since to anything which deviates from the social representation each society attempts to impose, by persuading its members of its universal value. He is more anxious than anyone yet to provoke this deviation in order to reveal the imposture of any social representation. He is impatient, as no one has been since, to proceed towards the limits to which deviation leads. It is from Silling Castle that Sade observes the social scene, just as he stands on the brink of that scene to observe the abyss of the human heart.

Equally constant in Sade's thinking, these two stages — the absolutely conventional one found in his theatre, and the utterly scandalous one of *The One Hundred and Twenty Days* — determine, by their incredible deviations, the fictional space which will be found in his novels. The co-existence of these two stages seems to me to be linked with childhood, with that innocent childlike ferocity so characteristic of Sade's gaze. André Breton is alone in perceiving what Sade's evocation of horror owes both to childhood and the fairy tale. As Breton writes in the *Anthology of Black Humor:*

> One of the great poetic virtues of this work is that it depicts social iniquities and human perversions in the light of childhood terrors and phantasmagoria, and this at the risk of causing an occasional confusion between the two.

This glaring light of childhood, emanating from the point where innocence and monstrosity meet in the same person, illumines both the stage of Silling and the stage of Sade's theatre. The two scenes should be considered together, not as stages reflecting their opposing images in mirrors, but rather as two yawning chasms tending only to diverge, though crossed by similar currents, with something organic forging a connection. To signify the efflorescence of this intermediary space, I propose we take the image of the "tree of crime," an image which has often and mistakenly been deemed emblematic of *The One Hundred and Twenty Days* itself. It may best be described by Valcour, that charming emulator of Jean-Jacques Rousseau, who says, of this fruit of his imaginings:

> I would like all men to have in their houses, not those whimsical pieces of furniture which never produce a single real idea, but rather a kind of tree in bas-relief, which would have the name of a vice inscribed on every branch, beginning scrupulously with the merest fault, and proceeding by degrees to crimes which stem from disregard of one's essential duties. Would not this sort of moral object have its uses? Would it not be worth at least a Téniers or a Rubens?

I choose to see this as an image of the living link between the surface, and the depths; an organic structure, from which will develop Sade's fictional space.

First and foremost, we cannot doubt that Sade's whole universe is rooted in Silling. We may have been able to experience the slow ascent to Silling as a gradual advance towards the heart of crime; but once we have reached the brink of the abyss, we are obliged to stop and stay there for as long as Sade's performance lasts, and for the time it takes to perfect this new means of seeing, which will itself determine how Sade subsequently conceives of movement. Even today, Sade is still the only writer who has managed to represent the formidable complexity of that motion of desire which determines all our modes of displacement. From this derives the confusing fictional freedom which Sade paradoxically acquires in the solitary and aloof atmosphere of Silling, where he has successfully created all the necessary conditions in which to learn discernment. From then on, a master of "delicacy," he is concerned only with watching for the slightest deviation to occur in social representation, a tiny deviation capable of taking him back down to the great fount of subterranean energy. In so doing, Sade discovers that the "tree of crime" conceals a whole forest. His fictional dynamics then become inseparable from this structure and its duplication.

Through a series of continual plunges linking the mechanics of convention with the effervescent state of nature, Sade develops the infinite scope of a fictional perspective identical with that of a perpetually changing world. Departing from mere circumstance, Sade rediscovers movement. From one deviation to another, his novels will return us to the brink of the abyss, as is his express wish in *Reflections on the Novel:*

> Nature, who is stranger than the moralists portray her, is constantly cascading through the dams their policies prescribe for her; uniform in her plans, irregular in her effects, Nature's bosom resembles the heart of a volcano, hurling forth in turn either precious stones to serve the luxury of men, or fireballs to destroy them; great is Nature, when she peoples earth with men like Titus, or like Antonius; frightful, when she spews forth Nero or Andronicus. But always sublime, always majestic, always worthy of our study, our paintbrush, our respectful admiration, for her designs are unknown to us; because, slaves of her whims and needs, we should never regulate our sentiments for her by what she makes us feel, but rather by her grandeur and her energy, regardless of their possible results.

Yes, on the brink of an abyss, where men count about as much as stones cast back by blind volcanoes. It is a gripping image, but more than that, it is unprecedented in its novelty. Sade seeks to discover man on the very brink of what negates him. In this connection, critics have spoken of an obliteration of the subject; but Sade is far from finding satisfaction in such problematics of deficiency, for neither he nor his heroes allow themselves to be effaced by their desires or their adventures. They acquire, rather, a passion for momentum which suggests a perturbation of the subject, a perturbation on which the subject is actually based.

CHAPTER FIVE

THE TURBULENCE OF IDEAS AND OF MEN

In her "Remarks on *Aline and Valcour*" of May-June, 1789, Madame de Sade reminds her husband that "Wisdom consists in submitting to what created us and in not exceeding the boundaries it has set upon our minds." She then continues:

> Our minds are the sap of our bodies. If that sap follows a thousand little branches, it deviates from the center, and the tree will be defective, more or less. The mind must incline towards truth, and truth is one and indivisible.

Consciously or not, and by means of these "thousand little branches," the Marquise de Sade is tracing an exact negative of the "tree of crime" imagined by Valcour. And whereas Sade's only aim is to show an infinite number of contradictory truths, his wife declares that truth is unique. Was she, therefore, the most addlepated and willfully obtuse of his readers? By no means. Her comments on the philosophical novel which her incarcerated husband manages to send her are far from being stupid. They even evince a certain open-mindedness, common to enlightened persons of that time, which leads her to agree that "the moral and physical constitution of persons is infinitely varied," even though this is because:

. . . people do not proceed from a true principle, and
which truth maintains whole; the passions being varied,
this extends the principles of these different persons, who
are guided by them brutally, without reflection, and produce these contrasts. The variety of these contrasts cannot
be seen as a conclusion in their favor.

The Marquise de Sade was not alone in holding this opinion; it
was shared by many fine minds of the day, whether theists or
atheists, anxious to find a moral foundation of Goodness and Justice
in man himself. It was an opinion which Sade's discoveries at Silling
would definitively prevent him from sharing. But if Sade — as he
so often does — stands aloof on this question of truth, why then
does he elect to debate it within the framework of the novel, an
area increasingly dominated by the humanism of the Enlightenment?

I do not much believe in studying literary genres, being convinced
that the singularity of any work of art has more to lose than gain
by such a study. Nonetheless, it is as a philosophical novel that
Aline et Valcour, alone among Sade's works, has acquired the
distinction of being deemed a reassuring book. This is not entirely
a mistaken conclusion, since Sade's own behavior — signing it,
claiming it as his, even boasting about being its author, unlike his
other books — has largely contributed to this state of affairs. But
that is not all. Critics have gone so far as to praise Sade for having
found, in *Aline et Valcour,* the means of escaping from the things
that disturb them in his other works. What is it then, that happens
in this novel, for it to seem so different from the ongoing monstrosity with which his various books are generally confused? In
romping with his reader across these different countries, political
systems and world views, with that encyclopedic lightness which
constitutes the philosophical novel's particular charm, doesn't Sade
appear to renounce all he has learned in the optical revolution of
Silling? Couldn't this whirlwind entry into the domain of fiction be
the effect of an abrupt retreat? And also, wouldn't the scandalous
victory of the particular over the general be possible only in the
experimental world of Silling, and therefore destined to vanish in
the free air beyond its walls?

This is certainly the impression one receives as one begins reading
Aline et Valcour. The novel's epistolary form cannot entirely dispel
the conviction that this meandering book is leading us into fresh
air, imaginative fresh air at that. First of all, unlike most contemporary philosophical novels of the time, which tended to have plots

that were stilted and inhibited by the idea they had to demonstrate, *Aline et Valcour* has the effect of a powerful fictional breeze. Sade makes full use of all the expedients of the genre, no matter how extravagant: kidnaping, murders, shipwrecks, sequestrations, baby-swapping, dramatic recognitions, piracy, theft, betrayal. . . . He both uses and abuses fictional freedom to the limit, creating characters in pairs or with doubles, creating situations and plots with parallel structures. The story of Aline and Valcour corresponds contrapuntally to that of Léonore and Sainville. As for the exchange of letters, when Valcour addresses his friend Déterville, he is writing to his mirror-image, just as Judge de Blamont writes to his alter ego, Dolbourg, to expound his foul intentions. Gradually, however, the play of mirrors causes the parallels all to converge, blocking off the horizon to create a closed chamber of reflections. Between the open air and air trapped by mirrors, what has taken place?

There is certainly no lack of journeying in *Aline et Valcour*. In no other book does one depart on such travels, as we are informed in the prefatory note:

> Those who like traveling will be well satisfied, and may rest assured that the two different world tours, which Léonore and Sainville undertake in opposite directions, are most accurately described.

There are also journeys into time, even into the future, since Sade boasts in his footnotes, which were probably written retrospectively, of having foreseen and prayed for the revolution of 1789. It is highly probable he altered certain passages between 1788 and 1793 — between the date of composition and the date of publication. This would have been to draw attention to the fact that:

> What is still unusual about this work is that it was composed in the Bastille. The manner in which our author, crushed as he was by ministerial despotism, foresaw the Revolution, is really quite extraordinary, and endows his work with lively interest.

It scarcely matters whether this was true or not, when this premonitory dimension swells the exuberant structures of a novel pirouetting in its own space, with episodes and characters that generate themselves. After the fixity of *The One Hundred and Twenty Days*, the extremely mobile aspect of *Aline et Valcour* is most intriguing, considering the book was written in the years immediately following the creation of Silling. Why does Sade suddenly deploy so much narrative energy? Could this be some sort of liberating process, as has been suggested, whereby Sade's imagination blasts to smithereens the dungeon of his phantasms? Then again, this hypothesis might contradict the serious tone habitually adopted when considering the book's political dimension.

According to the critics, the book's interest resides essentially in the presentation and confrontation of the three political systems with which the young protagonists, Sainvill and Léonore, become acquainted in the course of their adventures. These are: the despotic system of Ben Maâcoro, as defended by Sarmiento; the utopian communism of Zamé; and the anarchy practiced by Brigandos and his band. All the same, it remains very hard to believe that Sade would have constructed this narrative machinery in all its parts, merely to expound the relative merits of these three political concepts. Forgetting this problem for the moment, let us initially content ourselves with the "Lecture politique d' *Aline et Valcour*" of Jean-Marie Goulemot, delivered at the Sade colloquium of Aix-en-Provence in 1966. According to Goulemot, Sade proposes "three options in the face of tyranny: acceptance, reform, or individual revolt." It would also seem that:

> Sade wanted to show how three different religious attitudes could justify three political forms, it being admitted, once and for all, that fanaticism, whether Christian or idolatrous, was the best support for despotism.

Finally, Goulemot points to "another cohesive factor, the implicit reference to the political state of Europe which runs through these three episodes."

All this is perfectly true, but says nothing of the whirlwind at the center of *Aline et Valcour,* intimately shaping the book and dragging us into its vortex. Except that, unlike what he does with *The One Hundred and Twenty Days,* Sade operates under open sky, as if basking in the transparent clarity of an idyllic afternoon in heaven; one could also say, against a horizon expanded by the speed at which he travels. For the two contrary journeys Léonore and Sainville embark upon when searching for each other are far from being just a joke: they also determine the scope of the arena and the movement which Sade elects to give to his quest. For there is certainly a quest, in *Aline et Valcour,* a quest for something in this narrative abundance. Couldn't Sade be rushing to activate the natural momentum of the very thing he manages to immobilize before, thanks to the expedient adopted in *The One Hundred and Twenty Days?* Be that as it may, he opens something in this book which he closes in the other one. The very foulness which he had sought to isolate in the laboratory of Silling is now put back in circulation, unleashing, as it passes, creatures of prey who carry the disease. Built around an exchange of letters, *Aline et Valcour* is also a novel of interchange, almost in a chemical sense. This is what distinguishes this book from *Les Crimes de l'amour,* in which each story depicts the ravages inflicted by an unadulterated passion in a given world. One might be tempted to read the destiny of Eugénie de Franval as the negative of Aline's fate, since the former involves an acceptance of incest; the latter, a rejection. But the trajectory of Aline never approaches the black crystal in which our memory retains young Eugénie's delightful figure. This difference cannot simply be imputed to Aline's smaller scale. In *Les Crimes de l'amour,* Sade works with concentrated solutions that are about to crystalize; in *Aline et Valcour,* he is mainly interested in blends, and the diluted solutions which result.

Sade could easily narrate the separate stories of Aline, Léonore, Blamont, Zamé and Clémentine without connecting them in any way; however, he deliberately makes them interweave. He brings about meetings between characters who could easily remain ignorant of one another's existence. He causes mutually exclusive modes of living to cohabit, and presents opposing political systems within the same perspective. Why does Sade make all these moral, political, geographical, sensory and philosophical worlds communicate in this frenetic manner? Has he forgotten the principle of delicacy digested in the course of *The One Hundred and Twenty Days,* and which enabled him to exercise the subtlest of distinctions? Not at all. The method has simply changed. These accelerated exchanges offer two advantages: they make it easier to point to differences, while emphasizing parallels in structure. It is only when these parallels or structural analogies have been revealed that singularity can be perceived. This can be seen in the two political systems which Léonore and Sainville encounter while traveling in opposite directions. Beyond their immediately apparent differences, it is clear both systems essentially derive from the exercise of force. That this should evidently be the case in Sarmiento's despotic rule of Maâcoro is not at all surprising. What is stranger is that in the happy isle of Tamoé, everything depends on the good will of Zamé, the chief. As for the anarchist Brigandos, if he practices individual reprovals with a rough and ready charm, he shows great harshness in exercising power as a leader. As Léonore astutely remarks:

> This chieftain is an honest man, . . . his principles are sound, and I like his philosophy; he's a man who could command anywhere, and any society would be proud of his administration. But here he only heads a band of rogues, to which unfortunately we belong.

All this leads Jean-Marie Goulemot to conclude that "Sade, consciously or not, has distorted the reader's possibility of choice by presenting him with three options which are, at base, both incoherent and unclear."

I do not subscribe to this opinion, being more inclined to think that in showing these three options which are incoherent and unclear, Sade is, on the contrary, liberating his reader from ideological ascendancy. Refusing to expound these systems as coherent political programs, Sade exposes, in each case, the machinery of power which actually determines all of them. In fact, he goes further, since he shows us how, once put into practice, any of these schemes for organizing a collective life, be it liberal or despotic, ends up benefiting a single man. And so, Sade cuts away at the very roots of ideology, allowing his reader a hitherto inconceivable political freedom: he offers the reader a means of operating in the world of politics just as he does in the world of desire; he enables him to see through a political choice, and recognize the form taken by his own desire.

Once again, we should attempt to gauge the novelty of Sade's intent. Never before — and never since, for that matter — has politics been viewed in this way. Sade seems to have been aware of this, for in order to forestall the slightest logical objection that might sabotage his project, he feels it necessary to specify:

> Some readers will object: there's a fine contradiction. . . . Would these finicky persons be so good as to permit us to observe that this epistolary compilation is not a moral treaty whose every part must correspond and bind together? Formed by different persons, this miscellany offers, in each letter, the mode of thinking of the person writing it, or the persons whom this writer sees, and whose ideas he conveys: instead of endeavoring to untangle repetitions or contradictions, therefore, which are inevitable in such a

compilation, the wiser reader should amuse or occupy himself with the different political systems presented, whether for or against, and adopt those which best promote his ideas or his inclinations.

This holds true for both political and amorous systems in that Sarmiento's tyranny evidently corresponds to the dark debauchery of the Judge de Blamont, that Zamé's utopia parallels the virtuous feelings of Aline and Valcour, that Léonore's unruly passion finds an echo in the anarchy of Brigandos. Three amorous concepts, deriving from three attitudes towards desire: all three are simply modalities of the power of desire, just as the political systems in question, their differences notwithstanding, all derive from the fascination of power in three different modes.

We can already see that, beneath a narrative exuberance, beneath the swarming of ideas, systems and behavior, the sabotage of ideology is in full swing. There is not a custom, attitude or feeling which is not caught up in the incredible machine of this novel, which strips the most irreproachable comportment of its ideological camouflage. Consider the case of that model wife, Madame de Blamont, who supposedly submits to the whims of her husband and master, purely out of duty. Sade evidently enjoys allowing the debauched spouse to comment on this matter in a letter to his confidant, Dolbourg:

> What I find amusing is that the good woman ascribes all this to her own charms. . . . She should, nonetheless, be perfectly aware that these no longer count among the causes of my ecstasy. . . . Formerly, when I was rather more interested, there was far less enthusiasm: this is something that she ought to remember. What could possibly account for this new delirium? The impropriety of the act? For quite some time I have indulged in *eccentricities,* as she must know; seeing that none of this is what inflames me, she should wonder what it is that does . . . be astonished, even shudder. . . . It's a curious thing, the female sense of security.

Is Blamont, then, quite loathsome? Less than one might think, considering the prolix way in which the virtuous Madame de Blamont describes this renewal of matrimonial homage to her future son-in-law:

> Aroused and excited at my side . . . he began proffering
> fresh compliments . . . began demanding what I was re-
> lieved to go on granting, since I was determined to pre-
> tend. . . . Never had I seen him so ardent. . . . So de-
> praved, I should say; in souls such as his, love, or feeling,
> is only a disorderly excess. . . . "How beautiful you are!"
> he exclaimed, inspecting me unveiled.

What is left of virtue here, of its cohort of unshakable resolutions,
save a most disturbing complacency for vice?

This complacency is so deeply buried beneath the alluvium of
ideological justification that its practitioners are not even aware of
it; but Sade lays it bare to the point of obscenity. Not only does
he invite us to look closely at the wobbly undertones of Madame
de Blamont's virtue; we should also inspect the honesty of all
respectable persons in *Aline et Valcour,* since their submissiveness,
indolence, resignation and even cowardice combine to smooth the
path of vileness, if not crime. What is one to think of Valcour's
lofty soul, and his unexpected coldness, when the unfortunate
Sophie again falls prey to Blamont's schemes: "There are regrettable
instances when the prudent shepherd sacrifices a lost sheep, rather
than risk the entire flock by trying to protect the fugitive. . . ."
Then again, what are we to make of this sensitive young man's
comments to Madame de Blamont, perpetually in want of children
to recognize, and who thinks she has found, then lost, a missing
daughter:

> You have so sensitive a soul, it seems to fly in search of
> facts in order to transform them into tortures. . . . What
> does she matter to you, this daughter that you never met?
> It is bad enough to have to weep over real troubles, without
> regretting pleasures that one never had. Thinking as you
> do, one would find something painful in everything, and
> make oneself exceedingly unhappy.

How is one to react to a mother whose maternal instincts are so
highly developed that when providence sends her a second daughter, Léonore, all she can do is judge her severely, on the pretext
that the girl declares herself an atheist:

> When misfortune has not succeeded in fashioning the
> soul of this young woman, it must be feared that it has

made her wicked, and that the wealth she is shortly to enjoy will serve further to corrupt her.

Not that Sade prefers vice to virtue in this case. He simply encourages us to examine them both by the same light, and puts virtue back inside the system of universal exchanges from which our ideological habits invariably prompt us to extract it. We extract it the better to favor its effects, and thereby prejudice all other modes of being. When treated with no undue respect, virtue simply sinks back into the monumental chart of human behavior which Sade intends to draw in this philosophical novel. For the optical system he perfected in the utter solitude of Silling focuses on the whole world, and this explains the need for such varied situations, characters, ideas, feelings and desires — a panoramic, not scientific, need. In fact, Sade embarks upon the very same task as in *The One Hundred and Twenty Days,* except that in *Aline et Valcour* he focuses on what is accepted in society, whereas the material studied in the chill laboratory of Silling was by definition asocial. Here he looks closely at anything which has acquired objective status, whereas the research carried out at Silling was essentially determined by its extremely subjective nature. Common sense, in its diverse manifestations, is examined as closely in *Aline et Valcour* as the most criminal of passions.

How, then, can we not be struck by the similarity between the propositions Sade makes his reader in this philosophical novel and in *The One Hundred and Twenty Days?* Let's take another look at a passage I've already quoted: ". . . the wiser reader should amuse or occupy himself with the different systems presented, whether for or against, and adopt those which best promote his ideas or his inclinations." Doesn't this correspond to the banquet Sade proposes in his introduction to *The One Hundred and Twenty Days?* Doesn't Sade say exactly the same thing about ideological or political systems that he says about perversions? ". . . a few of them will arouse you to the point of costing you some sperm, and that is all we need." Even if it is not formulated as clearly in *Aline et Valcour,* that is indeed what we need to show us how unreal are the moral, intellectual, sentimental or political choices that we make; to show us at the same time how all too real is their erotic import.

This hopeless slide towards eroticism — the fate of every conceivable form of behavior — is what Sade depicts so splendidly in *Aline et Valcour.* Nothing escapes this principle, which makes the world go round and drives the machinery of this philosophical novel, inexorably drawing everyone towards the truth of his desire. By means of enormous, concentric whirling motions, Sade blasts clean every level of reality, then clears each situation of its ideological baggage. One is exceedingly naïve if one regrets, as some readers do, that this book does not occupy its rightful place in the annals of French literature. This supposed injustice becomes perfectly comprehensible when one considers that each person's reality is subject to Sade's terrible examination; when everything that causes the general to predominate over the particular is evaluated here in terms of the predominance of the particular over the general; when we are offered a means of seeing what is natural, savage and supreme, and which will help us put the greatest possible distance between ourselves and the world we're told is real.

Sade shows quite extraordinary mastery in using all the tricks of the adventure novel, proceeding by a series of adjustments. Each vicissitude brings about a systematic revision of all that is normally said, done, or thought in similar circumstances. This is more than just a detour. Sade sponges excessively from the forms of the adventure and the philosophical novel alike: he cheerfully confuses the two, exploiting the commodities of one to push back the limitations of the other, and vice versa. The hero of the traditional adventure novel is always astonished, even shocked and revolted by the mores of the country he is traveling through, and frequently encounters legal problems; Sade takes advantage of the momentum already acquired by the genre and increases the narrative dynamics. He does so in such a way that what was formerly an opinion, or a particular point of view, is transformed into a veritable trial of those values established by the different powers in order to enslave the individual.

Accordingly, he passes very quickly from a recognition of the relativity of customs to a criticism of justice, the very idea of which he questions. After denouncing prison, he pronounces negative and definitive judgment on capital punishment, ending up with a refutation of the notion of law. Basing himself on the authority of Montesquieu, Good King Zamé does not hesitate to declare:

> Your wretched laws, misshapen and barbaric, serve only to punish, never to correct; they destroy, and create nothing; they cause revulsion, not reform: now, you should never hope to have made the slightest progress in the art of guiding and knowing man until you have discovered the

means of correcting him without destroying him, of making him better without degrading him.

This, of course, is only one voice among many. It is nonetheless remarkable how, on such important questions as prison, justice, law, even religion, property and theft — to say nothing of virtue and vice — different characters frequently agree about the fraudulence of social structures, although using the most varied forms of argument. Regarding law, for example, Brigandos, Zamé, Léonore, Sainville and Judge de Blamont all have their different reasons for contesting it. After such consensuses, Sade's quest accelerates: along the way each of these characters upsets one or other of the established values, and together they end up toppling the totality of values on which humanity claims to be based. But there again, no one's role is predetermined.

It is intriguing, to say the least, that the virtuous Madame de Blamont — so virtuous it kills her — should be the one who suddenly declares:

> Is it possible, then, that fatal circumstances can arise in which providence is so hostile to virtue that it becomes impossible to wrest it from the arms of misfortune? May these fateful truths remain eternally unknown; too many young girls would conclude that it is useless to follow the thorny path on which their education sets them, since it only brings them sooner to the traps of intemperance and vice.

However, this does not stop Madame de Blamont from feeling offended when Léonore, her long-lost daughter, tries to show her the mechanisms behind decency and pity: ". . . there is no real greatness in the act of charity you just performed . . . a pleasure satisfied, and not the aspect of a virtue." As for pity, she declares: "It is a weakness, and not at all a virtue, since it only acts upon us in proportion to the impression we receive, and to the vibration set off in the fibers of our soul by the relative distance of the ill luck in question."

Everything is in motion in *Aline et Valcour,* everything moves vertically, more attuned to those vibrations of the fibers than the logic due to character or plot. One of the novel's more original aspects is that it shows us character tossed constantly about between vice and virtue:

> . . . like a ship at sea, sometimes avoiding reefs, sometimes foundering upon them for want of strength to draw away. We are like those instruments which, formed according to specified proportions, must render an agreeable sound or else a discord; formed with different proportions, we are nothing and possess nothing, everything belongs to nature; and in her hands we are no more than the blind instrument of her caprices.

Not for nothing does Sade choose wise King Zamé to tell us of mankind's constituent inner turbulence, a turbulence that fills *Aline et Valcour* with the uncertainty of a gathering swell, inwardly sapping its narrative structure. This inner turbulence increases as the social markers tend to disappear, shaken by the swell. There follows an acceleration of the general plunge towards erotic reality, and also a spectacular shrinking of the narrative space, for Sade has chosen to continue his risky pursuit — the study of the human heart — far beyond the territory of anecdote, far beyond psychology. He thus causes us to witness that most somber tragedy, the vanquishing of individual desire: the tragedy of Madame de Blamont's unsatisfied desire, the tragedy of Aline's unsatisfied desire, the tragedy of Judge de Blamont's unsatisfied desire. In transforming the novel into a tragedy, with its accompanying shrinkage of perspective, Sade then succeeds in penetrating, short of his characters' well-defined attitudes, their hidden erotic destinies — what Freud will later call the "destiny of libido."

The entire novel could well illustrate this observation by Judge de Blamont:

> What a strange thing is the analysis of the human heart! I'm perfectly sure at present that people make exactly what they will of it; quick to take in the impressions of the mind, the heart soon follows nothing but its movements, and thus the gangrene sets in from head to foot, with nothing to prevent the poison from circulating.

Even so the strongest, truest and most lively characters are those who become aware of an erotic fatality which can only be controlled by the consciousness one has of it. Could not the poison that Sade speaks of be this very consciousness? This consciousness, indeed, seems of definitive importance, considering that the schism between characters does not occur between the good and the evil ones, nor between aristocrats and bourgeois, as has sometimes been said; it occurs between those who have a brain and those who do not. It is hardly surprising that the novel's two brains belong to its two most accomplished characters — who are also the truest: Léonore and her father, Judge de Blamont. It scarcely matters that they belong to opposing camps; they are the only ones who harbor no illusions as to the nature of the world, knowing that everything obeys its own dynamism, that everything is driven by its own necessity.

From this point of view, I must emphasize how strongly the narrative dynamism compensates for characters' ignorance or lack of consciousness. Drawing each one to the limits of the self, it creates endless reversals capable of showing each, despite himself, what he cannot or will not see, extrapolating his destiny until it becomes a parody. Such is the subterranean reality governing the incredible thematic and stylistic pattern of this novel, which has been mistaken for a flight of fancy or a frolic on Sade's part, but which actually derives from the most rigorous reflections about change. From this point of view, too, it would be interesting to study the entrances and exits of the innumerable characters Sade introduces to us, each one remaining in the narrative arena just long enough to sketch out or suggest his plotted path. This is then added to all the other paths, making up an outline of the world.

Be it a short path, a long one, a path that is barely discernible or an extremely definite path, it is the relative degree of consciousness which counts, as Aline, most unexpectedly, manages to show Valcour:

> In the outbursts of temper which certain people provoke in me, I wonder if I'm not as fond of those who, like my dear sister, go far beyond propriety, through being too susceptible, as I am of those who feel nothing. At least the former make amends, by their pungent and extraordinary wit, for all the absurdities committed by their heart, while the latter can offer nothing in compensation for their apathetic dullness. They are like automatons which, it seems to me, have the same overwhelming effect on us as certain days in summer, when all our faculties, benumbed by the weight of air absorbing them, no longer even qualify as organizing powers. . . . Is not my comparison a fair one? Hasn't some imbecile ever made you feel a physical pain? Seeing him approach, or hearing him speak, have you not felt an upheaval like the one I'm describing to you?

Such is the phenomenon of numbness which imbeciles of every kind — the designated quarry of every type of prejudice — create all around them after falling prey to it themselves. It seems their resignation and submissiveness, their acquiescence to the world as it is, all have the effect — the physical effect, since Aline refers to the symptoms of oppression, asphyxiation, and even physical pain occasioned by stupidity — of slowing down the natural interaction between man and his surroundings, and thereby putting brakes on the running of the world. It seems as if prejudice — through which these automatons acquire, for want of moral science, a system of reflexes — has as its main function to conceal the true workings of the universe from men, perhaps even make them total strangers there.

This is at least what Léonore tries vainly to explain to her mother, first establishing the difference between impressions due to prejudice and those of free spirits. She then suggests the basis for a true ethics of perturbation:

> We are not less sensitive to this, either of us; violent events disturb our souls equally; but those impressions which reach mine are not of a kind suited to yours. Moreover, do we not frequently receive our impressions through the habitual form of prejudice? How then can the sensations of a mind accustomed to overcoming prejudice, and shaking off the chains of habit, resemble those of a soul given over to its influence? In that case, one would need only philosophy in order to receive the most unusual impressions, and in consequence, extend most astonishingly the sphere of one's pleasures.

In affirming this alarming consanguinity between eccentricity, truth and pleasure — which is another way of attesting to the supremacy of the particular over the general — Léonore provides one of the keys both to Sade's imagination and his ethic. By means of this passkey of commotion, Sade brings the different world into communication and returns us to the momentum of the universe. At the same time, he suggests the one means of not letting ourselves get carried away by it: metaphorically, one might say, since the relationship of eccentricity-truth-pleasure is paralleled by that of deviation-consciousness-knowledge. Here, as at Silling, this leads to an infinity of pleasure turning into consciousness and consciousness becoming pleasure. As Léonore explains:

One cannot conceive what might perhaps be found beyond the debris of these vulgar yokes; as long as we submit nature to our pretty views, as long as we chain her to our loathsome prejudices, confusing them with her own voice, we shall never learn to know her: who knows if we should not run ahead of her, to hear what she is trying to say?

After this splendid explanation Léonore concludes, to her mother's consternation: " . . . sometimes we should learn to treat her like a flirt, this unintelligible nature: in a word, we should dare to violate her, thereby learning to enjoy her." In other words, it is the relative degree of consciousness which allows one to join, or not join, in the workings of the world, and to participate in it. But this participation is inconceivable without some violence being done to the order of things, for only thus will we understand it. As Léonore adds, with fine intelligence: "Let us study nature; let us follow her to her furthermost boundaries; let us even work to place them further still; but never let us prescribe boundaries to nature." Only perturbation permits transition to another speed. But which speed? The speed we never stop losing, the speed of the imagination, which gives man an accurate idea of the time and space he has a right to claim for his desires. And that is the beginning of a moral.

CHAPTER SIX

BEING, HAVING, AND LACKING

W hat is desire? Not love, but desire? I believe Sade is the first
writer to have posed this question, posing it to the entire world,
brutally, as if driven by an ontological necessity. Today we can scarcely
imagine the irreparable hole this question tore in the horizon of the
Enlightenment, for the term "desire" has become a place of refuge
for all the insecurities and uncertainties of our declining century;
something which links libido and vital energy, via widely different
modes of social promulgation. Nor should we forget that Sade substitutes this interrogation of desire for *the* question posed by all
thinking persons of that time, persons increasingly concerned with
defining the human profile, as the notion of God progressively fades
from the horizon. The libertine tradition has some characteristics of
this search for human positivity: in systematically exploring the modalities of pleasure, libertine thought establishes new bases for a
command of the subject. But Sade, who links his quest to the freedom
of desire, casts doubt upon the very notion of identity. Here, perhaps,
is a measure of the true distance between Sade and his time, a distance
that determines all other distances, and brings about a definitive
change of perspective. For in asking, "What is desire?" instead of
"What is man?" Sade simply obliterates the supremacy of the human
subject, and puts it back into the system of universal exchanges. From
this derives a double scandal: first, of considering man in a way
that scarcely distinguishes him from the rest of the universe, and

second, of contemplating man in his particular motion, in his violent will to give form to something that is formless, to incarnate thought.

I am surprised no one has really noticed that in Sade one stands confronted with the most "physical" head in the eighteenth century. I mean, confronted with an exceptional way of conceptualizing the material reality of individuals, things, and situations. How can one forget this observation from *The One Hundred and Twenty Days:* "That evening she was dressed as a marmot, and was charming underneath this disguise"? Or his letter to Mademoiselle de Rousset, dated March 22, 1779:

> . . . New Year's Day has passed, and you did not come to see me. I waited in vain during the entire day; I had made myself attractive, with powder and pomade, I was closely shaven, I was wearing, not fur-trimmed boots but a fine pair of green silk stockings, red breeches, a yellow waistcoat with my long black tails, and a hat embroidered all in silver. In a word, I was a most elegant-looking aristocrat. The pots of jam were lined up like an army, and I had even prepared a little concert: three drums, four kettledrums, eighteen trumpets and forty-two hunting horns. . . .

How can one forget the sudden peeve of Eugénie de Mistival, when she thinks her libertine friends have inadvertently killed her mother: "Dead! Dead! What! Am I to be obliged to wear mourning this summer, after having had such pretty dresses made!" There is also the incredible scene in which Juliette gives herself the pleasure of assisting the libertine Moberti to change skins:

> How delightful I shall find this evening! Dress me in this tiger skin. All three women will be naked, in the bedroom, holding the corpse between them; I shall fling myself upon them all . . . I shall devour them. . . . And, he dressed in the tiger skin, its four paws armed with monstrous claws, its snout disposed so as to bite anything it touches — arranged, I say in this fashion, myself following naked, equipped with an enormous cudgel wherewith to rouse him from his laziness — we go in. . . .

Finally, there is this unforgettable insight into how Sade sees himself in Vincennes: "What am I here, Blessed Rousset, what am I here, if not a child?" A thousand excellent examples could easily illustrate this prodigious sense of presence, which Sade is surely the only person in the century to have possessed in such degree.

Could Sade's ideas so have shocked us that we've become insensitive to how they get inside us, endowed as they are with an almost physical weight? Or, on the contrary, could it be that we prefer to confine ourselves to the ideas alone, being unable to define their concrete power? Obviously, the customary Sadian coexistence of philosophical development and erotic disposition has been emphasized and analyzed, even though some critics have managed to write about Sade without ever mentioning his erotic side; consciously or not, they have hidden it from view.

This, however, is not really the question when at every level in Sade's work, we see a formidable and perpetually surprising objectivity, an endlessly perturbing savage innocence. Above all, one should not speak of style or "writing" in this context, when, once again, we are dealing with a way of being and thinking which makes Sade the greatest portrait painter in the whole eighteenth century and one of the true inventors of landscape, at a time when Europe is just beginning to discover nature. These talents do not always go together and, in the Enlightenment, seem rather to be mutually exclusive.

As an example of his portraiture, it would be hard to find an equal to this first appearance of Dolbourg, the friend of Judge de Blamont:

> Shortly before dinner was served there came a kind of short, square person, his spine adorned with an olive cloth jerkin, covered from top to bottom by an embroidered motif some eight inches high, of a design which seemed to be the same as that worn by Clovis on his royal cloak. This small person was the possessor of very large feet, rigged out in high-heeled shoes which propped up two huge legs. Looking for his waist, one encountered only a stomach. Should I describe his head? All one could see was a wig and a cravat; from between which there escaped from time to time a falsetto which left one wondering whether the gullet it proceeded from was indeed human, or the gullet of some ancient parrot. This ridiculous mortal, who looked just as I have sketched him, was announced as Monsieur Dolbourg.

This has nothing in common with the psychological portrait that was the glory of Prévost, Rousseau or Richardson — to name the writers Sade admires. Nothing could be less psychological than this likeness, with an evocative power equaling that of Charles Bovary. Here again, one could readily assemble an interminable and impressive gallery of portraits from the parade of characters Sade brings before us.

The same holds true of the landscapes Sade evokes, at the turn of a page or a path, in a chapter or a forest; landscapes which impress us as would people or new worlds: "Soon the shadows of night begin to fall, spreading through the forest that kind of religious terror which engenders fear in timid souls, and thoughts of crime in savage hearts." Thus, in *The New Justine,* night becomes a protagonist, affecting the subsequent course of action. As for Valcour, the thickness of darkness confronts him like a solid element, through which he must hew a path:

> I well knew it was becoming impossible to proceed further, and not wishing to bed down on the road, I plunged into the thickness of the wood. . . . Scarcely was I in it than the darkest night cast veils all across the forest; gradually the vault of sky was covered up with clouds, and increased the terror of the night.

At no time does Sade rid himself of this essentially concrete perception of landscape. It is a perception not found in any of his contemporaries, some of whom are actually the first to focus Europe's gaze on the forgotten wilderness surrounding it. For Prévost, as for Rousseau, nature is always the metaphorical expression of the human heart, endowing the psychological figure with a physical weight it here possesses on its own. One might say that portraits were like drawings to them, to which their evocations of nature add color, density and depth. We should remember how the eighteenth century discovers mountains, with *The New Héloise.* It all starts with this evocation of Saint-Preux' emotional state: "I had set off, saddened by my troubles but consoled by your joy, and this kept me in a languorous condition not without charm for a sensitive heart." That's all: the avalanche of abstract words is left behind as Saint-Preux leaves the valley, and it is his slow advance toward the summits that enables Rousseau to perfect this portrait of a sensitive soul, who is learning to recognize his own strangeness in the strangeness of the countryside:

Imagine . . . how pleasant it is to perceive around oneself nothing but objects that are utterly new: strange birds, unusual, unknown plants; to observe a kind of other Nature, to find oneself in a new world . . . this spectacle has something magical and supernatural about it, which delights the mind and senses; one forgets everything, one even forgets oneself, one no longer knows where one is.

In the same letter Saint-Preux will conclude: "Never have I noticed so clearly how I instinctively situate our common existence in diverse places, according to the state of my soul."

Obviously, such overflowing feelings are never found in Sade, even if he does succeed better than anyone yet in pointing out the alarming analogy between human and natural aberrations. This is doubtless why, being principally concerned with discerning the momentum which really controls people and things, Sade refuses any sort of participation — even at the level of lyricism — in the anthropocentrism of his contemporaries.

Thus, it was not at all by chance that I spoke of overflowing emotions. In Rousseau, the demonstrative human heart does indeed flow over the natural landscape until the landscape is completely submerged. In the more somber and rigorous writing of Prévost, the evocations of nature are recorded contrapuntally, alternating with the advance of passion and echoing the rhythm of its fatal progress. But, in both cases, the exchange between man and nature is effected in a single direction. The eighteenth century conceives its relationship with nature on the basis of this irreversibility, being careful not to damage the idea that man is superior to everything else. One might wonder if this new view of nature, seen first as a setting and often as a mirror, is not the lyrical consequence of extending the field of human capabilities, rather than the critique of the rational subject as we have grown used to seeing it. One might wonder also if it does not correspond to a symbolic appropriation of landscape connected with the historical accession of the bourgeoisie to land ownership.

Here, Sade does not equivocate at all: in total disharmony with his epoch, never at any time does he claim a privileged position for man within the universe, neither in his letters nor in his work, neither as a philosopher nor as an individual. The term "nature" is never employed in the sense of "landscape" and still less as a setting. If Juliette evokes the natural surroundings of Naples, she does so to convince us of their active power, without the slightest hint of anything picturesque:

> Nowhere in Europe is nature as beautiful and imposing as it is around that city. It is not the dismal, uniform beauty of the plains of Lombardy, which leave the imagination in a tranquility akin to torpor: around Naples, nature is on fire; her disturbances, her volcanoes — always *criminal* — plunge the soul into a perturbation which renders it capable of mighty deeds and stormy passions.

With this manner of depicting the world, Sade makes it quite impossible to view nature as a prop for sentimental effusions. At the same time, he shows us how its strength provokes and determines the course of events. But we can come back to this question later. In the meantime, having observed Sade's new view of nature — no longer seen as an aggregate of things, but as an aggregate of forces, and intensely active ones at that — one begins to conceive of Sade's intractable will to strip mankind of all its claims to be distinct from nature, to control or use nature at will. Sade's will is always constant: to extirpate lying, while trying to represent, as physically as possible, the nothingness of man relative to the universe:

> If there were not a single man left on earth, things would still continue as they are. . . . Nothing was created for us, wretched creatures that we are. . . . Nature could do without us as easily as she could do without ants or flies.

The same theme appears in *Aline et Valcour.* It is one Sade takes up time and again on the smallest pretext. This repetition would be incomprehensible if it did not lay the foundations for the paradoxical power that Sade simultaneously bestows on man: an enigma continually reabsorbed into the enigma of universal change, man according to Sade is capable of becoming everything that he is not.

This, indeed, is the terrible, disturbing work that Sade demands of the novelist when he designates him, in the *Reflections on the Novel,* as "a man of nature": "We want impulses from you, not rules; go beyond your plans, vary and increase them." No doubt this exhortation scarcely seems consistent with the idea Sade seems to have of a carefree human nature. But the contradiction appears only inasmuch as Sade's "man of nature" is the man who knows, or who has learned to know, just how indifferent nature is to human existence — with the corollary that man is not indifferent to nature. Accordingly, the novelist's first task should be to prove that if man, as a creature, is not important to nature, nature, for her part, is at work in every human cell. We must also notice how much power Sade bestows upon the novelist; it falls to him to change his contemporaries' relation to the world. Furthermore, to the bad faith of those sensitive souls who indulge in lyrical exploitations of nature, Sade opposes the brutality of a relationship based on transgression. The novelist must separate himself from nature in order to discover excess, which is all that links him to a nature herself essentially excessive. Nor does Sade content himself with recommending violence where nature is concerned. He uses the crude image of incestuous rape to explain what nature requires of the novelist, even if she expects nothing from him as a man. Indeed, nature has "created him to be her painter":

> . . . if he does not become his mother's lover as soon he is born, he should never write, for we shall not read him; but if he experiences this burning wish to depict everything, if he tremblingly probes into the bosom of Nature to search for his art and find his models therein, if he has the fever of talent and the enthusiasm of genius, then let him follow the hand that guides him: he has guessed what man is, and shall paint him.

I don't believe anyone has thought to compare these reflections with those expressed by Rimbaud, particularly in the poet's letters to Paul Demeny and certain parts of *Une Saison en enfer.* There is something so deeply analogous in what Rimbaud expects of the poet, that the two writers should be read in quick succession. We notice first the same scorn for the writer's profession, which corresponds to nothing in the intellectual drama that preoccupies them. As Rimbaud says: "The hand that holds the pen is no better than the hand that guides the plough. — What a century of hands! — I shall never have my hand." As Sade specifies further in his *Reflections on the Novel:*

> It's not worth taking up the pen: no one forced you into this profession; but if you undertake it, then do it well. Above all, do not adopt it as a means of salvation; your work would feel the effects of your own needs, you would infect it with your weakness; it would assume the pallid

air of hunger. Other professions are open to you; become a cobbler, and don't write any books. We shan't think any the less of you, and since you won't be boring us, we may even love you all the more.

This destroys the validity of any attempt at textual or literary interpretation, because writing, for both Rimbaud and Sade, is a matter of discovery: "Therefore it is nature one must capture when working in this genre, it is man's heart, the oddest of all her creations . . ." says Sade, while Rimbaud declares that, "The first object of study for anyone wishing to be a poet is his own knowledge, all of it; he seeks out his own soul, he inspects, tests and learns it." Sade goes on to say:

> One must see men of every nation if one is to know them well, and have become their victim if one is to understand their value; the hand of misfortune, in exalting the character of the person whom it crushes, puts him at a proper distance for observing men; he then sees them as a passenger perceives the waves break furiously upon the reef whereon the hurricane has cast him.

There again, Rimbaud remarks:

> Every form of love, suffering, or madness; the poet searches in himself, consumes every poison, retaining only essences. It is an ineffable torture, in which he needs all his faith, his superhuman strength; a torture in which he alone becomes the great invalid, the great criminal, the one accursed — the great Savant! For he has reached the *unknown!*

In my opinion, these similarities between Sade and Rimbaud cannot fail to disturb, especially the question of criminality, which both of them relate to knowledge. But is there any connection with what modernist pedantry, from Barthes to Marcel Hénaff, calls the "crime of writing"?

> The guile — or else the potency — of writing would be this: if the ultimate crime cannot be uttered, then one must make a permanent crime of utterance itself. If language is the form of law, if all sociality is constituted by it, if language is what this sociality produces in exchange, and watches with the greatest vigor, then the outrage inflicted

on language becomes the actual possibility of crime, its general matrix and pure model.

So one is informed by the pen of Marcel Hénaff in his essay, *Sade l'invention du corps libertin*. And why not? It's just that I would like to understand how this "outrage inflicted on language" can become the "pure model of crime," especially since Hénaff has just argued that:

> What Sade does not see is that language itself is the place of the forbidden, the absolute form of Law; but this is a revelation we owe Freud and Saussure. In the eighteenth century, people looked at language and read: Nature; in Discourse, only the Referent is meant.

Poor Freud! I should certainly like to hear his comments on how "people looked at language and read: Nature." But also, poor Sade, who is held hostage by a thought as hazy as it is contradictory. Indeed, if he does not know that "language itself is the stage of the forbidden," he cannot possibly be this criminal of writing that he is held to be.

It is interesting to see what manipulations this supposed unconsciousness of Sade has led to, when in reality his assertion that writers must "tell all" indicates a relationship with language that is far less innocent than our experts imply. For one has to be an expert, to extract a "crime of writing" from this "moral crime, to which one attains through writing," and which Juliette suggests to Clairwil in one of her friend's reveries:

> I should like . . . to find a crime with perpetual repercussions, which would continue even after I had ceased to act, so there would not be a single instant of my life, not even when I was asleep, when I would not be causing some sort of disorder, a disorder so extensive as to involve general corruption, or so absolute a disturbance that its effect would be prolonged even when my life had ceased.

One has to be an expert to substitute the idea of writing for that of moral science and totally exclude the real meaning of this desire for active corruption, expressed by Juliette's attractive friend. What's more, can Clairwil's dream so easily be sucked into the "telling all" of Sade? In any event, this maneuver serves only to strip both propositions of all sense. This sort of procedure is responsible for the enormous confusion of which Sade is a victim at the present time.

In wishing to "tell all," Sade does indeed confront the problem of all that cannot, will not, be uttered; of all that cannot, will not, be heard. Contrary to what some critics would have us think, this is not a literary problem, but an existential one. When he attacks the intolerable, the inconceivable, the unnamable — that is, everything that people cannot or will not tolerate, conceive or name — Sade is in no way concerned with the unnamable, the untellable, the unspeakable, which today's champions of writing all invoke, and which refer to the exclusively literary problem of the impossibility of telling. Not without reason, Marcel Hénaff quotes from Georges Bataille: "Violence carries in itself this disorderly negation, which puts an end to all possibility of discourse." But this is not at all Sade's problem; he has absolutely no difficulty in "telling," since all his problems start the minute that he "tells" what no one wants to hear. Even so, he says it.

Moreover, when as far as Marcel Hénaff is concerned, Sade's transgression is "of the order of *telling everything,* proving through literature that authorized language can say, materially, everything it must not say," one sees this misconstruction in its full enormity; one conceives, at the same time, what kind of negative relations these literary champions have with language. It is as if there existed an absolute "telling," short of which created beings are condemned to remain in insufficiency and want. Without insisting on the strong religious odor of this negative relationship with language, one can see it involves a problematic quite opposed to that of Sade. Sade does not want to prove that "authorized language can say, materially, everything it must not say." He has nothing to prove; all he wants is to tell everything, which is not the same at all. He wants to tell everything because he wants to know everything, just as Rimbaud does — not by violating language, but by inventing a language that is new.

In fact, Sade does not engage in any "crime of writing," but rather in an impressive flattening of language which has nothing literary about it. It corresponds exactly to the banquet in *The One Hundred and Twenty Days of Sodom,* and to the political, philosophical and amorous panorama of *Aline et Valcour,* in which Sade endeavors to put back into linguistic circulation all that is normally excluded. It follows that Sade attacks neither language nor what it may or may not "say, materially," but rather, the way it is used and

the ideological construction it serves. Thus, putting back into circulation terms that are excluded from the habitual course of language is inseparable from this flattening out. If, through functioning
from an ideological construct, with all its hierarchy of values, language becomes locked into a system of conventions, then Sade need
only bring all the words back into the same perspective — just as
he examines vice and virtue under the same light — for language
to be thoroughly shaken up again. The manuscript of *The One
Hundred and Twenty Days,* this famous roll of paper, clearly represents this flattening out. Thus, Sade unfurls language, stretching it
to the limit, exhausting all its possible meanings, to take the infinite
and terrible measurement of *what is.*

This, then, would be his real crime, certainly not a "crime of
writing," but a crime of thinking, of thought which rebels against
the laws of men. Even so, the term "crime" should be understood
in its strictest sense, not with that vague metaphysical exaltation of
today's knight errant of the referent, but more as Noirceuil puts
it, in a warning to Juliette:

> Be seated, Juliette, . . . I need to speak seriously on this
> matter, and if you are to understand me, I need your full
> attention.
>
> By crime is meant any categorical infringement, be it
> fortuitous or premeditated, of what men refer to as the
> law. As you see, this is yet another arbitrary and insignifi-
> cant word; for laws are relative to mores and climates.

Further on, he continues:

> There is nothing real, therefore, about crime; there is no
> veritable crime, no real way in which to violate a nature
> which is always on the move. . . . Laws are maintained
> through an absolutely equal mixture of what we term
> "crime" and "virtue;" nature is reborn through destruction
> and sustains herself through crime; in a word, death keeps
> her alive. A totally virtuous universe could not survive for
> even a minute; but the wise hand of nature creates order
> from disorder, and without disorder, would never accom-
> plish anything: such is the underlying equilibrium which
> maintains the stars in orbit, suspending them in vast areas
> of space, and causing them, periodically, to move.

This is precisely what Sade seeks and manages to say in wishing to "tell all." Can anyone imagine a project more radically opposed to that of Brecht, for example, whom Marcel Hénaff quotes in a footnote while developing the idea of writing as a crime, and who asks: "How can we obtain, we authors, a writing that kills?" Despite the fact that Kafka declares: "To write is to break rank with those who kill." How long, I wonder, will critics go on lying to us, attempting to persuade us that Sade and Brecht stand on the same side of the barricades? How much longer will they try to hide the fact that Brecht is on the side of the killers, with his ideological language that kills ideas just as it kills words, and words as it kills men? For if it is simply a matter of language, what on earth is Brecht doing — that bard of political virtue — if not cutting up, chewing and swallowing the facts, in order to impose his own false testimony and so exclude all other possible interpretations? What, indeed, is Brechtian distancing, if not an ideological distortion that blocks off every exit, petrifies action and coagulates the flow of language? But by the mere fact of examining what vice and virtue are, Sade, on the contrary, oversteps all ideological categories and at the same time enriches language, accelerating and freeing it, prompting us to reconsider men and things in the true, unlimited perspective of universal change.

This is why he requires the novelist to pay particular attention to change, in *Reflections on the Novel*:

> As fast as minds become corrupt and nations grow old, by virtue of the fact that nature is studied better, analyzed better, and that prejudices are overcome more frequently, so they should be made better known. This law holds true for all the arts; it is only through progress that they become perfect; they only reach the desired end through experiment. Doubtless, things should not have gone so far in those frightful times of ignorance when, bent beneath religious chains, people were put to death for wishing to appreciate such things, when the burning faggots of the Holy Inquisition became the prize of talent. But in our present state of things, we may always proceed from this principle: when man has tested the weight of his restraints; when he has looked boldly at the barriers and measured them with an audacious eye; when, following the example of the Titans, he has dared to raise his hand toward the heavens and, armed with his passions, as they are with the

lava of Vesuvius, he no longer fears to declare war on those who made him tremble in the past; when his very *deviations* seem no more than *errors* made legitimate by study — should he not then speak out with the same energy as he employs in his conduct?

As Rimbaud has said:

> I continue:
> The poet, then, is truly the thief of fire.
> He is responsible for humanity, even the animals: he must cause his inventions to be sensed, felt and heard; if what he brings back from *down there* has form, he gives form; if it is formless, he gives formlessness. A language must be found.

Finding a language: that is precisely where Sade succeeds. He smokes out its concrete aspects, giving rise to those inspirations so frequent in his letters: "As long as I'm not rehabilitated, there won't be a cat whipped in the provinces without someone saying: *It's the Marquis de Sade.*" To quote another example, he writes to his wife in July 1783: "You ride beautifully in the wrong direction, handle well, are strait in the gate and warm in the *rectum,* which means that we get on quite famously." Sade does not discover this language just by giving flesh to each idea — although he does this better than anyone — but he also uses every word in all its senses, so that its multiple meanings obliterate the idea behind the word and leave the concrete presence:

> Ignorant fools! Do you not see what I'm exposing here, and that, had you allowed me to continue, I was gently going to cause the story of destruction to flow out of that of construction, and that, by means of periods of calm, plump transitions and episodes cunningly sewn together, I was going to make a large part of the eloquence of Socrates shine beneath my quill? What good is it to interrupt me? And how do you expect me to resume?
>
> Well! Let us proceed directly to the point, since it is impossible with you to let forth spurts of wit, prove one has read Demosthenes, explicated Cicero and learned Vadé by heart! On then, to the point!
>
> *Trees cut down, and fruit-bearing trees at that!* Counsel,

you will find me rather hard, but misfortune does not soften one, quite the contrary.

In this dazzling letter addressed to Gaufridy on April 17, 1782, Sade is totally himself, particularly in the desperate flashes of humor he extracts from language, with its useless theatricality; humor appearing like unhoped-for fruit which despairs of plopping into nothingness. This kind of humor, indeed, is always borne by "trees cut down, and fruit-bearing trees at that," emerging from the same despair as Lichtenberg's "knife without a blade and with its handle missing." Herein lies the secret of the *presence* which Sade's language conveys. By eliminating all abstraction, which always threatens the singularity of people and things evoked, Sade succeeds in depicting them entirely. What more could be said about his miser, Du Harpin, who "only powders himself with grated walls," as Sade indicates in the notes for the first draft of *The Misfortunes of Virtue?* Or of the madness expressed by Vespoli, director of the prison of Salerno, when visited by Juliette and Clairwil:

> "Good God!" he exclaimed from time to time, "What joy it is to come inside a madman's bum! And I'm demented too, and doubly fucked, by God; I bugger madmen, I discharge in them, I turn giddy when I see them, and in the whole world I would fuck none but them."

Immediately after this, Clairwil stands up, flushed with an enthusiasm it is impossible not to imagine:

> "This spectacle arouses me," she told us, "do as I do, friends, and you, wicked man, have your jailers take off our dresses and lock us, naked, into cells; imagine we are madwomen, we'll initate them; you'll have us tied to the cross, on the side without spikes, your madmen can whip and bugger us all afterwards. . . ."

Then again, how can anyone not be convinced by Aline, or by Valcour, when he declares: "She is never as pretty at one moment as she becomes at the next"?

But above all, how can anyone not feel the presence of this thought as it takes shape? That, literally, is what Sade urges us to do when he disposes of bodies according to the dictates of desire, in such a way that its successive waves supplant the working of his theories. The resulting motion is organic, like the undertow of surf, and it expands in quite an inverse ratio to that overflowing which seems to characterize Rousseau's relationship with nature. Through his outpourings, Rousseau's sensitive man devotes himself to a rather limp conquest of nature, which he continues to perceive as something outside himself. Sade, on the other hand, causes the troubling reality of bodies to well up precisely when the greatest control has been attained (permitting a continuance of philosophical reasoning); he makes it spring from a nature which controls man at the deepest level, although man himself is utterly unaware of its laws.

It is hard to imagine two more contradictory procedures. Rousseau creates a lyrical impasse that effectively seals off the reality of the human heart and uses nature, when all is said and done, as sole prop for the "something" that results from this deliberate blindness — or at least from the remasking operation which his deism aids and abets. Sade, on the contrary, tracks down everything that is vague, indeterminate or absent — tracking it down everywhere and on every occasion — as a deficiency of being which must be resisted. One such example would be the matter of his detention, which is made more intolerable for being of uncertain duration: "This frightful uncertainty plunges me into a sadness that no words can convey." Another example concerns clear and unclear ways of saying things, a subject of frequent irritation with his wife:

> Does there exist anywhere an amphibology or a logograph resembling this one, and if so have you sufficiently warmed it in the forges of the infernal demon who gave you this inspiration? . . . Will this never end, then? And will it always be the same thing! To put it briefly, what do you mean to say in this sentence?

Sometimes, on the contrary, this deliberate tracking shows in the way of "telling everything" which eradicates the systems operating in licentious jokes and even in licentious behavior, both being equally dependent on the ambiguity of the non-said: " 'My dear brother,' said the prelate in a strangled voice, 'Your discourse smacks of sperm.' " or, to take another example: " 'Your Honor,' said the Bishop, 'Your voice has a certain interrupted quality which informs me that you're hard.' " Sade is, in fact, striving to make us hear this same voice loud and clear, strangled, interrupted and censured as it otherwise always is: " 'Come, come, my child,' he continued, 'Show me your buttocks, perhaps it will divert me.' " Sade introduces it into every domain, this voice which smacks of sperm, beginning with the psychological: " 'His soul is as hard as his bum is wide,' said Ferdinand, speaking of Francaville." There is also the domain of ethnography:

> "The Sybarites buggered dogs; the Egyptian women pros-
> tituted themselves to crocodiles, and American women to
> apes. Finally, it came to statues: everyone knows that a
> page of Louis XV was found discharging on the rear of
> Venus of the Lovely Buttocks," explained Noirceuil to
> Juliette.

And, of course the domain of philosophy:

> "By what authority do you control me?" Justine asked
> Bandole. "By this one," said Bandole, revealing his prick,
> "I'm hard and I want to fuck."
> "Can this appalling logic of the passions be related to
> humanity?. . ."
> "Here's a creature who can reason," said Bandole, pull-
> ing up his breeches; "Being accustomed to so very few of
> this species, I wish to chat with her."

Precisely by making this voice speak, the one that smacks of sperm, and by making us aware of the sperm behind the voice, that causes this voice to vibrate, Sade attains to the *integral literalness* which is the mark of his genius. Because of it, the sentence yields up every sense it can, just as the licentious picture is made to render all its hidden postures and the body all potential pleasures; just as thought is milked of every drop of sperm. It is a will to saturation inseparable in Sade from the consciousness of nothingness; insep-arable too, from the very simple system of communicating vessels to which his lucidity reduces the human condition. As he explains to Mademoiselle de Rousset on April 17, 1782:

> Man has tried vainly, has striven vainly to improve himself;
> there are always two fatal moments in the day which
> remind him, in spite of everything, of his sad bestial con-
> dition. . . . These two cruel moments are — forgive me
> these expressions, Mademoiselle, they are not noble, but
> they are true to life — these two appalling moments are,
> therefore, the moment when he must *be filled* and the
> moment when he must *evacuate*.

His lucidity is integral, and to escape from lying it demands integral literalness, as if the only way of capturing being is to assault deficiency.

To accomplish this task, Sade searches desperately and magnificently the concrete aspects of everything supposedly not concrete. We have already seen the materiality of language (and how pleased he was to get letters from Mademoiselle de Rousset, studded with Provençal expressions!), but there is also a materiality of feelings, of passions, of ideas, and of thought. All this explains his primordial hatred for God, who is the epitome of absence and deficiency, the ultimate chimera and phantom: as he announces in his poem *La Vérité:*

> What indeed is this execrable ghost,
> This good-for-nothing God, this frightful host,
> Whom nothing offers to our eyes or mind,
> Whom madmen fear and wise men mock in kind,
> Nowhere present to our senses, whom no one understands,
>
> . . .Vainly do I analyze this rogue on high,
> Vainly do I study him; my philosopher's eye
> Sees no other reason in your religions
> Than the foulest mess of contradictions
> Which does not bear examination.

Throughout his life, Sade was scandalized by this cult of absence, and devoted himself to pointing out what an aberration it was:

> If your hearts absolutely must adore something, let this adoration be offered to the palpable objects of their passions; something real will at least satisfy you in this natural homage. But what do you experience after two or three hours of divine mysticism? A cold void, an abominable void which, having provided nothing for your senses, necessarily leaves them in the same state as if you had been worshiping mere dreams and shadows!

That is what he was to write in *Fantômes,* some twenty years after *La Vérité;* it appeared among the literary notes of the *Cahiers personnels* between 1803 and 1804.

Astute observers have never failed to be astonished at the vehemence and constancy with which Sade rebels against something inexistent. The more perspicacious among them have even gone so far as to discern the beginnings of religious conscience in this blaspheming force. This remains to be proved, especially when one lends some attention to the paths which this religious consciousness might take, in *La Vérité* for example:

> As for me, I admit, so strongly do I hate,
> My horror is at once so just, and so great,
> That with pleasure, vile Deity, and in tranquillity,
> I would masturbate upon your divinity,
> Or even bugger you, if your tenuous existence
> Could present a bum to my incontinence.

I am quite aware of what miracles we may expect from sophistry and that its workings never cease to astonish; but isn't it more probable that the violence inherent in Sade's interminable "discourse against God" is directly proportionate to the ravages that Sade thinks his existence, monstrously conferred upon his inexistence, inflicts upon men's lives?

> Chimerical and vain being, whose mere name has caused more blood to spill upon the surface of the earth than any political war will ever shed, may you return to the nothingness whence the deluded hopes of men and their ridiculous terror regrettably extracted you!

Fantômes, this text written in Sade's final years, attests to the fury with which he sought throughout his existence to "eradicate" from men's hearts this "execrable runt." He perseveres in this task because he sees that God's revolting lack of being gives rise to a deficiency of human being that is more revolting still. Not only does God not exist, but the mere idea of his existence prevents men from existing, as Madame Delbène explains to a very young Juliette:

> This very idea is responsible for the bitterest misfortunes in men's lives; it constrains them to renounce life's sweetest pleasures, because they have such fear of displeasing this disgusting fruit of their delirious imaginings. Therefore, my dear friend, you must free yourself as rapidly as possible of the terrors inspired by this phantom.

Hence the vital necessity Sade feels of continuing to denounce this "vain divinity" who, not content with depriving men of what is best in their lives, divests those lives forever of all sense. Addressing his newly republican compatriots, Sade does not miss an opportunity to remind them of the principle of atheism:

> Make one more effort; since you are striving to destroy every possible prejudice, allow none to remain, if all it takes is one to bring back all the rest. We may be all the more certain that they will indeed return, if the one you leave alive positively fosters all the others!

Diverging at this point from a logical refutation of God's existence, Sade is the first to express a theme which has become central to modern atheism. When he asserts that "God is the one mistake I cannot pardon man," it is because he essentially sees God as the "eternal thief of energy" whom Rimbaud will denounce scarcely a century later. It is not, therefore, surprising to find Nietzsche using almost the same argument in the *Twilight of the Gods* when developing his thesis of "imaginary causes." Sade has already denounced the facility with which God "harks back to an imaginary origin which neither explains nor helps anything." *(Frenchmen, another effort . . .)* Nor are we surprised to find in *The Antichrist* Nietzsche, who sees in the "Christian conception" a "God who has degenerated into the antithesis of life," and blames mankind for "Having, with God, deified Nothingness and sanctified man's aspiration to the Void!"

Such disturbing similarities deserve a comparative study of their own. All coincidence apart, it should reveal a violently physical dimension to Sade's struggle which Nietzsche's "imprecations against Christianity" seem to me to lack, their grandeur being apparent rather in the abstract lyricism of his metaphysical rage. And yet, "in every phrase he utters" Nietzsche does not fail to accuse every theologian, every priest, every pope of deceiving himself and others, just as Sade devotes himself to tracking down imposture and impostors — everything and everyone who profits from the formidable diversion of energy accomplished in God's name. To quote again from *Fantômes:*

> Weak, absurd mortals, blinded by error and fanaticism, cast off these dangerous illusions wherein you are maintained by tonsured superstition, consider what powerful interest it has in offering you a God, reflect upon the powerful hold such lies have given it over your possessions and your minds, and you will see that knaves of this sort

could only herald a chimera; and, conversely, that so degrading a ghost could only be heralded by rogues.

Nonetheless, while engaging in his innumerable attacks on the
"tonsured rabble," Sade never stops searching for the cause of such
aberrations in mankind. Each diatribe progressively becomes a pretext for wondering why man allows himself to be duped so easily,
or more exactly, why he so strongly wishes to be duped:

> How, you will ask, was it possible to persuade reasonable
> beings that the most difficult thing to understand was the
> most essential one for them? It's because they were terri-
> fied; because, when one is afraid, one cannot think; be-
> cause, they were told above all to mistrust their reason and
> because, when the brain is troubled, one believes everything
> and analyzes nothing. Ignorance and fear, you will say again
> to them, those are the twin bases of all religions. The
> uncertainty in which man finds himself with respect to his
> God is precisely what attaches him to his religion. Man is
> afraid in the shadows, morally as well as physically; fright
> becomes habitual in him and changes into need: he would
> think something was missing if he no longer had anything
> to be afraid of or to hope for.

Here, indeed, is that monster of monstrosities that Sade analyzes
in *Frenchmen, another effort* . . . : the fear that something is lacking
giving rise to the tyranny of lack. Here, too, we find the difference
between Nietzsche and Sade. The former seeks to determine the
symbols of lack through the refusal of knowledge, self-abasement,
moral and intellectual cowardice — forms of behavior which link
it to the notion of decadence. For his part, Sade does not determine
anything and does not judge. Instead, he frenziedly accumulates the
symbols of lack, discovering in them the fraudulent mechanism
whose most perfect product is certainly the notion of God, although
this is but one of the forms taken by a system of general deceit.

All the Christian virtues Nietzsche will late denounce as willful
self-deception are examined one by one in the different stories
which comprise *Justine*. Modesty, the horror of evil, piety, good
deeds, prudence, love of good and truth — these qualities determine
Justine's succession of adventures, adventures serving to reveal the
deception that such virtues represent materially. I say, materially,
because Sade has chosen Justine as the most innocent being possible, in order to try out on her virginity the values proclaimed by

our world, and examine what sort of material trace these virtues leave upon the whiteness of her innocence.

How does this work out? From the point of view of the user — Justine — the results are catastrophic. No sooner does she attempt to put into practice even one of these virtues than it unfailingly produces an effect quite opposite to what it is supposed to do. Consider, for example, what Sade has planned under the heading "Pity," in the notebook that contains an early sketch of *Justine, or the Misfortunes of Virtue:*

> A young man of her condition falls in love with her and marries her, then himself falls upon hard times; she works night and day to ease his wretched state and the monster sells her to an old lecher who rapes her, and thus she is doubly punished for taking pity on her husband.

The heading "Prudence" scarcely fares better:

> She seeks her fortune once again near a gushing river; she sees two ways of crossing, one involving an extremely dangerous boat, the other being a bridge; out of prudence she walks over the bridge, which collapses while she's on it.

So it continues with all the socially respected values which Sade enumerates here. Contrary to what Justine and similarly deluded women might think when faced with such a chain of mishaps, the system functions very smoothly, forcibly confronting us with the reality each virtue tries to negate — the reality of bodies. Unlike Nietzsche, who hurls a system of countervalues in the face of Christian values, Sade is not content to set blasphemy against piety — as certain critics have eagerly believed — immodesty against modesty, or vice against virtue. . . . What he shows us in each case is an idea vanquished by the material reality it attempted to deny. The funniest and most striking example, in all senses of the word, is the fifth item in this rough draft:

> *Piety.* Free again, she continues on her way and goes into a church to hear mass, which she has not heard for some time; the vault collapses at her feet, and she is seriously injured by a stone.

What Sade dramatizes here is the intolerable deceitfulness of ideas without bodies, the intolerable deceitfulness of any system which denies human and material reality. The adventures of Justine could also be read as the story of the body's dreadful vengeance, inscribed in Justine's life despite her reluctance: the expression "over her dead body," indeed, has never received such literal illustration. Moreover, in functioning so well *a contrario,* all these virtues that Justine proclaims actually reveal their affiliation with a system entirely different from the soothing values of ordinary morality. And this is true to the extent that:

> . . . there is so great a distance between the way one lives and the way one ought to live, that he who abandons what is done in favor of what ought to be done will sooner learn the means of his own undoing than his own preservation; for whoever would profess himself entirely a good man cannot avoid destruction, among so many others who are wicked.

This quotation is not from *Justine,* nor any of its commentaries; it is one of the key passages in Machiavelli's *The Prince,* which Sade actually refers to in *Juliette.* No one will be particularly surprised by this new coincidence when Machiavelli, revealing that part played by self-interest in human comportment, is the first to have shown us the materiality of this behavior. Even so, the similarity seems to me far more deeply woven than those which I have mentioned up to now. Perhaps the day will come when *Justine* is viewed as an exact negative of *The Prince.* This is why it is so surprising that critics have carefully refrained from making any connection between Sade and Machiavelli, when we know from Madame de Sade's letter of May 20 that Sade read *The Prince* as early as 1780. Borrowings from Machiavelli are frequent in his works, and are not just limited to the five or six quotations appearing in *Justine* and *Juliette;* they attest on the contrary to a profound knowledge of the Italian thinker.

We can begin with the essential fact that Sade, just like Machiavelli, is always more concerned with "pursuing the material truth of a thing than its imagination," by which is meant, the image or idea men have of it. What else is Sade looking for, if not this "material truth," even if he looks for it beyond the limits of the historical materialism where Machiavelli finds it? The resemblance may go even further. Doesn't Sade want to know the "material truth" of his situation, when he harasses his correspondents as to the terms of his various detentions, declaring himself ready to hear the worst, rather than have everyone continue to "amuse" him? Isn't he concerned with the same "material truth" when he asks, with respect to the immortality of the soul: "But can the desire for a chimera ever become the incontrovertible proof of the reality of that chimera?" Or when he asks, also in *The New Justine:* "If we can only acquire ideas through material substances, how can we suppose that the cause of our ideas may be immaterial?" Isn't this still a matter of "material truth," when, in both his life and thought, Sade's principal concern is not to be deceived? When he does his utmost to ensure that everybody else refuses to be deceived, too?

In view of this, Jean Paulhan's sprightly thesis, according to which Sade is purely and simply Justine, does not hold up. It holds up even less after re-examination of the texts, that is, letters and the various novels. For even before becoming a victim, Justine is dupe to every stereotypical idea and prejudice, and proud of being so. But what is more, she cheats, deceiving herself and others: to avoid lying, she betrays; pious, she gets raped by a monk; virtuous, she falls in love with a poisoner. . . . Entirely unlike Sade, who sought throughout his life the *verità effettuale* of our criminality and opposed capital punishment in the middle of the Terror, at considerable risk to his own head. As he writes to Gaufridy: "They wanted to make me commit something inhuman. I would not." Unlike Justine, Sade finds his dignity precisely in not deceiving others, as he informs his wife on February 17, 1779:

> I add and certify today, after two years of this horrible situation, that I feel a thousand times worse than I did when I arrived, that my temper has become bitter and cantankerous here, my blood boils a thousand times more easily, my head is a thousand times worse — in a word, I shall have to go and live in a wood when I get out, for my present condition would make it utterly impossible to go back to living among men!

Unlike Justine, Sade goes on to add, in the same letter:

> *Others were deceived by them,* you tell me, *and did not say a word. . . .* They are animals, and they are imbeciles; if they had spoken, if they had revealed the horrors and shameful deeds of which they have been victims, the King would have been informed; he is just man and would never have permitted it; those rogues enjoy impunity precisely on account of that silence.

Quite unlike Justine, Sade explains to Madame de Montreuil, as early as March 13, 1777:

> For some time, Madame, I have been your victim; but do not think you can deceive me too. It is sometimes interesting to be a victim, always humiliating to be deceived, and I flatter myself on being as shrewd as you are false.

After reading that it is difficult to take seriously, even for a second, the paradox advanced by Jean Paulhan in his famous preface to *Justine,* in which he suggests that Sade, tired of his freedom, behaved in such a manner as to ensure reincarceration for the last fourteen years of his life:

> The lover of liberty goes back to prison. Thoroughly disgusted.
> Yes, the explanation is a plausible one. All the same, I can't say it enchants me.

So, at any rate, concludes Paulhan. Literature is certainly one big happy family, to which Sade will never belong.

It is difficult, too, to believe that none of Sade's commentators have read Machavelli. But then, why have none of them seen fit to point out the analogous procedures of Sade and Machiavelli, both preoccupied — and for the same reason as Spinoza in his *Ethics* — with distancing themselves from normative thinking, in order to conceive "human deeds and appetites the same way as if one were dealing with lines, perspectives or bodies." I myself have no hesitation in seeing this critical omission as an unconscious censoring of Sade's thought, intended to prevent it from uncovering the fallacy of bodiless ideas.

Why then attribute to Sade, as critics habitually do, certain ideas of Machiavelli? I am thinking particularly of his ideas on energy as a means of correcting the inequities of birth, or on how to reach the summit of the social hierarchy and on the extreme vigilance needed to remain there, whether one has reached this pinnacle by chance or a persistent effort of the will. These are Machiavelli's chief ideas, not secondary considerations which one might easily find passed on from one author to another. In that case, why not recognize the energy Sade's heroes all invoke as an exact translation of Machiavelli's *virtù*? Juliette's downfall, a consequence of her not being sufficiently energetic to poison all of France, as Saint-Fond had wished, is typically Machiavellian. Why then does no one notice this? The omission must surely be intended to confine Sade's thinking to a purely erotic realm, whereas he strives, on the contrary, to show the reality of desire and the body beneath all human conduct.

More seriously, in obscuring this connection, critics fail to see how magisterially Sade intervenes with respect to that strange trans-mutation of passions into simple self-interest which the eighteenth century is in the process of perfecting, and whose progress Albert O. Hirschman has traced in his remarkable study *Les Passion et les intérêts* (P.U.F., Paris, 1980.) For people were actually beginning to suppose — unlike Machiavelli, who thought all passions could be governed — that only a few of them are capable of serving the public good and that all the rest must be severely tamed. Is this a change of perspective, or just of mentality? Certainly both, for the world is in the process of changing: the notion of self-interest, like the society in which it takes root, is assuming a progressively more economic coloration. Gradually the observation of passions is obey-ing this change of perspective, becoming more and more selective in its search for peaceful and lucrative passions, capable of coun-terbalancing and neutralizing the more dangerous ones. There re-sults a considerable shrinking of the horizon in the economic field, preventing political reflection from attaining the scope it has known with Machiavelli or even Montesquieu, when he affirms, for exam-ple, in *The Spirit of the Laws:*

> And it is fortunate for men to be in a situation where, even if their passions prompt them to be wicked, it is nonetheless in their interest not to be.

Finally, the very fact of thus wishing to subordinate selfish pas-sions to sociable ones, and sociable ones to the general interest, allows the establishment — in terms of the economic axis which henceforth runs right through society — of a hierarchy of passions that founds a new social morality (as much the basis of Rousseau's social contract as of Holbach's social pact), just at the point where Machiavelli's absolute social pragmatism had offered the inestimable advantage of excluding any idea of good and evil. This constitutes a veritable moralization of cynicism via the field of economics, and could well be seen as a perfect example of what Sade never ceases to rebel against. For here begins a spectacular dematerialization of human conduct, with effects that we still feel today. At first, the notion of interest, vague as it is, and suggesting different points of social insertion for the various passions, simply conjures up the singular dynamics of an individual or a state. There is nothing moral about this, just an intriguing conjunction of reason and passions enabling a person to find an effective way of asserting his individual being. Interest then manifests itself as a sign of constancy in change, and the forms it assumes are all the same: wealth, power, influence. Except that henceforth, ever greater effort will be made to adapt this key to social goals — the key of self-interest, which helps in deciphering individual conduct through being at the origin of its dynamics. The notion of interest then gradually loses all individual content, until the point is reached where interests and passions are set against each other. This opposition provides the basis for the new ethics by which we still live, good being on the side of the many, and evil on the side of eccentric individual passions.

Everything suggests that, thanks to this development, money became the vehicle by which particular interests moved towards the general interest, and acquired, historically, the dignity it did not formerly possess. The moralization of the idea of interest goes hand in hand with that of money. And in both cases, it is remarkable that this moralization is accomplished at the cost of a most deceptive dematerialization. Now, this is precisely what Sade shows us — and he is absolutely the only person to do so. Completely at odds, yet again, with his time, his genius will plan that stinging counterattack of materiality which constitutes *Justine,* in which each moral value is in turn negated by a concrete reality — just at a time when the bourgeoisie, gaining power through money, is trying morally to justify its material power and the means of acquiring it, precisely through this notion of interest. One might even wonder if the three successive rewritings of the story of *Justine,* each one being more violent than the one before, are not dictated by a growing need to answer the intensive moralization engaged in by the moneyed bourgeoisie, and which reaches its dual peak in weepy sensibility and revolutionary virtue. This moralization is accomplished at the cost of a systematic dematerialization of the body. From this point of view, the orthodox art of the revolutionary era can be said to anticipate the future horrors of socialist realism. Whether one is viewing the bundle of tetanized Horatian muscles which qDavid's painting amounts to, or the petrified gestures characteristic of so-cialist realism — emprisoning its heroes in a mortal statuesque heaviness — one encounters the same violence: a violence perpetrated against the individual body to transform it into anonymous human material for nourishing the ideological machine. From Greuze to David, from the *Fils naturel* to *La Marseillaise* or the Feast of the Supreme Being, one finds the same disembodied moralism, a moralism of monstrosity which first pulverizes individual bodies in order to affirm itself. This bears upon the deep significance of the Revolution of 1789 in that the pathos of revolutionary representation, its principles and sentimentality, is determined by that most efficient of machines for obliterating bodily reality: the guillotine. The various, aggravated stories of *Justine* should also be viewed in this white light of triumphal abstraction, triumphal to the point where it entirely effaces the reality of bodies and cheerfully engenders the most moral of killing machines.

From one *Justine* to another, in fact, Sade always shows us the same body, mutilated by ideology; but in each successive version, that body's integrity is more severely damaged. In his *La Philosophie dans le pressoir,* (Paris: Grasset, 1976) Philippe Roger devotes attention to the three different paths taken by the flash of lightning which ends Justine's life. Thus, in *The Calamities of Virtue (Les Infortunes de la vertu)* of 1788:

> The thunderbolt had entered through the right breast, scorched the bosom, and emerged through her mouth, disfiguring her face so badly she was horrifying to behold.

Bosom, mouth, face: the attributes of traditional femininity are obliterated here. In *The Misfortunes of Virtue* of 1791:

> . . . the thunderbolt had entered through the right breast; having consumed her face and bosom, it emerged through the center of the belly.

Bosom, face, belly: this is a very real woman who gets felled. In the final version of 1797: "The lightning, having entered through the mouth, had emerged through the vagina." Vagina, mouth: in this case, the sexed body is what gets destroyed, run clearly through by lightning. One cannot help but see that it is lightning which sexualizes this body, spectacularly linking the mouth with the vagina. By means of this obscene shortcut, nature takes control of the outrage, revealing what Justine denies: a gaping sex, from head to foot. At this point, Justine is completely violated by her own *verità effettuale.* For in Sade, outrage always occurs when the concrete reality of bodies intervenes, demolishing the fallacy of ideas which have no bodies. If one remembers the death of Don Juan, who is also struck down, but by powers divine, one can appreciate the incredible audacity Sade shows in thus reappropriating lightning, causing it to boomerang against any transcendental force. Justine's death is surely the best possible vengeance for the fate of Don Juan, especially when Sade tells us:

> Our four libertines surround the body; and although it is entirely disfigured, the scoundrels still conceive appalling designs upon the bloody remains of the unfortunate Justine. They remove her clothes; Juliette shamelessly excites them. The lightning, having entered through the mouth, had emerged through the vagina: appalling jokes are made about the route taken by this fire bolt from above.
>
> "People are quite right in praising God," says Noirceuil; "See what decency he shows: he has respected the bum. It's still beautiful, this sublimest of bottoms, the cause of such expenditure of sperm! Doesn't it tempt you at all, Chabert?"
>
> And the wicked priest responds by penetrating this inanimate mass right up to his balls.

One outrage succeeds another, turning this scene into the most perfect embodiment of violations Don Juan could ever have imagined. We see outrages of sexualization committed to the utmost limit of all that had opposed it, to the point where death itself resexes Justine. This is perhaps the worst outrage of all: once dead, the body finally reclaims its rights. But in all this Sade is only showing us what we are. Blasphemy and outrage are duties that he never shrinks from, availing himself of any pretext for teaching people to avoid deception, so numerous are the occasions when deception may prevail.

From this point of view, too, *The Story of Juliette* may be read as the reconquest of all that Justine loses, at least to the extent that *The Story of Juliette* constitutes the first attempt of any consequence to set self-interest toppling in its own sphere of passions. But also, the first attempt to define the vague notion which moralists, economists and philosophers of that time saw as the driving force for all human conduct, and which they sought to socialize. By putting himself once again at a magisterial distance from his era, Sade begins a revolution in the history of passions: *The Story of Juliette* is also the story of an individual renewal of the idea of interest, which Sade transfers from the field of economics into the field of eroticism. Freed of any moral repercussions, this notion of interest will disturb the erotic field by revealing its excesses. For in Sade, there are neither ideas without bodies nor bodies without ideas.

Part Three

CHAPTER SEVEN

TECHNIQUE IN THE BOUDOIR

There is another profound link between Sade and Machiavelli: their common genius for landscape. On August 12, 1760, the young Marquis, then aged twenty, and with his own command, writes to his father from the camp at Obertistein:

> I ride very often to examine the enemy's position and our own. We need only be encamped for three days, and I know where the smallest ravine is, as well as the Field-Marshall.

For his part, Machiavelli advises the prince to go hunting often; it is a means, he says, of

> . . . learning the lay of the land, knowing how the mountains rise, the issue of the valleys and the extent of the plains, of knowing how the rivers and the marshes lie; one must pay great attention to this.

The similarity in their behavior is of more than passing interest. In both cases, one perceives the same necessity for knowing places as thoroughly as men. Since neither Sade nor Machiavelli treats himself to words, preferring things, it may be useful to look closely at the influence this "knowledge and practice of landscape" exercised on their thinking.

In my opinion, Jean Giono's introduction to the complete works of Machiavelli (Paris: Gallimard, Pléiade, 1952) draws its beauty and its considerable accuracy from showing us the importance nature held for the author of *The Prince*. Giono begins by showing us how different Machiavelli is from Hobbes, "who will discuss man and his soul without ever once pronouncing the word *rain*." Could not one say as much for Sade? Giono continues:

> Often, when speaking of a revolt, a conspiracy, a battle, a barricade, some cavalry struggling to emerge from heavy ground . . . Machiavelli will say: "Night, rain, mud, marshes, wind, copses, bridge, sunshine, plain," as if the aspect of the landscape leaps out at him in bits and pieces, through history and politics.

Sade, too, when speaking of a vice, a passion, or a destiny will often say, "night, storm, ravine, forest, rocks, lightning." Of course, it isn't the same landscape: Machiavelli addresses a nature whose orchards, vines and fields all indicate man's presence, whereas Sade and his heroes always ride towards a nature void of man. But Sade and Machiavelli are both capable of seeing that the sky can suddenly grow dark, that the wind can change direction, that a bird has flown off over on the left, or that the silent countryside takes on the hues of murder. It is probably because they have the same way of seeing that they both consider men with so much rigor.

Nonetheless, this view of nature is not at all the one habitually held by the moralists to whom Sade and Machiavelli are sometimes compared, though without at the same time being compared to each other. Indeed, moralistic thinking would seem to exclude exterior reality by its very principle, since it seems to see human nature as comprising all of nature. It would be too simple, however, to view this as myopia relating from overspecialized observation. More likely, a feeling of man's radical strangeness in the world, reinforcing an incontestably anthropocentrist will, contributed to this deliberate ignorance of the remainder of the universe. It was a weakness, or a luxury, which Machiavelli could not allow himself. For Machiavelli, who did not believe in heaven, studied men's movements here on earth, where everything becomes important as soon as no other theatre of activity exists. But, then, why does Sade view nature the same way, more than two centuries later, believing neither in man nor in God, and having nothing either to gain or to lose? Why, all by himself, does he maintain this steady, separate gaze upon the unforgettable landscapes produced by natural efficiency, in the middle of the eighteenth century, when people are indeed turning from the psychological abstractions of the moralists, but only to plunge into countrysides that correspond to outbursts of emotion?

Just like Machiavelli, who understood the importance of weather and the seasons in political affairs, Sade remarks on the morning of the fourteenth day of *The One Hundred and Twenty Days of Sodom:*

> It was noticed on that morning that the weather was becoming even more favorable to the shameful projects of our libertines, screening them, even better than did their precautions, from the eyes of the universe. There had fallen an appalling quantity of snow.

From Sade too, nature is seen as the only theatre of activity; but a theatre whose every element may suddenly assume a decisive importance in the drama being played. Consider how lightning affects the destiny of Justine; consider the role played by forests, caves, paths and storms . . . which quite literally become the mainsprings of the action. For when did a storm ever acquire the importance that it has for Juliette and her companions?

> They waited for a stormy day, and came to fetch me in a gondola, just as flashes of lightning were streaking through the heavens. We reached the open sea; the storm broke, and thunderclaps were heard.
>
> "Come on," exclaimed these mischievous girls. "The moment has arrived to masturbate; let us lose our juices while braving the thunderbolts."

For that matter, when did the night ever inflame someone's imagination as it does here:

> Night had fallen. The silence of the woods, the darkness which enveloped them, all combined to exacerbate desires he now saw he could satisfy. While growing hard the rake conjured up lascivious memories of the delightful young person's charms, recalling those which chance or her deception had hitherto masked from him. He no longer contained himself.

Who, one might ask, is Justine's aggressor here, the night or the rake? This is an example of Sade's inventiveness when compared to Machiavelli, in whose work nature appears as the perfect materialization of chance in the physics of confrontation. But also, when compared to his contemporaries for whom, as we have seen, any natural setting becomes the virtual container of their sentimental outpourings. For this steady gaze is as strange today as it was in the eighteenth century, or as it might have been in the sixteenth century, in that no traces either of sentimentality or of strategy help constitute the Sadian landscape. This is for the very simple reason that Sade is the first, if not the only, author to have seriously conceived of a universe without God, and never to have forgotten it: "Mankind," he writes, "could totally annihilate his species without altering the universe in any way at all."

We can readily imagine that there results from this a revolution in the way things are seen. It is harder to conceive what flaws this revolution reveals in the order of representation. But before pursuing it, I shall emphasize in passing the extreme coherence of Sade's thought. This concept of the universe without mankind results directly from his atheism. Once God seems nothing more than a projection of man's notion of himself and of his anthropocentrism, the disappearance of this chimera leads to a reconsideration of the central position man has usurped in the universe. This is exactly what atheistic thinking does not do, falling back into an ideological mire for want of Sade's stark gaze — a unique gaze of unbelief pushed to the point of lyricism.

From the universe without man to man thrust into the indifferent momentum of matter, there results a spectacular autonomy of elements brought face to face. In Sade, the accidents of landscape certainly rival human characters we meet. The volcano of Pietra-Mala, which Juliette visits, is a neighbor worthy of the giant Minski; they could vie in immensity. And Sade carries this equivalence between human conduct and natural phenomena so far that his characters — unlike ordinary men who try to identify with their peers — model themselves on lightning, volcanoes and earthquakes. . . . Which are successive creations of a perpetual mutation, some disappearing into others, vicissitudes of matter that "merely changes form." In this connection, I recall the famous confidence uttered by the monk Jérôme in *The New Justine:* "One day, observing Mount Etna as it was vomiting flames, I wanted to become the celebrated volcano." Judging by the evidence, Sade considers the machinations of man and nature with the same cold, but passionate eye.

He goes about representing these machinations by setting up a formidable imaginary machine. I use the word *machine* in all the senses it possessed in the eighteenth century, distributed according to three semantic principles:

— the deposition of natural or unnatural means with a view to obtaining a result. Organism;

— an instrument serving to transform a natural force;

— a means of action. An invention, ruse or illusion.

For if Machiavelli turns landscape into one of the elements of the *war machine* he is constructing, Sade scarcely proceeds any differently, combining natural forces into a system of representation which will function as a *theatrical machine*. By this I mean, as an ensemble where everything is representative, people and places alike, objects and words, even Aline's little spaniel, Folichon:

> . . . a spaniel of the rarest kind, which Valcour had given to Aline. He had trained it to take his mistress love letters, concealed in a seed-cake: Aline would receive one and give the dog another cake, also filled with a letter which the spaniel then carried to his master just as faithfully. They wrote to each other in this way for two years, concealing this innocent deception by the sobriety and cunning of the little dog, who fetched and carried in this manner, without ever damaging an object which must certainly have tempted his greed.

The apparently harmless nature of this stratagem paradoxically attests to the extreme concern with efficacity which governs the construction of the Sadian machine. For psychological observations become useless when a little dog — but also the shape of a sex, a piece of clothing or furniture, a blasphemy, a sexual obsession, a storm, a philosophical dissertation — can be made to function as a cog in the mechanism of human behavior: the "assemblage of movements" which constitute life, according to Sade. It scarcely matters that he hesitates, like most minds of his time, between a chemical interpretation of these movements ("the principle of life is but the result of four elements," the Pope declares to Juliette), or an electrical one (" 'Animal spirits' is the name given this electric fluid which circulates in our nerve cavities; there is not one of our sensations which is not caused by a disturbance in this fluid," as someone states in *Aline et Valcour*).

Sade's originality lies in his having used materialism's concern with schematization as a principle for representing the world; a principle as manifest in La Mettrie's *man-machine* as in d'Holbach's cherished notion of the giant mechanism of the universe. It was his genius to make this image of the machine coincide with the philosophical weapon which the concept of the machine had in other respects become, serving to reveal the machinations of social and religious authority. As a result of this philosophical *bricolage,* so unique in its time, Sade succeeds in constructing the optical machine we are familiar with, allowing him to wreak havoc with existing perspectives.

In the first place, one must keep in mind what a weapon the concept of the machine has then constituted, for about a century, in philosophical combat. Just at the moment when the machine gives access to the material world, thereby becoming both a powerful instrument and an instrument of ruling power, intellectual contestation takes hold of it and uses it to make manifest the material reality of everything which, in man, is supposed to remain immaterial. From there it goes on to reveal what hidden strategies of the human heart this supposed immateriality serves to conceal. Sade, too, possesses this reductive concern, and one can see him quickly assimilating the technique which corresponds to it, as an indispensable preliminary to his plan for studying the human heart. The gaiety of the *Dialogue between a Priest and a Dying Man* owes much to this technique of ideological scouring by means of brutal simplification. We can see it operating when a vault collapses on the pious Justine; when, having been honest, courageous and unselfish way beyond the call of duty, she ends up being arrested as a thief. As early as *The Misfortunes of Virtue,* the systemization of this reductive concern determines the mechanics of the adventures of Justine. But this systematization is accomplished — as is always the case in Sade — by a passage into literalness which then asserts itself as a brutal objectification. Each time this occurs, it marks the point of rupture with his contemporaries. Such is the case with his use of lightning in the killing of Justine: no atheist of that time would or could have wanted to justify it. Sade goes further than the others in this application of this reductive mechanism, even if the Sadian machinery sometimes seems very sophisticated. Its sophistication is linked to the sophistication of the human heart, which is the subject on which Sade strives to operate this radical reduction. In fact, nothing could be simpler than Sadian mechanics, modeled on the workings of the universe, which drag everything along to its eventual void.

From this, we can see that Sade's genius meets his contemporaries just where they lose control of their thinking, at the point where it catches fire and ignites, in the darkness which surrounds the scene of the Enlightenment, a most disturbing hotbed of subversion. Thus, it is quite possible that the reductive machine may have played a decisive role in the epistemological rupture spotted by Michel Foucault at the end of the eighteenth century in Europe. If the machine functions primarily as a materialization of movement and the chain of causes and effects, couldn't this be why we are increasingly tempted to abandon the representation of evidence, leaving visible forms behind as we plunge into the heart of things, towards their organizing principle?

But there again, with the figure of God becoming ever more blurred, faced with an invisibility now turning into absence, wouldn't people be impelled to seek out the reality of those mechanisms behind the working of the world? No one has yet measured the degree of skepticism inherent in the concept of a God who is a sort of universal watchmaker. The mere idea of demonstrating a mechanical organization mortgages the concept of God, even if this vision of the world only accounts for the organization of what is visible and seems to oppose, in its reassuring distribution of forms and forces, the vertical momentum so disturbing to the thought of the time. For this vertical impulse drags it irresistibly towards that inner and paradoxical space which determines and foments the very essence of our reality. Even so, as early as 1725, in his *Discours sur les motifs qui doivent nous encourager aux sciences (Discourse on the Reasons for our Studying the Sciences),* Montesquieu explains the superiority of great nations over the primitive peoples by the fact that: "The effects of nature are only a consequence of laws and the communications of movement." Relying on the image of the machine, this encomium throws light on the machine's contradictory power of materializing an abstraction which itself establishes the materiality of beings and things. This is a fact without precedent in the history of representation: here is an object over which the square dance carried on by proper and figurative meanings will have no influence at all. Moreover, they will be able to give only the most deceptive idea of it, since the image of the machine not only represents a functioning, but also suggests the principle of functioning as a mode of representation. And so, at a time when the sky is growing empty, when the classical system of representation is sinking behind the horizon with the idea of God, the eighteenth century lets itself be flabbergasted by the emergence of the machine as a model of representation which installs itself in front of the stage and sends thought back into the depths.

First of all, scientific thinking was fascinated by a mode of representation capable for the first time of grasping the decisive articulations of time and space as they occur in every phenomenon. It therefore embarked on an immense reflection as to its past conduct, with effects still felt today, since it began at this point to wonder as much about its limitations as its proper functioning. And it is astonishing that Sade, as early as 1782, and from the depths of his solitude, instinctively finds the energy to carry out this reversal of perspective. In his *Etrennes philosophiques* to Mademoiselle de Rousset, we can see how this reductive concern prompts his endless inquiry: "You want to analyze the laws of nature, and your own heart, where nature is imprinted, is itself an enigma you cannot hope to resolve!" Sade is already conscious that "There never having been a creation, and nature being everlasting, impulse is eternal as long as there are people," as he will put it fifteen years later in *Juliette*. It is then equally stupefying to see him engaging in this real and definitive desertion of classical order — this alone being a mode of representation prefiguring those of the modern era — when this immense detour of thought returning to its origin is brusquely halted wherever its developments are capable of threatening the integrity of the human subject.

It is as if the death of God and its unforeseeable consequences in the order of changes were only too sufficient. As if in order to mitigate them, man's best bet was to slip into the place God had vacated and become a sort of metaphysical intermediary, declaring himself ready to disappear, but at the same time doing all he could to stay there, until in the end he puffed up into an ideological being, a capitalized creature: Man. It is a usurped place and an illusory one, but it remains privileged, because it stays immobile in a world often described as being in perpetual agitation. The only urgent consideration is to stay there, in order to avoid being definitively swept away in the universal tide whose inner rumble will cause such constant alarm to western man. It is equally important to do everything possible to furnish and consolidate this position of withdrawal. In the end the only way of regaining control is to submit to the thing which made one lose it: the machine.

Once again, the model of the machine will play its part in the game which is played out here, but in an inverse manner. Through its reductive action, it had served as an accelerator in comprehending the world; now it will serve as a brake. The same thing happens in the machine for destroying "deified chimeras," which the atheist tradition had perfected to such a point that it could denounce the interdependence of religion and tyranny on every occasion. This machine — certainly one of the most effective in thwarting the machinations of the ancien régime — has been transformed with incredible speed by atheist philosophy; as soon as the idols seem safely overthrown, the atheist machine is made to conform to the model of the industrial machine, churning out new values and particularly those of efficiency and productivity which still dominate us today! The fabrication of humanism and of revolutionary ideology derives directly from this perversion of the atheist machine, a wonderful instrument for destroying values, which suddenly starts producing them. In my opinion, *Frenchmen, another effort . . .* — the political reflection which is at the heart of *Philosophy in the Bedroom* — should be read in this light: as a desperate effort by Sade to return the atheist machine to its primary function of cleaning up ideologies and to prevent it, once it has been perverted, from sewing fresh values in the still-free terrain of a world without God. It is also significant that Sade takes religion as his point of departure, setting the atheist machine back in motion by simply recalling the collusion between altar and crown: "Let us not lose sight of the fact that this puerile religion was one of the best weapons in the hands of our tyrants." Immediately thereafter, he makes it function at full speed:

> O you who carry scythes in your hands, strike a final blow at the tree of superstition; be not content to prune its branches: but pull up by the roots a plant whose effects are so contagious; realize above all that your system of freedom and equality so contradicts the interests of the ministers of Christ, there will never be a single one who does not either adopt it in good faith or try to overthrow it, if in so doing he manages to regain some hold over men's consciences.

He continues:

> And so you must abolish forever anything which might one day destroy your own accomplishments. Remember — since the fruit of your labors is reserved only for your

nephews — it is a matter of duty and integrity not to leave them any of those dangerous germs which could plunge them back into that chaos from which we have emerged with so much difficulty.

In conclusion, Sade declares:

Frenchmen, I say again, Europe is waiting to be delivered by your hands both from the scepter and the censer. Remember that it is impossible for you to set it free from royal tyranny, without at the same time breaking the yoke of religious superstition: the ties of both being far too intimately linked for you to leave one of them without very soon falling back under the yoke of the other, which you neglected to dismantle.

In the course of this implacable text, Sade proves that the new republicans are indeed using the same machine; the same, except that it is now equipped with a safety catch. It is a capital text, in which Sade's appropriation of the atheist machine effectively sabotages the machine of social representation, itself in the process of developing out of a fundamental lie, as much with regard to the machine's functioning as with regard to what it will produce. For one only has to obstruct the atheist machine's function of unmasking, for the image of the machine — which continues to materialize abstraction, but now does nothing else — to fall back on the reality of the productive machine, now transformed into an instrument of domination. Once the thing seems to have conquered its imaginary side, the imaginary mimics it and begins to produce positive results and goes on producing them. Thus the war machine of atheism ends up producing the Supreme Being; the rationalist machine ends up producing bourgeois morality; and the machine of revolutionary rhetoric ends up by producing the guillotine.

If I emphasize this idea of the machine, it's because it is always present, in all its different meanings, in Sade's innermost thoughts. Not as a result of some mechanistic obsession, but because its emergence into the realm of the imaginary is inseparably linked to atheism. The fact is, too, that we are not through with the machine, nor with its fundamental fascination, even if its actual functioning is now less interesting than what it produces. And this is exceedingly important because through the imaginary side of the machine, whatever it may be, the question of meaning continues to be posed.

Once again, Sade is the first to have raised the problem in its full seriousness. After all, doesn't he show us in *Frenchmen, another effort* . . . that in turning the weapon of machinery against the impulse of thought, an effort is being made to suppress the disturbance which God's disappearance has just caused in the human mind? And also, to end the infinitely prolonged interrogative impetus, which the actual function of the machine as a model had first begun to represent and reflect in the depths of the imaginary? From this point of view, the extraordinary speech made by the Pope when he explains universal instability to Juliette, by means of his theory of the three reigns, could become emblematic of everything which atheist thinking, humanism and revolutionary thought was messing up, and would mess up for quite some time. Again, how can we fail to see that it is by means of a series of maneuvers around the idea of functioning (camouflaged as productivity, usefulness or social good) that an inversion of meaning is always obtained? The notion of functioning has thus far served to accelerate and radicalize the process of disclosure, currently being substituted, in scientific and philosophical thinking, to the taxonomic will of the classical world. It is enough to emphasize functioning a little more, to make it spectacular, for this new spectacle — because it is so strong and fascinating — to henceforth close all other perspectives. Indeed, this is where the optimism of the Enlightenment takes root, together with progressive stupidity and rationalist blindness.

Clearly, there is nothing deliberate in this vast motion of ebb and flow, thanks to which the model of the machine will henceforth serve two antagonistic thoughts, leading to a confusion we still feel. But once atheist subversion has carried out this progressive movement of occultation, the evolution of thought takes place, and continues to take place, between these two imaginary modes of the machine; between a machine that unveils machination, and a machine that weaves machination; between a machine that destroys illusions and a machine that constructs them; between a machine that diminishes and one that amplifies; between a machine that empties, and one that fabricates; between a machine that negates the system of values and one that not only produces values, but also produces values that produce other values. These values are always new, but have in common that they derive from an image of the well-functioning machine. In this way, they help affirm the spectacular power of the idea of functioning, whose incontestable advantage is continually to project the question of meaning, today more than ever.

New values, or new chimeras? For a long time, Sade was the only writer of his time to ask the question. All the others, progressively more embarrassed by the infinite materiality which reveals itself by the intermediary concept of machine, in effect went on trying to decide how and with what to replace the grand watchmaker. In the meantime, Sade did not yield an inch. He even went on the attack, scandalously, voluptuously and with considerable humor. Just when the thought of his time was succumbing to the productive reality of the machine, Sade staked his outrageous all on the luxuriously unreal invention of pleasure machines. There is the curious cutting machine belonging to Bernis, "A sort of steel slab comparable to the seat of a pew, of which the part touching my belly was as sharp as a razor blade," as Juliette describes it. There is also the incredible machine for using victims to squash each other, of which King Ferdinand is so proud; and Bandole's voluptuous machine for procreation. All these are pure creations which in no way derive from the numerous pleasure machines to be found in the erotic literature of that time, as can readily be seen from the feminine part of the mechanical dildo dreamed up by the dandy Francaville:

> A new and far more singular mechanism was at work beneath the belly of the woman. In sitting down on the part of the chair destined for her use, this woman sank, inadvertently as it were, onto a soft and flexible prick which, by means of a spring, filed constantly away at her, discharging every quarter of an hour into her vagina waves of a warm and sticky liquid, whose smell and viscosity caused it to resemble the purest and the freshest sperm. The head of an extremely pretty girl — of whom one saw nothing but this head — her chin pressed against the prick, was masturbating with her tongue the clitoris of the woman bent above her, and was even replaced by means a trapdoor, as soon as she was tired. Near the woman's head, several round footstools had been placed, which could be changed according to her whims, and on which could be seen either cunts or pricks.

Like all Sade's machines, no matter how immense, this erotic construction disappears, as soon as it starts functioning, behind the flesh that it makes tremble, and the bodies it disturbs. Since these pleasure machines are all vying in ingeniousness, vertiable inspirations of erotic intent, why is it they are always effaced, in the end, by the intimacy of the bodies they expose? Not only does the machine become eroticized, in Sade, like every other object; but its functioning also becomes eroticized, turning into one of the modalities of erotic order, the continual quest for which gives rhythm to Sadian time. Between these machines and the paintings where the postures are disposed, desire, that great investigator of forms, is always in charge. By the same token, there is not a person, object or place which cannot be conceived as a possible element of its ephemeral constructions. It constitutes a formidable neutralization of the machine, equaling in efficacity all possible negations. For if the Sadian machine shows us the nothingness of bodies, desire, in appropriating the machine just long enough to find an order and desert it, exposes the nothingness of the machine, just when everyone is fascinated either by its function or its product.

In this respect, the organization of Justine's misfortunes as a mechanics of unmasking acquires an even greater violence. The materiality of bodies, as if moved by a spring, cuts down all moral values in this veritably atheistic game of massacre. And while ineradicable human pride succeeds in appropriating the image of the machine, which has now become an instrument of domination producing positive values, Sade uses it here to continue — against all expectation — the work of "demolishing the hero" (Paul Bénichou, *Morales du grand siècle,* Paris: Gallimard, 1948) begun by Jansenism. That Sade should rediscover, in considering men's conduct, the rigor of the seventeenth-century moralists, is scarcely surprising. There are numerous comments on human vanity in both La Rochefoucauld and Pascal which could have been made by Sade, and vice versa. But it is interesting to point out that the story of Justine, which Sade conceived as a chart of "vexed virtues," could be read as an illustration of the list of disguises assumed by self-esteem, according to La Rochefoucauld. As Bénichou remarks, self-esteem

. . . is confused with all the chivalrous virtues: illustrious nobility, love of glory, disinterestedness, magnanimity or "moderation" in success, loyalty, sincerity, friendship, gratitude, faithfulness to past memories, stoic firmness, disdain for death, valiance, and refined, spiritual love.

The coincidence is interesting, and becomes even more so when one recalls that in *Aline et Valcour* the characters are divided up as aristocrats — Aline, Valcour, Madame de Blamont — or as bourgeois — Dolbourg, Judge de Blamont — and that this rift is less political than economical. For *Aline et Valcour* is also very obviously a novel of confrontation between two economic orders: on one side, the aristocracy with its spectacular scorn for money, and on the other, the bourgeoisie with its avowed love of money and advancement presented as a virtue. Here again, Sade joins the moralist tradition: we've already seen La Rochefoucauld hunting down self-interest in all those splendid performances directed by self-love. But Sade adds to that tradition by carefully refusing to amputate the notion of self-interest from its new economic acceptance. He then takes advantage of this increment of meaning to reveal the brutality of erotic interest, just when the moralization of money has reached it highest point.

In *Aline et Valcour,* therefore, the confrontation between two ways of relating to money reveals a still more violent confrontation between two ways of relating to pleasure. The erotic energy, moreover, is all concentrated in the bourgeoisie; the tempestuous, likeable Léonore is very much her libertine father's daughter, and in no way resembles her victimized mother, Madame de Blamont. The revolutionary value of *Aline et Valcour* certainly lies more in its condemnation of the aristocracy, dying out for not daring to assert its desires, than in all the professions of good revolutionary faith Sade apparently felt obliged to add afterwards, in notes. But this is only one of the consequences of the mental upheaval that begins with *Aline et Valcour,* for the unmasking of erotic interest beneath economic interest is a sort of Copernican revolution in man's observation of himself. After all, haven't we had to wait until Freud to envisage the true implications of this altered point of view?

Sade arrives at his discovery by seeking the mechanism which binds each notion to a body. If this is not the case, why doesn't he just stick with the notions of self-interest and self-love that Machiavelli and the moralists flush out from under charitable deeds, for example? Don't such notions help unmask that imposture which absorbs all his attention? Without a doubt; but that is not enough for Sade, and therein lies his genius. In this connection, we should carefully observe how each of Justine's interlocutors, contesting, as one might expect, her moral positions, gradually — one might almost say unconsciously — discovers the erotic implications of those very ideas he is using to contest these positions. And so when Bressac attempts to persuade Justine to help murder his mother, he attributes man's strange reluctance to kill his fellowmen to mere pride. He then proceeds to find in this denunciation a philosophical voluptuousness which anticipates the other sensual pleasures. Justine need only look convinced for Bressac to pull up her skirt and be ready to renounce his nonetheless confirmed homosexuality: "Come, child, you are an angel, I don't know how it is you're causing me this instant change of taste." Sade is once again the first and only writer to make us witness this sudden erotic wave that wells up during thought. And this is most important, since it involves the actual workings of the mind. We may note in passing that this is what distinguishes his thought from that of Bernard de Mandeville, for example, whose *The Fable of the Bees* was as famous as it was scandalous in the second quarter of the eighteenth century; in it Mandeville declares that "private vices constitute the public good," and situates the origins of human conduct in the field of economics. We know how much Karl Marx owed Mandeville, borrowing the famous eulogy of thieves and criminals, who create a livelihood for judges, executioners, locksmiths and jailers. But if Sade has not the slightest difficulty in recognizing this reality, his reflections nonetheless lead him to the other side of the mirror, where he returns to the origins of passion and deciphers its meaning, flying in the face of every social, economic and intellectual convention.

In the same connection, we should listen once again to Saint-Florent as he tries to explain to the Justine of *The Misfortunes of Virtue* how he finds himself obliged to sacrifice two children every day; he finds himself praising avarice, and imagining previously unthought-of imbrications between lewdness and cupidity:

> I go further, Thérèse: activity, industry, a modicum of comfort would work against my corruptions and deprive me of many of my subjects; I oppose to these dangers the credit I enjoy in this town, I stir up *oscillations* in commerce, or high prices for food which enlarge the poorer classes and, by on the one hand, depriving them of work, and on the other hand making life more difficult for them, increase in proportion the total number of subjects which poverty delivers to me. This ruse is well known, Thérèse: these scarcities of wood, corn and other comestibles, from which Paris shuddered for so many years, had no other aim than those by which I live; greed and debauchery,

there are two passions which extend a multitude of threads,
from gold-leaf panels to the poor man's humble roof.

A curious vertigo soon overtakes anyone who starts to reason in
Sade. Of course, critics have resorted to the thesis of madness,
working away beneath the mask of reason, to find what causes the
most hardened libertines to be disturbed in this manner. But one
has to be extremely insensitive to this disturbing disturbance, to be
content with such an explanation.

What then is the cause? Why does the "mental orgasm" so dear
to Sade not spring immediately to mind? And why are Sadian
heroes the only characters in fiction to experience and communicate
it? Let's take another look at Saint-Florent, the voluptuous econo-
mist, and what is going on inside him: wanting to explain to Justine
the causes and effects of his particular passion, he notices that the
effects get muddled up with the causes while, at the same time,
the aims eroticize the means, and the means eroticize the aims, and
that in the end, this is the only mechanism controlling him. This
holds true for all Sadian heroes, since this over-excitement of the
mind is what distinguishes the libertines from other men.

Mental over-excitement, eroticizing of the mind: such are the
points of departure and return for a general eroticizing of everything
else. What Sade shows us here — and will continue to show us,
with an ever more dazzling extravagance — is the unprecedented
spectacle, never before seen or imagined, of this general eroticizing,
and eroticizing of every idea, every attitude, every reasoning, every
thought. In this sense, *Aline et Valcour* can be considered an
adventure leading to the discovery of the erotic dimension. But in
the story of Justine those perturbations, which leave crevices in the
theories developed by all adversaries of virtue, prefigure an erotic
disturbance which will henceforth overtake all Sade's characters and,
with them, the fictional body in general. In all three *Justines,* these
crevices seem caused directly by the growing violence accompanying
the revenge of the bodies. In the successive versions these crevices
will deepen, like graven portents of the unprecedented mental
revolution shortly to occur with *The Story of Juliette.*

Sade prepares this revolution — apparently with the utmost
precautions, examining his mechanisms one by one, reassuring himself as to their precision *in vitro* — in *Philosophy in the Bedroom,*
which is a highly accurate account of this experiment. For a guinea
pig, he chooses a small and charming animal, Eugénie de Mistival,
whose only qualities, at the outset, are that she is very lively and

bouncy, and who will be subjected for several hours to this process of general eroticizing. It is doubtless on account of all these reasons that *Philosophy in the Bedroom* is a very jolly book. Of course, it is a closed-off space, this "delightful boudoir," so cunningly uphol- stered that "one could slit a bull's throat in this cabinet, and nobody would hear its bellowings." Critics have even remarked upon the unity of place, time and action of this dialogue, conceived like a play. But it is four in the afternoon, the doors open into the garden, Madame de Saint Ange is twenty-six, her brother, the Chevalier de Mirval is twenty, her friend Dolmancé is thirty-six, Madame de Mistival is thirty-two and Eugénie, fifteen; they are all young, rich and good-looking — even the gardener is handsome, aged between eighteen and twenty, and liable to be picked like a fruit in a kitchen garden as soon as he is needed.

There is no resemblance, then, with *The One Hundred and Twenty Days of Sodom,* even though both texts are announced as having a certain pedagogical value (*The One Hundred and Twenty Days* has as its subtitle *The School For Debauchery; Philosophy in the Bedroom, The Immoral Schoolteachers*); both are presented as accounts of experiments which seem to have been conceived less to propound a new object of study than a new discipline. A new discipline in all senses of the term, since, in both cases, Sade's discourse bears simultaneously on the subject matter, method and rule of conduct which may be deduced from it. Not least among the paradoxes of these curious pedagogical enterprises is the fact of being led, each time, inside a theatrical setting; that is to say, into the most spec- tacular and least scientific form. As for the scientific side of things, thanks to which, despairing of their cause, well-intentioned ratio- nalists — and there are some — attempt to save Sade, it is preferable to dispel all ambiguity by limiting ourselves to a vigorous remark of Curval:

> "Oh! What and enigma is man!" exclaimed the Duke.
> "Yes, my friend," said Curval. "That is why a certain very intelligent gentleman once said it was better to fuck him than to understand him."

In comparison with this basic principle, the well-known dictum of Karl Marx — that is better to transform the world than understand it — appears rather pale.

It is, furthermore, from this irrefutable basis that *Philosophy in the Bedroom* proceeds, having, in the purest libertine tradition, the initiation of a young person as pretext for covering a most complete erotic course, with theoretical explanations and practical exercises, it being always understood that:

> We shall gloss over all that concerns the commonplace mechanics of population, devoting ourselves principally and uniquely to the libertine pleasures of which the mind is no mere populator.

A most classical beginning, since the genre presupposes that "A pretty girl should only be concerned with fucking, never with giving birth." Right at the start, however, the beautiful Madame de Saint-Ange informs her brother of the quite exceptional scope of the project which will subtend this crash course in debauchery:

> Dolmancé and I will instill into this pretty little head the principles of wildest debauchery; we shall inflame her with our heat, we shall feed her our philosophy, inspiring her with our desires; and as I wish to add a little practice to the theory — as I wish us to both demonstrate and dissertate — I have chosen you to harvest the myrtles of Cythera, and Dolmancé the roses of Sodom.

This alters everything, and especially for Saint-Ange herself. As she explains:

> I shall have two pleasures at once. . . . Of myself enjoying this criminal sensuality, and of giving lessons and forming the tastes of the sweet innocent I'm trapping in our nets.

For the stakes are proportionate to the performance:

> It is of course certain that I shall spare no effort to pervert her, to degrade and thwart such false ideas of morality as may already have benumbed her; I wish, in two lessons, to make her as wickedly artful, as impious, as debauched as myself.

A strange mechanism indeed is set up here, that functions in the reverse manner of the libertine tradition. To begin with, there is the extraordinary fact that Saint-Ange expects no prerogatives for having provided this education, desiring only to make little Eugénie as "wickedly artful, as impious, as debauched" as she herself is. This means she acquires no power from this transmission of knowledge and, as gratification, hopes only for the infinite pleasure of corrupting her. Here surely resides the principal immorality of these immoral schoolteachers, seeking and finding their main pleasure in the information they dispense. Furthermore, in the working of this boudoir, one does not come across any of the devices which habitually ensure the success of the libertine machine: neither surprise, suggestion nor seduction can function in this boudoir where everything is shown, named, analyzed, explained, manipulated, or tasted, and where the instruments of pleasure are always studied twice, at rest and in motion:

> EUGENIE, *feeling at Dolmancé's testicles:* "Oh! how annoyed I am, my dear friend, with the resistance you oppose to my desires!. . . And these two globes, what are they used for, and what is their name?
> Mme. DE SAINT-ANGE: The technical word is balls . . . testicles is the artistic term.

As we can see, this is exactly the sort of education Madame de Saint-Ange announced to her brother in their earlier conversation. It is an education whose tempo is determined by the progress of an exceptionally gifted pupil, whose body opens up to pleasure at the same time as her mind is opened to philosophy. Decency, virtue, charity, piety, good deeds — all these virtues disappear with the first fruits. But there is more than a mere simultaneity of functioning in this connection of the mind and body, so speedily displayed: false ideas and prejudices are forcibly penetrated like so may hymens blocking off the path to pleasure. Each discovery of a new route to enjoyment corresponds to the discovery of a new route for reflection. Unlike the traditional libertine project of conquering and exploiting bodily space with the intent to increment erotic returns, the teachings of Saint-Ange and Dolmancé seem to have as their one goal — once the body has been taught to function perfectly in bed — to activate exchanges between the mind and the body, so that the voluptuous disturbance extends as far as possible. Instead of the libertine's proprietary tour of the known boundaries, Sade presents a grand voluptuous adventure, in the course of which bodiless ideas are killed off so that bodies without ideas can better be chastised. This is why it seems so hard to ignore the terrible symmetry determining the philosophical perspective of this delightful boudoir.

Before embarking on this education, Madame de Saint-Ange is careful to specify that she requires Dolmancé's help:

> . . . so that the poison of his immorality, circulating through this young heart with the venom I, too, shall inject, succeeds in rapidly eradicating such seeds of virtue as might germinate therein without us.

What does Madame de Saint-Ange subsequently propose, after Eugénie's unfortunate mother falls into the hands of the four libertines and is raped in every way possible by Dolmancé's syphilitic valet?

> Mme. DE SAINT-ANGE: I think it is now most essential for the poison circulating in your veins not to be exhaled; and consequently, Eugénie must carefully sew up both your bum and your cunt, so that the virulent humor, becoming more concentrated and less likely to evaporate, burns your bones more promptly.
> EUGENIE: An excellent affair! Quickly now, some needles and a thread! Spread your thighs, mother, so that I can sew you up, and then you shan't provide me with any more brothers and sisters. *(Madame de Saint-Ange gives Eugénie a large needle containing a thick, red, waxed, thread; Eugénie sews.)* . . .
> EUGENIE, *from time to time pricking the inside of the labia and sometimes the belly or the mons:* That's nothing, mother; it's just to test my needle.

One could dissertate at length upon the actions committed by Eugénie who, in sewing up her mother, completes her own deflowering and scandalously denies her own origins: as if in opening up to pleasure, we must first close off our own dependency on nature. This deed, accomplished by a little girl — in other words, by one of the beings supposedly most dependent on nature — is of stupendous violence. "In this way the mother's gift is given back to her: death and life together . . . and slowly, so that nature's own action is imitated: nature, whose greatest cruelty appears not in the sudden jolts, but in the pain and death which she distills, little by little, right until the final drop," as Simone Debout puts it in her enlightening study of Fourier and Sade *(Sade et Fourier, Libre* no. 4, Paris: Payot, 1978). By means of this supreme outrage inflicted on woman, who gives birth in pain, Eugénie acquires the sovereignty of her own birth, becoming the first "daughter born without a mother" in our history. The feminists should have read Sade better. But while we vainly wait for that to happen there is, in the meantime, this poison circulating all around the boudoir, this corrupting substance which must in one case act upon an innocent heart — that of Eugénie; and in the other, upon an innocent body — that of her mother, Madame de Mistival.

What is this corrosive substance, which, by means of the theme of corruption, continues to circulate in *Frenchmen, another effort . . . ,* binding this political reflection strongly, one might almost say organically, to the lesson in the boudoir? I tend to emphasize this question because I find it impossible to agree with Gilbert Lely when he states, in his *The Marquis de Sade: A Biography,* that:

> . . . this long pamphlet, arbitrarily inserted into an exqui- sitely constructed whole, rather compromises the harmony of *Philosophy in the Bedroom.* Having first intended it for independent publication, Sade may quite possibly have felt obliged to include it in his work, so as to rejuvenate the fiction and its mores, too redolent of the old régime.

In the same connection, I don't really understand how Maurice Blanchot could have presented this text without really pointing out that it's inserted in a boudoir whose atmosphere, heavy with the scents of love, only increases the curious vertigo of the political reflection. I understand it even less, considering that a reading of this pamphlet in no way interrupts but, if anything, prolongs the odd hilarity dispensed by *The Immoral Schoolteachers.*

Corruption and mirth — isn't this connection a trifle disconcert- ing? And even more so, when this theme of corruption in politics — developed here by Sade via the problem of a corrupt nation wanting "to pass from crime to virtue," a problem he will return to with Chigi's criticism of the law in *The Story of Juliette* — has already been broached by Machiavelli in his *Discourse on the First Decade of Titus Livy,* section III, wherein he treats of "how, in a corrupted state, one might preserve a free government if it was already in existence, or introduce one, if it was not." Or when the question has just been asked even more dramatically by Robespierre himself, in the speech delivered on December 3, 1792, entitled *On the Judgement of Louis XVI,* in which he declares: "When a nation has been forced to resort to the right of insurrection, it returns to a state of nature with regard to tyrants." And so, with the corruption of the preceding state justifying, in Robespierre's eyes, the right to insurrection, therefore the absence of any social pact, therefore the absence of a constitution, he is drawn to ask:

What are the laws which replace it? Those of nature and that law which is the basis of society itself: the welfare of the people. The right to punish a tyrant, to dethrone him — both are the same. The first right comprises the same forms as the second; the trial of the tyrant becomes insurrection; his judgment is his fall from power; his sentence, that demanded by the freedom of the people.

If Maurice Blanchot has sensibly compared certain phrases of Saint-Just to the thesis of *Frenchmen, another effort . . . ,* it may prove useful — after this text of Robespierre grounding revolutionary virtue, as it were in the murder of Louis XVI — to read Sade on the subject:

Insurrection . . . is not a *moral* state; but it must be the permanent state of a republic; and therefore it would be both dangerous and absurd to require that those who must maintain the perpetually *immoral* motion of the machine should themselves be highly *moral,* for the *moral* state of a man is a state of peace and tranquillity, whereas his *immoral* state is a state of perpetual agitation that unites him with the necessary insurrection, in which the republican must always uphold the government that he belongs to.

As with Saint-Just, the comparison yields as much through the differences as through the similarities which suddenly appear: there is the same form of argument, up to a certain point, and then the distinction between Sade and Robespierre becomes evident — and it is far more disturbing than the areas in which they coincide. For this distinction is of a moral order. In Robespierre's case, the end justifies the means: the king's death need not be justified before any tribunal — and the absence of laws scarcely matters, since it serves to establish republican legality! Sade, on the other hand, shows that the means justify the end for the obvious, irrefutable and indisputable reason that "those who must maintain the perpetually *immoral* motion of the machine," cannot "themselves be highly *moral.*" Then and there, Robespierre becomes immoral and Sade becomes moral, announcing with his ferocious innocence a manifest fact of morality still scandalous today: that men are what they do, and not what they aspire to be.

We have come a long way here from naughty little Eugénie de Mistival — and yet, not as far as it might seem. For if Sade is the only writer of his century to entertain this moral observation, it's because he knows the lesson taught in Madame de Saint-Ange's boudoir: there are no ideas without bodies and no bodies without ideas. Moreover, one cannot justify the execution of the king while proclaiming an opposition to capital punishment, as Robespierre calmly proceeds to do in this same speech of December 3, 1792:

> I personally abhor the death penalty meted out by your laws, and have neither love nor hatred for Louis: I hate only his crimes. I demanded the abolition of capital punishment, standing before the Assembly which is still termed Constituent. . . . Yes, capital punishment in general is a crime, and for this reason alone, according to the indestructible principles of nature, it can only be justified in those cases when it becomes necessary to ensure the safety of individuals or the social body.

This is a remarkable document, in which one sees how ideologies are made. We all know what happens next: the Terror, the death of Robespierre himself. After quoting this text in which abstraction follows abstraction until it becomes easy to justify any sort of extortion, I cannot help but quote this letter of November 19, 1794, in which Sade informs Gaufirdy that he has been moved to four prisons in ten months:

> . . . the fourth one was an earthly paradise; a beautiful house, splendid garden, select society and pleasant women when, all of a sudden, the site of executions was moved to right beneath our windows and the cemetery of the victims was placed in the middle of our garden. In thirty-five days, my dear friend, we buried some eighteen hundred people, of which one-third came from our wretched house. My name finally appeared on the list and I was to have been guillotined on the 11th; but the previous day the sword of justice descended on this latterday French Sylla.

It is a fearful contrast: one hears death speaking through the cold, white, cutting tones of Robespierre, and life breathing in Sade's letter. Sade is fully aware of the physical horrors of capital punishment because he can see that the women are rather pretty and the gardens, quite superb. So which of the two do we call moral? Robespierre, for whom the end justifies the means? Or Sade, showing that the means justify the end? Sade, who is opposed to capital punishment and who risks his head so as not to break faith with his principles; Sade, who writes to Gaufridy on January 21, 1795: "With all this, I'm not very well: being detained by *the nation, with the guillotine before my eyes,* did me a hundred times more harm than all the Bastilles you can imagine." Robespierre, who does not know that ideas have a body, builds a machine to make them socially disincarnate, placing the guillotine there where he thinks the Supreme Being reigns. In this respect, there is no difference between Robespierre and Saint-Just, and it is significant that Maurice Blanchot prefers to emphasize the similarity between Saint-Just and Sade, rather than casting light upon the moral breach dividing them — as if it's better to put Sade on the side of revolution, despite his utter solitude. One might almost think that Blanchot's ideological interest is similar to that of Robespierre and Saint-Just, not so much through their manifest political commitment as through their common denial of the body. This is actually quite feasible, since Blanchot's whole theory of writing rests on the exaltation of a bodiless idea, much like the revolutionary rhetoric of 1789 endowing the "spirit of the revolution" with its legislative shape.

On the other hand, everything suggests that Sade's contemplation of the machine of social disincarnation erected by the Revolution is what causes him to ask the French to make another effort. And the tiny effort he proposes is simply to put back a bit of body in the principles affirmed; a tiny bit of body, just to see the reality of means grimacing underneath the laurel wreaths of ends:

> Are there crimes in politics? Let us be courageous and admit, on the contrary, that crime is one of politics' major devices. Was it not through numerous murders that Rome became the mistress of the world? Is it not through numerous murders that France is free today?

Once again, the body comes back seeking justice:

> Strange blindness of mankind, which publicly instructs in how to kill, rewarding those who do it best and punishing the man who, for his own private reasons, rids himself of an enemy!

And the body continues to advance in Sade's thinking. Equality is an abstraction; Sade tries to see, in physical terms, what this might mean. As for liberty, this is even vaguer, even more obscure, more abstract still. But Sade has a secret lunge for skewering abstraction, and that is through the feint of literalness, which is actually the body's untimely return into language. Thus liberty is that which knows no limit, otherwise it isn't liberty at all. Sade then imagines everything it's possible henceforth to do. That is why this text conveys such great hilarity, not because one or other of its propositions is absurd, but because of the physical subversion busy damaging the order of its principles. In this sense, *Frenchmen, another effort . . .* is a text which takes revenge for all of us on the grand ideas we have accepted and continue to accept, even now "over our dead bodies."

However, it is also a text which perturbs us, by making us witness the extraordinary sight of a social machine running amok, wildly out of control as a result of this physical subversion, then turning into an imaginary machine. Just as ideas come and subvert the libertine machine which *Philosophy in the Bedroom* might otherwise have remained, the same ideas reappear in *Frenchmen, another effort . . .* as if reflected in the mirror of bodies. The construction of this whole, into which *Frenchmen, another effort . . .* has been inserted like a kernel of trouble in the very heart of thought, probably provides the best possible illustration of how intimately the reciprocal subversion of idea and body is effected in Sade. Paradoxically, the intervening text of *Frenchmen, another effort . . .* reminds one of the weight of bodies both in philosophy and in the boudoir, so much so that the boudoir is modified thereby. Everything becomes more serious, and if laughter is still heard in it, the lights are growing dimmer and night is closing in. We are forced to admit that the naïve mechanisms of the libertine machine are no longer appropriate: the winches, pulleys and springs that organize contemporary erotic constructions no longer have the slightest efficacity. As a result of transformations which we do not notice at the outset, and which end up equaling a veritable mechanical diversion, other gears are set in motion, other drive-belts put in place, another mechanism starts to work — in fact, a new machine begins to function at the expense of the preceding one. In this machine, as in *Frenchmen, another effort . . .*, chemistry appears with this corrosive substance that changes everything, that ends up changing the composition of the social body, just as, inside the boudoir, it ultimately changes the lives of Eugénie and Madame de Mistival. And it may well be that the full text of *Philosophy in the Bedroom* was conceived as a laboratory for isolating this substance and studying the effects it has on both the social and individual body.

And that is how we first perceive this substance, generated by the effective communication brought about between the head and body. This is an essential observation which dissipates all doubts as to its real nature: this corrosive power is the direct result of the imagination giving ideas to bodies. Such is the unadulterated venom which Saint-Ange and Dolmancé inject into little Eugénie, one fine spring day. Could anyone think of more favorable conditions for conducting an experiment: the medium is stable, the subject a virgin? Its effects will soon be felt: as early as the third dialogue, Eugénie, already quite contaminated, understands that her future will be profoundly affected by this:

> . . . the more we wish to be exited, the more we desire to experience violent feelings, the more rein must we give to our imagination on the most inconceivable matters; our pleasure will then increase in proportion to the progress made by the mind and . . .
> DOLMANCE, *kissing Eugénie*: Delightful!

Yes, delightful and prodigious Eugénie who already knows that everything depends on "progress made by the mind," keeping in store for us the most disturbing surprises. First among them is Sade's savage poetry, luxuriant and deep, growing on this mental path like weeds in wild delirium. Indeed, one hardly knows if the weeds or the path determine the way ahead.

CHAPTER EIGHT

EXCESS AS A MEANS OF TRANSPORT

I have no experience of happiness, but a few people and a few books have given me so precise an image of it, albeit rather fleeting, that thanks to them, life sometimes seems almost acceptable. I do not mean mere commonplace happiness; I mean the quintessential happiness of seeing an order of things appear, so luxuriously necessary that there is nothing left to say, because everything has been expressed, just as Sade would wish — or just as poetry would wish. Who could dispute that the presentation of Eugénie de Franval by her father to Valmont, her lover of the moment, is one such instance of delight:

> There, in the ornate room, Eugénie sat naked on a pedestal, acting the part of a young savage tired by the hunt, leaning against the trunk of a palm tree, whose soaring branches concealed an infinite number of lamps placed in such a way that their reflections, shining only on the charms of this lovely girl, emphasized them most artistically. The little theatre in which appeared this animated statue was surrounded by a moat some six feet wide, which acted as a barrier protecting the young savage from any possible approach. Beside this circumvallation an armchair had been placed [for Valmont]; a silk cord connected it: and by pulling on this thread, he could maneuver the pedestal in such a way that the object of his adoration was

visible from any side, and so arranged that no matter how she was directed, her pose was always pleasing. Concealed behind a decorative shrub, [Franval] could observe both his mistress and his friend, an examination which, according to the last agreement, lasted half an hour. . . .

If happiness were but a matter of being able to turn the figurations of desire with a silk cord, with silk cords of time we're holding in our hands. . . . And if happiness were but the quivering luxury of such vengeance wrought upon the void, then Sade would be a writer of happiness; indeed, the greatest of all writers of happiness, for the festivities to which he summons us always have the fatal charm of opening onto something far beyond our desire.

Festivities of the instant: how could anyone not dream of a friendship or a love beginning with the first words Madame Delbène utters to the very young Juliette: "You're blushing, little angel; I forbid it; modesty is just a dream." Festivities of the present, which "electrify": how could anyone resist the same Juliette when she suggests, to the omnipotent Saint-Fond:

> It's so warm today. . . . I would like you to dress up as a savage, with your arms, thighs, buttocks and prick all uncovered; on your head you'd put a snakeskin hat, your face would be daubed with red paint, we would change your moustaches, and a large belt could hold all the weapons needed for the tortures you'd inflict upon your victims; and when they saw this costume everyone would be afraid. . . .

Festivities in which time disappear into the space of wonderment, as in the interior at the palace of Minski, plunging like an excessive enclave into the bowels of the earth. But let us listen to him as he makes us

> . . . closely observe the composition of this furniture. You see that this table, these chandeliers and these armchairs are entirely composed of groups of girls, artistically arranged; my dishes will be placed, still warm, upon the backs of these creatures; my candles are embedded in their cunts, and my bottom, together with your own, in finding niches in these chairs, will soon be supported by the soft face or white titties of these young women: for this reason, ladies, I must beg you to remove your skirts and you,

gentlemen, your trousers, so that, in the words of the Scripture, *flesh may rest on flesh.*

I think only André Breton and André Pieyre de Mandiargues have succeeded in conveying the joy experienced by Sade; a child-like joy in depravity which offers us, head-on, just when we had almost forgotten what forbidden delights are like, everything that fairy tales used to promise us but never actually delivered.

> He's a man, yes, who gives parties. How can we not
> take pleasure in obliging him, if he invites us to his plays?
> How could so rare a dandy have passed, in the eyes of
> fools, for a laborious pornographer?

This splendid remark by André Pieyre de Mandiargues in his preface to *The Story of Juliette* raises another question. Why have most of Sade's commentators been unable to give us even a feeble idea of the way in which this thought — tracked down, appalled, threatened in its equilibrium — invents its freedom and finds it in answering, against all expectations, the savageness of desire with that sense of wonder in which our ferocious childhood always manages to find nourishment?

What are we to think then, when Bataille proposes to discuss, in *Literature and Evil:* ". . . the obvious monotony of Sade's books, a result of his decision to subordinate literary play to the expression of an inexpressible event." Immediately thereafter, Bataille adds: "Boredom emanates from the monstrousness of Sade's entire work; but this tedium is itself the meaning of the work." How should we react to Maurice Blanchot, when he affirms, in *L'Inconvenance majeure:*

> . . . the major impropriety is deferred to the simple power
> of repetition, the impropriety of a narration which does
> not encounter interdiction because there is no longer any
> interdiction (this entire work-limit tells us so by the mo-
> notony of its appalling murmur) except the time of the
> interdiction, this absolute suspension which no one can
> attain except by never stopping speaking.

What is this "inexpressible event?" What is this "time of interdiction" which can only be attained by "never stopping speaking?" If Sade never stops talking it is, on the contrary, in order to fill in and saturate the time of telling, to inaugurate the time of telling all." If Sade bets on the luxury, the luxuriance, the extravagance of

beings, objects, situations, ideas, demonstrations, and comport-
ments, while furiously straining his wits to put order into disorder,
to formally uphold the logic of a line of reasoning, to find the
maintenance of postures, to think out the grouping of a picture, it
is only to ultimately threaten this excessive order by the excessive
principle of luxury, of luxuriance, of extravagance. This panting
succession of unstable balances can of course be assimilated into
an equivalent number of successive negations, as long as one is
careful to remember that it is excess, and never insufficiency, which
always tips these equilibria.

Without for a second questioning the negative impact of Sade's
thinking, can we really be content with this opinion of Bataille:

> . . . it is not permissible for anyone to wish and hope
> clearly for what Sade obscurely demanded, and obtained.
> It's that the essence of his works is destruction: not only
> of the objects and victims brought into play (and which
> are only there to answer his rage to negate) but of the
> author and the work itself.

Can anyone really accept Blanchot's thesis when the latter perceives
in Sade's "infinite power of negation," "the truth of disordered
movements looking for themselves in an enormous work"? Unable
to escape from the dominion of rationality, unable to imagine a
radically different way of thinking which could not simply be
reduced to terms of reason or unreason, isn't it rather that Blanchot
finds himself constrained to speak of an "excessive reason," revealing itself essentially through a "madness of writing" which refers to
nothing more than an unqualifiable textual vagueness into which
disappear both Sade's reason and Blanchot's point of view? We
may judge of this when Blanchot tries to be more explicit:

> Something more violent becomes clear in this rage to write;
> a violence which all the excesses of a proud or ferocious
> imagination can neither exhaust nor appease, although the
> imagination is always inferior to the transport of a language
> which does not tolerate a halt, any more than it conceives
> of limitation.

What does this mean? What has become of excessive reason?
How can this "proud or ferocious" imagination always be inferior
to the transport of language? Why wouldn't this transport of language reflect, on the contrary, the heat of the imagination? The

only possible way that it can be as Blanchot states is to postulate the autonomy of language and substitute language for reality, and to affirm the absolute reality of language against all the rest, as Blanchot indeed does. "When I speak, I deny the existence of what I say, but I also deny the existence of the person who says it," as he declares in *La Part du feu*. That the metaphysics of Blanchot's language rests on a founding murder, on this "differed murder which is my language," all right, we accept. But it remains to be known how this obliteration through language concerns Sade.

However this may be, it is most useful to resort to this linguistic metaphysics in order to erase the enigmatic parts of Sade's procedure, to neutralize his thought by tossing it about in the problematics which obtain for *any* writing. And so, when Blanchot observes in *L'Inconvenance majeure* that: "Sade's way of *telling all,* understood in his books as the prodigious reiteration of an eternal word, eternally clear and void, goes even further," one is entitled to expect that this "even further" leads us somewhere. Not on your life. It's there to bring us back to the transports of language:

> The violence is all the stronger for being simple, asserting itself through an unambiguous word, free of any afterthought, which always expresses everything straightforwardly and leaves nothing to pretend, speaking thus so purely, pure indeed of this dishonest obscenity by which the majestic emotions of Chateaubriand will shortly disturb language, without being denounced by any law.

In light of this purity which certainly illuminates the circular nature of the undertaking, language simply brings us back to language to catch Sade in the trap of writing, like any commonplace writer, and with all the more impunity in that:

> . . . in the end writing has no connection with life, unless it is the necessary insecurity which writing receives from life, as life receives insecurity from writing: an absence of connection such that writing, although it gathers and disperses in life, never returns there to itself but to the *other than itself,* which ruins, or even worse, disturbs it,

as Blanchot further states in *L'Amitié*. Applied to Sade, who spent more than thirty years in prison, aren't such opinions rather useless, not to say, ridiculous?

There is worse to come, however, when one considers that the mad effort made by Blanchot, Bataille and their followers to enable words to live without things is realized at the cost of a general demetaphorization itself utterly opposed to Sade's approach. This demetaphorization is implicit from the moment when, taking language as the sole reality, one negates the possibility of a strong organic bond linking thought with concrete things — a link which it is precisely in the nature of metaphorical impulse to discover, even if it always carries us beyond what actually exists. So what connection can there be with Sade, perpetually seeking to reveal the link between thought and the body, and between the body and thought? For Bataille and Blanchot's concepts of language-fall, language-renunciation or language-expiation hope to suppress images and see death as a metaphor (the only one allowed) for the act of speaking. Could these concepts be more strongly contradicted than by Sade's way of thinking, which finds its momentum in the savage joy of saying, words that have the extraordinary power of evoking beings and things, even of arousing and transporting them: "I would certainly astound you if I told you that *all those things,* and their remembrance, are what I summon to my aid whenever I try to forget my present situation." This also explains Sade's blasphematory power, since words have power to affect the body, as Dolmancé vigourosly states in *Philosophy in the Bedroom:*

> . . . as soon as God has ceased to be, what point is there in insulting his name? It's because it is essential to utter strong and filthy words in the drunkenness of pleasure, and those of blasphemy are most useful to the imagination. Nothing must be spared; these words must be ornamented with the greatest luxury of expression; they must scandalize as much as possible; for it most pleasing to scandalize.

For his part, Blanchot declares:

> Language as totality, is language replacing everything, postulating the absence of everything and at the same time the absence of language. It is in this primary sense that language is dead, the presence within us of a death which no particular death can satisfy.

How can this absence of absence have any possible connection with Sade's fury against ideas without bodies or bodies without ideas;

how can this ideology of deficiency prove anything but deceptive when applied to Sadian excess?

The Sadian excess is not an excessiveness of reason, but a metaphorical excess. Far from being a rhetorical figure, it asserts itself as a mode of being in that, for Sade, excess is itself a metaphor for the momentum of desire. His strangeness and poetic force owe much to this, saying everything in order to say more, concerned only with bringing each person, object, passion, situation or idea to its point of excess, as if to invest the singularity of metaphorical omnipotence. There again, Sade has brought about a revolution of which, even now, we are scarcely aware. By means of this metaphorical excessiveness. Sade invents what we might call the *autometaphor* — each being or object concealing its own excessiveness inside itself — which is perhaps the first radical, poetic criticism of the ideological deviation which any metaphor, in the uncertainty of passing from one state to another, risks not being able to avoid. For in Sade's work, metaphorization seems to have the particular quality of taking place without the external detour — without passing through the other. His intense use of literalness further constitutes a model for this autometaphorization that transports each image to the limits of itself. Thence come these incredible metaphorical chains that extrapolate each poetic being towards its own infinity — seemingly towards the derision of its own infinity. Unlike the traditional practitioners of metaphor, Sade never loses sight of his initial point of view, never deceives himself or us as to the singular character of singularity: that is to say, as to wretchedness and grandeur, the all and the nothing of each being, of each thing. In my opinion, this is a case of unprecedented poetic novelty. This implacable return of lyrical impetus to the void of its own point of departure, this infinite derision of the temptation of infinity, sweeps the board clean as never before. In so doing, they exclude the approximation and indetermination which normally favors the establishment of ideological grids. Then, like a voluptuous magician, Sade is able to produce styles, colors, manners, temptations and voyages from any situation. That, in fact, is Sade's poetry, freeing in each person the erotic possibilities that he conceals. There is, for example, the baroque possibility:

> "Come," said Chigi, "Since you're all linked in a chain, the monkey will have to bugger me, while the dwarf, astride the little boy, offers me his buttocks to be fucked."

If colors are desired, here is an unforgettable cameo in white: "He buggers a swan, by putting a host in its bum, and strangles the animal as he discharges." I think Sade is alone in practicing this autometaphorization of the world, which casts doubt on the metaphorical principle of lying about individual solitude, since metaphorical comparison presupposes a recourse to something else, to the other. It is highly likely that violent pleasure, which yields Sade's poetic inventions, is linked to this truth, which we find so hard to recognize, but from which Sade molds his heroes. For if the excessiveness by which they live tends only to lead them beyond themselves, outside any connection with the other, can we not say that they are walking Sadian metaphors?

But let's get back to the facts. Initially, there is excess, and nothing else. Excess, indeed, is the one condition necessary for the Sadian hero to exist: durable excess, repeated excess, excess practiced to a greater or lesser degree, corresponding to a greater of lesser degree of resistance in the character. Resistance should here be understood in its physical sense, as referring to the solidity of the original building materials, and their ability to resist the process of universal destruction; also in its electrical sense, as a conductor and transformer of universal energy. All Sadian libertines are assiduous in the daily practice of excess, as much from taste as from survial instinct. As it happens, this sense of excess is what distinguishes the libertines from their victims; a kind of sixth sense which, in the Sadian universe, can alter a person's destiny. And if Sade's victims are indeed characters who do not resist excess, falling by the thousand before the excessiveness of libertines, isn't this more on account of their inability to conceive of excess, than their inability to tolerate it physically? In Sade, anyone becomes a victim whose head can't tolerate excess — as they say of alcohol. Even Juliette proves no exception to this inexorable law: simply because she hesitates at something suggested by Saint-Fond, because she fails the principle of excess, she risks becoming a mere shadow, one of those thousands of women "made to be painted," one of those thousands of young men "handsome as Hercules or Mars," whom Sade throws to the wind of images.

Henceforth, one can see how Sade opposes metaphorical excess to traditional metaphor. For if these girls with "skin as white as lilies" and boys as handsome as Greek gods all disappear so easily, it is certainly because nothing excessive inhabits them; because there is nothing excessive in them to prevent their being swept off in the universal drift. One need only compare them to the giant Minski, whose qualities of excess impose him absolutely on the rest of the world:

> "As for the member all this comes out of, here it is," said Minski, revealing a sausage of about eighteen inches long and sixteen inches round, topped with a vermilion mushroom as wide as the crown of a hat. "Yes, here it is, it's always in the state you behold, even when asleep, even when I walk."

Clearly, we are confronted with an ogre whose "ejaculations are as tumultuous and abundant the tenth time as they were at the first," and who never feels "the day after, the exhaustions of the day before," who is the possessor of two harems, one containing "two hundred little girls, aged from five to twenty," and the other "two hundred women aged from twenty to thirty." His own walking metaphor, achieved by virtue of his giant stature, Minski is perhaps the only Sadian hero to have the means of contenting his desires. This does not alter the fact that all are driven by this same process of autometaphorical extension.

The case of Justine is quite to the contrary, although of all Sade's victims, she is the one who best resists excess. Endowed with the same constitution as Juliette, she has, initially, all that is needed for a grand career. On several occasions, the subtlest of the libertines she meets — Rodin, Bressac, and also Jérôme — recognize in her this exceptional power of endurance which makes a Sadian hero. Sensitive to this gift of excess, which has been put to such bad use, they even break the silence habitually observed with victims and try to persuade her to fulfill the great destiny for which her constitution fitted her. But Justine is the perfect example of a dramatic misuse of this sixth sense of excess. She illustrates marvelously well the ravages committed by this redoubtable power on those who fail to control it. It is no accident that in her course on atheism, Madame Dèlbne denounces this perversion of excess as being among the more overwhelming manifestations of religious feeling:

> . . . the adoption of this phantom is filled with reefs which we shall but bump into if we are wise, but on which we shall founder if our minds become enthused; and chimeras never fail to enthuse.

For it is not enough to praise the kind of imagination which generates excess, as does Dolmancé in *Philosophy in the Bedroom*:

> Imagination is the stimulus of pleasures; in those of this kind, it governs and motivates everything we do; is it not through the imagination that pleasure finds its height? That the most piquant pleasures come?

> Mme DE SAINT-ANGE: Agreed; but let Eugénie beware; imagination only serves us when our minds are absolutely free of prejudice: a single prejudice can be enough to chill it.

The warning is a slight one, but nonetheless prefigures the dread law to be enunciated by Madame Delbène as she explains to little Juliette the need for an excessive relationship with nature:

> But one single sign of resistance, I repeat, a single one would make you lose all the benefit of your most recent lapses; you might just as well know nothing at all if you have not known everything; and if you are so shy as to desist with [nature], she will escape from you for ever.

It would seem that the imagination is the excessive principle allowing man to oppose nature by exceeding it. And so, if one only wishes to see, like Maurice Blanchot, in this continual overbidding nothing more than:

> . . . an infinite power of negation [that] in turn expresses and rescinds, by means of a circular experience, the notions of man and of nature, finally to affirm man in his entirety. . . (*L'Inconvenance majeure*)

one simply misses the specificity of the relationship with nature from which the Sadian hero constructs himself. The Sadian hero never really denies this specifity, but seeks to draw away from it according to a process of excessive affirmation. Doubtless, all that can be retained from this overbidding are the successive negations it implies. But these negations are only secondary effects of the excessive impulse which, for Sade, affirms what is specifically human. Madame Delbène is at particular pains to explain this process to Juliette, as soon as they first meet:

> That's when you will recognize the weakness of what were formerly proposed to you as nature's inspirations. When

you have dallied for a few years with what foes term nature's laws, and when, in order to grow used to breaking them, you have taken pleasure in trampling on them all, you will see unruly nature, delighted at having been violated, smoothly bending to your nervous desires, coming of her own accord to bear your chains . . . offering you her hands, the better to be captured. Then, having become your slave instead of your sovereign, she will give fine instruction to your heart as to how to outrage her even further, as if she took pleasure in debasing herself, and as if it is really only in showing you how to insult her excessively that she is skillful enough to reduce you to her laws.

Henceforth, it becomes obvious that if deviation is imagination's only gauge, imagination is what enables man to duplicate nature. Duplicate it, in all senses of the term, until the relationship of the initial forces is reversed, implying a transition to another speed, the speed of the imaginary, which I have already discussed. This accounts for the fact that the Sadian hero continually risks losing everything, once he acquires his momentum through excess alone. The slightest halt or hesitation not only causes him to fall back into a simple relationship of submission to nature, but also hurls him into inexistence. The only characters to survive in Sade are those who duplicate nature. Should they be so unfortunate as to slow down, nothingness immediately claims them. This is how the friends acquired by Juliette all disappear, one by one: the slightest weakness is fatal to them, the slightest sign of love, pity or humanity immediately precipitates their death sentence. Even the frenzied Princess Borghese perishes in this manner. Juliette and Clairwil actually help destiny a little in this case, deciding to push the princess into the flames of Vesuvius, under the pretext that she: ". . . still clings to her prejudices, and is capable of being converted at the first misfortune. . . . This weakness alone renders her unworthy of two corrupt women like ourselves."

In prematurely ending this existence, Juliette and Clairwil to some extent remedy their friend's want of energy, accomplishing through her murder the excess which she herself evaded. Thus, it is tempting to perceive this concept of the Sadian hero duplicating nature as a means of affirming the potential autometaphorization of each being. Similarly, couldn't Sade's taste for large numbers — whose sado-anal origins have been much and seriously emphasized — rather be the metaphor for a connection with reality, entirely dictated by this double movement of acceptance and surpassing with regard to nature? For, seen in this light, there is a disturbing resemblance between the Sadian hero and Alfred Jarry's Supermale. What does the latter do, except follow a dynamics of excess which aims at exceeding the limits of human nature and also at unmasking the unmeasurable excessiveness in man? In the celebrated "ten-thousand-mile race," isn't it the Supermale himself, that solitary cyclist, who will overtake the quintuplet, a scientific machine for all that, conceived in order to "proclaim the human motor superior to mechanical motors over in long-distance running"? In this mad race between machine (the locomotive), man acting as machine (five champion cyclists fixed to the quintuplet who set off at a hundred kilometers an hour) and man alone, it is man who wins, casting a most unexpected shadow over the human horizon before returning to the night whence he emerged.

In just the same manner Juliette suddenly appears, as the unforeseen shadow in all races run by Sadian heroes. One is reminded of Durcet, admitting in the middle of *The One Hundred and Twenty Days:*

> . . . my imagination has always exceeded my means in this respect; I have always imagined a thousand times more than I've accomplished and I've complained of nature who, having endowed me with the desire to outrage her, invariably bereft me of the means to carry it out.

What Juliette intends to explore is precisely this region that lies beyond satiety. She is aided only by her imagination which returns continually to her body, then transports her continually beyond it. This is very much like the Supermale, wondering about the nature of excess before embarking on his truly mad performance with young Ellen Elson, simply to find out if "love is an unimportant act," since it can be done indefinitely:

> "STILL MORE?" said Marcueil, as if dreaming. "What does that mean? It's like the fleeting shadow in the race . . . *Still more,* that's something that's no longer firm, it recedes further than infinity, it's intangible, a ghost . . ."
> "You were the Shadow," Ellen said.
> And he clasped her in his arms, mechanically, in order to take hold of something firm.

Here, as in Sade, numerical excess never exhausts the swarm of appearances but exalts it, on the contrary, before making it reverberate into the depths of being. The same fascination with number reveals the same derision for numerical power on which is founded — with the rise of the merchant, rationalist bourgeoisie — a libertine tradition bent on conquering all beings, occupying all erogenous zones, controlling all the paths to pleasure. From Sade to Jarry, like the blackest and most brilliant vein of modern sensibility, there runs an opposing tradition. It is one of the most rigorous: according to its terms, accumulation does not aim at mastery but leads to dizziness; systematization guarantees no equilibrium, but on the contrary, destabilizes; mechanical excess, instead of returning to the laws of number, opens up onto the infinite possibility of lyrical excess. It is one of the most subversive traditions, opposed as much to the conquering imaginary of the productive machine as to the reductive imaginary of the mathematical machine. Such is this tradition, beginning with the establishment of an imaginary conceived as a "machine to inspire love," invented by Sade long before Jarry, and on which everything important in modern art will depend.

Obviously, at the tender age of fifteen the playful Eugénie de Mistival can scarcely know what she's asking when she begs Madame de Saint-Ange to tell her "the most extraordinary thing" she's ever done. "I made myself agreeable to fifteen men; I was fucked ninety times in twenty-four hours, both in front and behind," replies Saint-Ange. To which Eugénie retorts: "That's nothing but debauchery, all that; just *tours de force*. I bet you've done more unusual things than that." Despite her youthful age, one could say that Eugénie instinctively opposes eccentric excess to numerical excess. This does not prevent her from trying to find out, by every possible *tour de force* during this long studious afternoon, how to attain to "unusual things." Is this mere inconsistency? Absolutely not. Is she fixated at a certain stage of study? By no means. Eugénie has far too many talents to admit of any possible defect in her pretty head. So what is happening here?

Curiously, critics have composed lengthy dissertations on Sade's fascination with large numbers and on his "obsession with repetition," without ever wondering if there might not be a connection between these two aspects of his thought, both of which play upon the dizzying effects of cumulation. What Eugénie attempts to interiorize is precisely this connection, so as to control, delay or hasten the passage from numerical excess to eccentric excess, and so as to derive full and conscious enjoyment from this transmutation. Such is the lesson of *Philosophy in the Bedroom,* such is the homily of Sadian apathy, which is not assimilated as quickly as one might suppose. Eugénie must wait until the final dialogue to see her efforts crowned:

> Ah! you cry out, mother, you cry out when your daughter fucks you! And as for you, Dolmancé, you're buggering me!. . . Here I am then, committing incest, adultery and sodomy at the same time, and all this in a girl who was only just deflowered today!. . . What progress, my dear friends!

Yes indeed, what progress, allowing one to provoke at will the moment when repeated arrangements of ideas, just like arrangements of positions, necessitate the transition into eccentricity. Sade constantly repeats this procedure, as much to make this necessity more urgent as to deploy the numerical infinity, which will enable everyone to recognize, or discover, his own singularity.

It is not surprising that we should here rediscover the structure of the sumptuous banquet of *The One Hundred and Twenty Days.* It differs in one detail: instead of seeing one's singularity exposed on a plate as at the feast of Silling, one now has to discern the path which leads to singularity. Naturally, this will be different for each person, even if the means of determining it lead back to precise laws which are valid for everyone. For this passage from numerical excess to eccentric excess is always effected from a point of saturation. Although this point varies from one individual to another, it nonetheless indicates, each time, that the slippage towards the imaginary is indissociable from concrete reality. More exactly, it only occurs after violent and gluttonous assimilation. It seems reality must first be known, explored and taken stock of, before immeasurable excess can appear, like a superfluous reality which suddenly decides excessive singularity and opens up imaginary perspectives.

But isn't this really how we function? Considering that all it takes is an erotic detail (which might be anything, for that is Sade's lesson too — a glance, a knee, a hesitation of the hand, a wrinkle, a scar, a smell, the way the lips close over teeth . . .) for our lives to start swaying, and with them, the horizon?

Such is Sade's great discovery about the paths taken by desire: its persistence in the imagination depends on the extent to which it is rooted in concrete reality. This is what Sade shows in *a contrario* through the character of Justine. We should always remember that her exceptional power of endurance sets her apart from the hundreds of boys and girls who disappear at the turn of a page. Justine remains. But she passes into time bearing a disembodied memory and a body that has no memory at all. She passes into the implacable time in which ideas deteriorate through the body, and the body deteriorates through ideas. The passage of this time is engraved on her virginity, tracing her story at the whim of successive retractions that are both physical and symbolic. Justine may lie to avoid being raped, betray others to avoid becoming a thief . . . her moral conduct can be confused with a series of retractions; but in the same way, her body contracts with each erotic assault and retracts until its final fulgurating obliteration. A novel of time from which desire retreats, and retreats absolutely, the story of Justine constitutes the most formidable challenge yet to the adventures of sensual pleasure. No one but her sister Juliette could possibly accept this challenge.

It has become customary to read *The Story of Juliette* as a formative novel which is simultaneously the negative and the negation of the story of Justine. I am more inclined to see it as a challenge and a sequel to *Justine*. For whatever anyone may say or think, Juliette studies absolutely nothing, assimilates nothing, and does not alter in any way at all. From one end of the story to the other she is splendidly herself. She manages this feat even while devoting herself completely, as a model student should, to her successive teachers: Madame Delbène, Noirceuil, Saint-Fond, Clairwil and Madame Durand. Actually, there is something very aggressive in the pedagogical submission Juliette evinces with respect to each of the above. She only listens to them in order to rob them of their mode of thought. With each exchange, Juliette does not learn something, she recognizes herself; her professors helping her reflect upon her conduct are like so many theoretical mirrors in which she seeks her own reflection. In reality, Juliette is not so much thrilled by her lessons as she is eager to find the secret of the fascination they do hold for her, so as to free herself from it at once. Thus, if Juliette learns anything, it's how to break off something. But break off what? And why does she break precisely with the only persons she admits to resembling?

To be completely fair, one must observe that each of Juliette's break-ups is prefaced by an act of withdrawal on the part of her professors. One might even think that on some occasions they initiate the break, if Juliette, now totally familiar with their way of thinking, did not divine their intentions and forestall them, thereby covering herself with all the glory of the rupture. But once again, why? What does Juliette gain in this game of breaking up? Not freedom, it would seem, since she enjoys practically unrestricted liberty with each of her mentors. No, the freedom sought and obtained by Juliette through her untimely breaks is the freedom to disappear within herself, the way a glistening fish will disappear into the depths. One must understand that there is not the slightest trace of psychological complacency in these strange plunges Juliette performs, after each theoretical advance, into organic anonymity, into the shadowy quicksands which surround the splendor of her frail silhouette. For it is this dazed condition of the body that Juliette seems to be continually trying to recover, when she withdraws from the successful mode of thinking offered by one or another of her masters, even if the thought she solicits satisfies her expectations. And so I ask again, what lies behind these frenzied and spectacular desertions?

It can surely not be a simple affirmation of sensation against reflection, as certain critics have thought. On the contrary, in fact, since Sade's entire work and, *a fortiori, The Story of Juliette,* illustrate this observation by Madame Delbène:

> It's not everything just to experience sensations, one must also analyze them. There are times when it is as pleasant to speak knowingly of them as it is to enjoy them, and when one has exhausted one's enjoyment, it's divine to plunge back into speech.

So much so, indeed, that when Juliette visits the Pope, she tells him: "Listen, you old ape, I did not come here to be a vestal virgin." She then informs him of her conditions for going to bed with him, the most important one being this:

> The second thing I want is a philosophical dissertation about murder: I have often soiled myself with this deed, and I would like to know what to think of it. What you tell me will determine my opinions for ever; not that I believe you are infallible, but I have some confidence in all you must have studied, and since you know my philo-

sophical aptitudes, I'm sure you will not dare to deceive me.

In fact, Juliette's unquenchable thirst for knowledge is equaled only by her sense of its physical origins, which Madame Delbène instills in her like a basic principle:

> I can't see my soul. . . . I can only see and feel my body, which feels, thinks, judges, suffers, rises to the height of pleasure and . . . all these faculties necessarily result from its mechanisms and organization.

It is as if the darkness of sensation conjures up the brilliance of thought; as if the dazzling nature of the mind summons an organic opaqueness; as if the one is inconceivable without the other.

This, doubtless, is why Juliette abandons all the modes of thinking adopted by her friends. She does so as soon as she feels their coherence is proving detrimental to the disturbance which originates in the body or returns to it; as soon as she feels their thinking is about to run the major risk of being fixated in a form. Even if she has to wait a long time, the moment always comes when she spots, in the reflection of her masters, that critical point where thought gets jammed into a system, even a negating one. For the force which transports Juliette beyond herself also carries with her the most splendid negative constructions. I'm thinking here of the astonishing character of Clairwil who does not ultimately resist Juliette, even though Juliette has never hesitated to admit that, in addition to her "imperious graces," Madame de Clairwil possessed a superior mind:

> . . . she was highly educated, astonishingly opposed to prejudice . . . which she uprooted even in her childhood; no woman had proceeded further in philosophy. She had, moreover, many talents, being fluent in both English and Italian; she acted divinely and danced like Terpsichore; she knew chemistry and physics, was an accomplished poet, knowledgeable about history, drawing, music and geography; she wrote like Madame de Sévigné, perhaps carrying a little too far the extravagances common to a gifted mind, which normally resulted in an intolerable display of pride with those she did not deem at her own level, such as myself . . . the one creature, as she used to say, in whom she had really recognized a mind.

The fact is that Juliette aims beyond negation, duplicating everything and everyone, hurling herself into every situation and at every person, in order to perceive the secret order and intimate organization that give them form; but above all, to release the energy which form contains. Is this any different from the Pope's own explanation?

> . . . you can vary the forms, but you cannot annihilate them; you cannot absorb the elements of matter: and how could you destroy them, since thay are eternal? You change their forms, and vary them; but this dissolution helps nature, since she reconstructs things from these destroyed parts.

Immediately, one can see that Juliette's attitude to her friends is only a dramatization of her concept of the world: by passing through ideas and words, bodies and desires, Juliette damages the finitude of their forms and links them to infinity. She actually acquires her extraordinary traveling speed from this liberation of energy: as a being in search of its form beyond forms, Juliette is the embodiment of the finest idea of freedom that one can possibly acquire. What is more, she knows no other means of locomotion than this way of drifting through the full modalities of order. Haven't we seen her traveling through life like a perpetual temptation, of the most disturbing sort? Naturally, Juliette is young, rich and beautiful. But her irresistible charm is that she instinctively perceives that intolerable truth of desire so endlessly terrifying and fascinating to men, and which the curious personage of Moberti formulates so clearly: "I wish the whole universe would cease to be when I'm hard." Juliette's strength is that she has never been deceived by this desire from which derive all others, and has always acted accordingly. That is to say, she has always played on the paradox of an erotic omnipotence dependent on the extreme fragility of eccentricity. One might add that our sense of wonder at the supernatural has this same origin. For such is Sade's second great discovery: he unmasks monstrosity at the very root of wonderment. This explains the staccato aspects of *The Story of Juliette,* a story without a story, in which we constantly perceive this omnipotence re-emerging from a series of collapses, when a pretention to absolute sovereignty presupposes the continual risk of nothingness:

> If I were king, Juliette, my greatest pleasure would be to
> have myself attended by executioners, who would instantly
> massacre everything that I was shocked to see. . . . I would
> walk over corpses, and be happy; I would discharge into
> the streams of blood flowing at my feet.

This erotic brutality is far from being an attribute of Noirceuil
alone; it concerns us all, and Juliette is the first character in the
whole world who dares to confront it, just as Sade is the first and
only writer to dare state that this brutality is found in him, in us,
and that it marks human desire. Juliette knows this, right from the
start, and that is why she has nothing to learn, since she already
knows what men strive not to know. It is with full knowledge of
the facts that she seeks out the most ferocious desires, without even
pausing for the warnings of Noirceuil:

> No, let me be; you might be sorry if you aspire to the
> honor of making me discharge alone; my passions, all
> concentrated on a single point, resemble rays of sunshine
> focused by a magnifying glass: they immediately burn what-
> ever object finds itself within range.

It makes no difference. Juliette still rises up from this charred
landscape. Her childhood has known no other garden but this ashen
prospect, against which the flames of passion sometimes bloom in
an extravagant bouquet. In vain does she travel with this disconcerting ease — the magic wand of her sexual cynicism enabling her
to pass through countries, bodies, doors — in fact, she never leaves
her own scorched spot, a spot found in the "sands of love." And
so, alone against everyone, Juliette forges for herself a shining
breastplate of flesh, and Sade gives us the rare privilege of being
present at its preparation, an event implying a new kind of alchemy.
One may expect any transmutation, even the transmutation of the
erotic fierceness of wishing to be everything, turned into the poetic
fierceness of wanting to be other.

CHAPTER NINE

FRESH PIGLET OF MY THOUGHTS

"**A** being of whom nothing is yet known, detached from humanity, who will grow wings and renovate the universe" — I have never much cared for Guillaume Apollinaire's definition of Juliette, it has too many wings and halos. Apollinaire was nonetheless the first to point out the utter newness of this character, which leads me to think that the Joan of Arc-like aspects of his description would not greatly bother Sade. Aided by derision, he might even be quite pleased, since he grants Juliette a certain privilege of treatment. To begin with, she is unlike any of his characters, differing even from her closest libertine friends, despite their mutual pledges of concordance, complicity and trust. At the end of his novel, Sade informs us that Juliette "is quite unique" — a quality not bestowed on any of his other heroes, for only Madame Durand makes such a claim about herself, and her qualifications as the world's finest poisoner do permit her to aspire to an exceptional position. But Juliette, who has no qualifications and has specialized in nothing, has no especial weirdness or strange tastes like all her friends, Juliette is the one whom Sade points out as unique.

What is it that makes her more remarkable than the various exceptional people she takes pride in being with? For one can hardly say that Sade conceived Noirceuil, Saint-Fond, Clairwil, Brisa-Testa, the Princess Borghese, Queen Charlotte and Pope Pius VI according to some common model. None of them is just a simple libertine: exceptional in their excesses, they all possess the talent of being able to analyze the same. The more prestigious among them even have a system, principles, method and practice which they can lucidly expound at any moment, being able in this way to demonstrate the logic of their slightest peculiarity. In short, they possess the rare gift of being able to invent order in disorder, and control the changing structures of the form of their desires.

All this they possess, which Juliette will never do to such a degree, and that is why they fascinate her. They are what Juliette will never be: specialists of the highest order. They are what Juliette does not need to be, for Juliette has a secret. It is a secret she confides one happy day to the Comtesse de Donis, "The richest, most beautiful, most elegant and Sapphic woman in all Florence," Juliette tells us, "who was rumored to be keeping me, and not without foundation."

This is how Juliette explains her secret to her elegant friend:

> Spend two weeks without performing any lewdness, distract yourself and think of other things; you must not, to the very end of those two weeks, allow a single debauched thought inside your head. Once the fortnight is ended, go to bed alone, in utter darkness, calm and silence; recall to mind everything you've banned during this interval, and then indulge, in indolence and nonchalance, in that mild defilement which nobody performs, alone or with others, as skillfully as you. Allow your imagination to conjure up, by slow degrees, different perversions; dwell on them, reviewing each in turn; convince yourself the earth is yours . . . that now you have the right to alter, mutilate, destroy or overthrow whomever you think fit. You have nothing to fear from this: choose whatever pleases you, making no exceptions and suppressing nothing; have no regard for anyone; let no link bind you, let nothing hold you back; leave all the fruits of the experiment to your imagination, and above all, make no hurried motions; let your hand obey your head, and not your temperament. Without your noticing, one of the varied pictures that has been parading in your imagination will hold your attention far more strongly than the rest, so much so that you will be able neither to banish nor replace it. This idea, produced as I describe, will dominate and captivate you; delirium will overtake your senses and, thinking yourself really at the task imagined, you will suddenly discharge like

Messalina. As soon as that is done, light the candles once again and write down the kind of frenzy you have just experienced, omitting none of the details which may have contributed to the effect; then go to sleep, read your notes next day, and begin the operation again, adding everything that your imagination — now a little *blasé* with respect to this idea, which has already caused you such paroxysm — can suggest to increase your next arousal. Next, compose a body for this notion and, while giving it a clear outline, continue to add whatever episodes your head may advise. Execute the whole, and you will find this to be the deviation which best suits you, and which will cause you the most delight. My secret, I confess, is rather wicked, but it is absolutely sound, and I would not advise it had I not experienced its success.

Apart from the beautiful countess, who is madly in love with Juliette and fired up by these words, no one really listens to the incredible secret which sets Juliette apart from her libertine acquaintances. No one has noticed that this secret, this stupefying recipe, is the first and only answer to the question that haunts all Sadian heroes, and of which Juliette is careful to remind the Comtesse de Donis before beginning her exposé:

"Have you never found, my dear friend, that your desires exceed your capacity?"

"Oh, yes indeed!" replied the lovely countess, with a sigh.

"I know that frightful state, it's the torment of my days," continued Juliette.

That is why she has sought and found a remedy. But the remedy is only the result of long endeavor, slow preparation and a secret period of gestation, which I shall try to describe.

Before confessing her secret — never to turn to it again — Juliette seems to have absorbed and appropriated her professors' recommendations as to the degree of apathy needed in the practice of debauchery which, as they see it, is intense, transgressive and unbridled. At first, their suggestions have a preventive value, cautioning against the transports of excessive sensibility, as Clairwil advises Juliette:

Imperceptibly, your sensibility will lose its edge; you will not thereby avert any great crimes, since, on the contrary, you will have caused others to commit them and will even have committed some yourself; but at least it will be done phlegmatically, with that sort of apathy that allows the passions to conceal themselves and, by putting you in a position to plan their consequences, preserves you from all danger.

This amounts to killing two birds with one stone, since apathy here serves to take the preliminary precautions for the deviations it requires. At the same time, as Juliette reminds the Princess Borghese: "It is through insensitivity and depravity that nature begins to reveal the key to her secrets, and we only guess at it when we outrage her." Such is the ascesis of excess which no Sadian hero can avoid. It gives him the feeling of reality, of being alive.

It can also make him feel unreal, when the detachment assumed while experiencing sensation seems to turn into an irreversible schism between mind and body. The seductive Belmor explains to Juliette:

> . . . you must have noticed that my most delightful paroxysms with you are those in which we give free rein to our two imaginations and create beings so lubricious their existence is, alas, impossible. Agree, my angel, that we have no idea what we create or invent in these heavenly moments when our souls on fire no longer exist, save in the impure organs of lubricity.

This preamble entirely justifies Juliette's approving words: "Few men, doubtless, had been as far as he had, and few men were more lovable." At the same time, few men are more tormented:

> In truth, Juliette, I do not know whether reality is worth as much as chimeras, or if paroxysms from what one has not are worth a hundred times as much as those with what one has: behold your buttocks, Juliette, here before my very eyes; I find them beautiful, but my imagination, which is always more brilliant and artful than nature, if I may say so, creates even finer ones. And is not the pleasure I derive from this illusion preferable to the peak I shall derive from truth? What you offer me is simply beautiful; what I am about to do with you is nothing more than anyone

could do; and yet it seems that what I would do with the bum of my imagination, the gods themselves could not invent.

But Belmor's case is not the only one: none of Sade's libertines escapes the hold of this absolute desire which asserts itself at the expense of bodies and intensifies as scorn for them increases. When a rascal on the scale of Saint-Fond finds himself in the aberrant impossibility of "denying [him]self the possibility of another life," why else would he imagine — on the advice of a libertine alchemist — constraining his victim to sign a pact with the devil, being most careful to "then push the document right up his arse with his prick"? In consequence, the victim "thus destroyed will never go to heaven. His sufferings, identical to those you caused by ramming the document inside him, will last for ever." Why else would the ferocious Clairwil imagine the "perpetually effective crime" I have already mentioned? Why else would they all get so excited by the little calculation done by Juliette and Belmor, who have "reasoned out this matter," this kind of "moral murder":

> A libertine who decides on this line of action can easily, in the course of a year, corrupt three hundred children; after thirty years, he will haved corrupted three hundred thousand; and if all the children he corrupts imitate even a quarter of his depravities, which is more than likely, and if every generation acts the same way, then after thirty years the libertine, who will by this time have witnessed the birth of two corrupted generations, will have corrupted almost nine million people, either in his own person, or by example.

Why are all Sade's libertines, except for Juliette, so tormented by this need to exceed the boundaries of pleasure? In guarding so carefully against excesses of sensibility, they have perhaps omitted to beware of excesses of the mind, which are just as hard, if not harder, to control. Perhaps, too, they all are so concerned with committing crimes in cold blood they are unable to avoid the dangers of overintellectualizing? One day the Princess Borghese confides to Juliette what a nuisance excesses of the mind can be, developing in emptiness:

> I was counting enormously upon the parricide I've just committed; I was a thousand times more excited in plan-

ning it than by the actual execution: nothing is at the level of my desires. But I have analyzed my fantasies too much; it would have been a hundred times better for me never to have thought them out; in leaving them the envelope of crime they would at least have diverted me; but the simplicity which my philosophy bestows on them means they have no further effect on me.

In fact, each of Juliette's friends could make these disillusioned speeches, with the possible exception of Madame Durand, whose profession as a poisoner puts her into daily contact with actual substances, and preserves her from this kind of misfortune. All the others — with Clairwil as a dazzling example — become obsessed by this apathy which, instead of remaining a means, becomes an end for them, and so allow themselves to get caught in the trap of negativity. But how do they come to such a pass?

First, we should listen to Clairwil's perpetual complaint regarding Juliette:

> . . . I always find the same flaw in her: she only commits crimes out of enthusiasm, as if having an erection; and one should never indulge in crime except in cold blood. One should use the torch of crime to light up the torch of passion, whereas I suspect her of only using passions in order to light up the torch of crime.

This is first of all an intellectual criticism which Clairwil develops from a completely negative point of view. When she indeed demands that her friend's conscience become "so *twisted* she can never straighten it again," it is to give virtue a bad knock as soon as it recovers: "This habit of positively molesting it, just when the calm of the senses makes it want to reappear, is one of the best ways of destroying it for ever." That, in fact, is Clairwil's secret, which, as she assures Juliette, is "certain" and "infallible." Clairwil has nothing to offer but this essentially negative design. Reading it, one immediately understands Juliette's reticence — not to say, resistance — with respect to the injunctions of her friend. For Juliette has always been elsewhere, working in quite a different field from Clairwil. For Clairwil is concerned only with breaking the resilience of virtue, and overcoming all restraints within herself. This always brings her the same unsatisfactory pleasure. Juliette, on the other hand, seems impatient to venture beyond this complete blank. One can feel how much she is opposed to her friend's ideas when, becoming impatient one day with so many sententious remon-strances that lead nowhere, she reminds Clairwil:

> Remember, Machiavelli said it is better to be *impetuous* than *circumspect,* because nature is a woman one can only get the better of by tormenting her. He goes on to say that with experience, one can see she grants her favors more readily to fierce persons than chilly ones.

This divergence is by no means accidental, for Juliette's impetuous-ness fascinates everyone who meets her, beginning with Clairwil herself. Clairwil vainly tries to dominate Juliette by means of her intellectual power, but remains unable to analyze her phenomenal friend. For the phenomenon of Juliette is a poetic one, and that is Juliette's true secret.

To begin with, *The Story of Juliette* is really a fairy tale, perhaps even the first and only fairy tale that is utterly erotic. For the first time, a little girl comes into the world purely for her own pleasure — and ours — and takes her first steps within a universe where sexes are as big as houses, where houses open up like sexes, where gestures unfold in the whirling space of pleasure. It is a universe where duration is measured by a fine erection, where objects of desire outnumber actual desires but where desire, once satisfied, returns to prowl like a haggard and fierce shadow in the silent fields of the unthinkable.

Herein lies the drama of this fairy tale, and, at the same time, of all fairy tales. Except that normally one cheats, hastening the outcome so as to finish off the story quickly, before desire can come prowling back to the scene of wonderment like an insatiable wild beast. In *Juliette* there is none of that, for once again, Sade does not cheat; he is too intent on seeing and showing both sides of wonderment, too intent on showing the actual trajectory of members, darting like lightning through silky mucous textures.

But there is only one way not to cheat in fairy tales; and that is to speak directly to the fairy. Even better, one should first observe and follow all her movements, and eventually try to make her speak. This is exactly what Sade does with Juliette: he approaches her when she is just a little fairy, watches her grow up, and then observes her playing with her own desire as if it were a talisman. But a talisman she never stops perfecting, to make it more functional, as we would say today. This essential condition of wonderment was utterly ignored until Sade left Juliette to tell the tale. For Sade invents the first fairy tale narrated by the fairy herself. This capital innovation allows Juliette to show us her work as a fairy and to reveal her secrets. This, surely, is a poetic enterprise, beginning with a refusal to tell lies, a refusal to be taken in by one's impulses.

Thus, when Juliette spends a night with Saint-Fond's delightful daughter, who is also Noirceuil's future wife:

> I admit I viewed her in so philosophical a manner, with such satiety of senses, that I am scarcely able to tell you of the pleasures I received: enthusiasm would be needed, whereas I scarcely felt emotion at all. So confirmed were my opinions, the moral side of my being so dominated the physical, my indifference was so pronounced and my calm so assiduous that, whether from satiety or depravity or constitution, I was able, without becoming aroused, to keep her naked for ten hours in my bed, masturbate her, be masturbated by her, suck her and titillate her, without feeling the slightest mental arousal. This, I am so bold as to declare, is one of the happier fruits of stoicism.

This kind of stoicism, aided by her humor, evokes a technical prowess Juliette might well be proud of, especially as she is too lucid to attribute this serenity to any system, or to endow it with any ideological value. What Juliette may boast about exclusively is that she possesses a true champion's virtuosity. Her remarkable honesty leads her to conclude, with axiomatic rigor, that only this physical excessiveness can set imaginary excessiveness in motion:

> In stiffening our souls against anything that can excite them, in acquainting them with crime by means of debauchery, in allowing them only physical pleasure, and in obstinately refusing them all delicacy, one enervates them; and in this state, wherein their natural activity does not permit them to remain for very long, they pass into a kind of apathy soon changing into pleasure a thousand times more heavenly than those procured by weakness.

What Juliette discovers here, at the end of the first part of her story, is the inexorable law of the "deserts of love": namely, that the object of desire always appears as the betrayal of desire. All Sade's heroes must learn this law, which is the cause of their torments. But whereas all the others strive to deny this flaw in the object, incessantly obliterating it to endow it with a negative existence, Juliette, with her terrible lucidiy, departs from this betrayal of the object to elaborate her secret against the blankest possible backdrop. We must not forget the two weeks of abstinence with which her secret begins. She transforms this want of an object into the principle of her erotic solitude: "Go to bed alone, in utter calm and silence," thus completely reacquiring her own physical power. Juliette is first and foremost the body of this erotic revery; in the beginning, that is actually all she is, so as to assert her solitude physically. And so, entirely for herself, slowly and without words, Juliette strives to accomplish the passage from physical excess to imaginary excess: she does so once, twice, three times, more . . . : "Allow your imagination to conjure up, by slow degrees, different sorts of perversion; dwell on them at length." She transforms the betrayal of the object into the principle of her thirst for an erotic absolute: "Convince yourself the earth is yours . . . that nothing binds you; nothing holds you back." And this is to continue until one image stands out "far more strongly than the rest, so much so that you will be able neither to banish nor replace it."

What is this, if not the determination of an erotic arbitrariness which could well be confused with poetic arbitrariness? Isn't Juliette here redesigning for herself the mental structure of *The One Hundred and Twenty Days of Sodom?* Isn't she offering us tickets to the spectacle of thought, in its actual functioning, being mixed up with desire? And what is she indulging in, if not this autometaphorization I've already discussed? Poetically and erotically, it seems Sade always takes individual solitude as his point of departure. It seems that every procedure, either poetic or erotic, which denies that solitude is necessarily deceptive and inane.

Once again, Sade touches on the heart of the problem: in poetry, as in other things, dressing up and camouflaging the void constitutes the deception which authorizes all other deceptions. Erotically, the wager is exactly the same. Everything that comes to mask the individual's solitude — *a fortiori* — all amorous ideology betting on the feasibility of union — has, for Sade, something revolting about it. He might say it was a scandalous misuse of the one weapon we dispose of for getting near the truth, that weapon being desire.

What is Juliette actually looking for, if not the truth? Hence the savage concern with erotic accuracy which seems to dictate her whole life. Doesn't her two-week withdrawal help her to acquire that keen sense of precision indispensable to her fairy-like endeavors? In this determining aspect of Juliette's secret we discover the progressive precision so essential to a grasp of poetic reality, just as it is for a grasp of erotic reality (isn't orgasm a kind of a mad accession to the precise nature of what haunts us?). "As soon as that is done, light your candles once again and write down the kind of frenzy you have just experienced." Thus does Juliette set about fixing the unstable forms of her desire, just as poetry seeks to fix the forms of the unthinkable, just as pleasure is the particular form snatched from the indeterminate nature of the orgasm. "Next, compose a body for this notion and, while giving it a clear outline, continue to whatever episodes your head may advise." Giving bodies to ideas, giving ideas to bodies: that is what the fairy does.

Is it erotic or poetic work? Juliette's genius lies in her confusion of the two. This, too, is her strange secret, which may well reveal the way Sade wrote his books, continually searching for the deviation which best suited him — and everybody else — just as Juliette says. In her fairy-like labors, Juliette also shows us how thought and desire are indissociable, how the erotic imagination is exalted by the act of writing, and how the act of writing is nurtured by erotic exaltation. I myself see no other meaning in writing, and if I prefer poetry, it's because I see it as a more radical means of causing and prolonging this propagation of disturbance.

Like Juliette, Sade is concerned with nothing else. Departing from the general erotization implicitly intended by fairy stories and erotic books, he offers us a most extraordinary journey across all possible erotic objects. At the end of this journey we are greeted by desire, appearing for the first time in its most primitive state. Quite simply, Sade succeeds in freeing "the amorous imagination from its own objects," as Paul Eluard foresees in *Donner à voir*. In other words, *The Story of Juliette* is this race of desire beyond accepted forms to find its own unstable, improbable, lively and perpetually changing form. It is also a criticism of the fairy tale by its own fairy, a critique of wonderment effected by contingency.

An erotic revolution, or a mental one? How should we describe it, this discovery Sade makes, through Juliette and her secret, of how to overcome the disaster of satiety? There is deviation duplicated through the act of writing, augmented by the act of reading, repeated once again in writing, and thus repeatable until the mind and senses go quite wild — all this comprises the great value of Juliette's strange secret. It seems that in order to avoid that natural satiety resulting from a series of aberrations, one must detach oneself from nature, and artificially detach oneself from nature's deviations.

Especially as this technique of deviation artificially renewed is like a curious replica of the volcano of Pietra-Mala, a "natural" artifice which seems to have fascinated both Sade and Juliette, in the course of their respective visits to the site.

In both his *Voyage d'Italie* and in *Juliette,* Sade gives detailed descriptions of this volcano, declaring in the former that "the flames proceeding from its center are exceedingly intense, they burn and instantly consume whatever one throws into them and are colored purple like the soul of wine." With a few minor changes, Sade repeats this description in *The Story of Juliette.* Nonetheless, in both texts we sense he is more deeply impressed by what goes on nearby:

> To the right of Pietra-Mala lies another volcano, which burns only when fire is put inside it. I was most amused by an experiment we did: by means of a candle, we set fire to the whole plain. With a mind like mine, my friends, one should never see such things, I do agree; but the candle I presented to the ground caught fire far less quickly than my mind, set ablaze by the evaporated flames from that terrain.

This confession, which is far more dramatic than the corresponding description in the *Voyage d'Italie,* shows how excited Juliette is by this "natural" possibility of imitating nature through artifice. Even rainfall, filling up the center of the second volcano, adds to the oddness of this volcanic double, since the water then "rises up boiling, without losing any of its coolness. Oh, Nature! how whimsical you are!. . . And yet, you do not wish to be imitated by mankind!" as Juliette exclaims, promptly proceeding to do just that: "By means of a candle, we set fire to the whole plain." In terms of humor and naïveté, Juliette's confession certainly equals the chemist Almani's "secret for effecting an earthquake." One can, he affirms, "imitate a volcano," and "by the seething of the factitious volcano [produce] the same effects as does and earthquake." He even adds that the "procedure is a simple one."

Indeed, the procedure is a simple one. This is what we learn from Juliette as she systematically abandons the known regions of the amorous imaginary, dragging us to the distant territory where man discovers how terribly far his own erotic aspects set him from the world. Through being the only person to realize this great distance and to make every possible use of it, Juliette becomes the first erotic dandy known unto this day. Her story recounts the formidable labors she carries out upon herself. It is certainly no accident that Sade has chosen a female character, mired in every natural, social and moral contingency, to rise up as this ferocious little "vulvovagant" dandy.

Daughter, wife, mother; Juliette's first move is to hurl the cast-off accoutrements of traditional femininity into the devouring flames of her own passions. Or rather, she uses them to fuel the furnace which provides her with her energy. It is to this savage rejection of traditional roles that she owes her own inimitable style, as she herself declares after several incestuous encounters with the author of her days: "Once the child begotten by my esteemed father was buried in the latrines, I re-appeared with a prettier and cleaner waistline than I ever had before."

A prettier and cleaner waistline than before — that is what constantly sets her apart from all the other women, spouses or whores, all fatally imprisoned in their flesh, and whom Sade never finds attractive in the least degree. Like a sculptor, Juliette chisels away unmercifully, shaping her own nervous style from the raw material of female flesh. Applying herself night and day to discovering its weaknesses, surprises and betrayals, she never prejudges her resistance, but continually tests it to increase its limits. Therefore, when still fascinated by Noirceuil, she does not hesitate to tell him:

> "As for the submission you demand, it shall be absolutely total; do as you wish, for I belong to you; I put myself in woman's proper place, knowing that my fate lies in dependency."
>
> "No, not necessarily," Noirceuil replied; "The freedom you enjoy, your mind and character, detach you from such serfdom. I only require it of *wives* and *whores,* and in so doing follow the very laws of nature who, as you can see, allows such beings to do nothing else but crawl."

This does not stop Juliette from subsequently indulging in regular treatments of "whoring," so as never to lose contact with the matrix of her nature; from this she extracts the increasingly subtle matter that adorns her, rather in the manner that downy complexions are obtained from mud baths.

If contemporary feminists had anything in view besides the promiscuity of womanhood, they might be able to perceive *Juliette* as a searching reflection on female freedom. Examining women both savagely and lucidly, Sade offers them no model, but suggests the one mode of functioning by which they might evade the traps of femininity. *At no time does Juliette react like a woman:* on the contrary, she constantly invents her freedom, abandoning with assiduity and *brio* the ready-made behavior that is expected of her. In this respect, her meeting with King Ferdinand, an ordinary, stupid man, is most enlightening. Arriving as a courtesan, "embellished like the goddess who obtained the golden apple," Juliette begins to undeceive him as to the honor he thinks he's done her in inviting her. She then proceeds to analyze the political situation of his States:

> Ferdinand, who had listened most attentively, asked, as soon as I had finished, if all Frenchwomen discussed politics as I did.
> "No," I replied. "The vast majority analyze powder puffs better than they do kingdoms; they weep when oppressed, and become insolent as soon as they are freed. As for myself, frivolity is not my vice; I cannot say the same for debauchery . . . which I enjoy excessively; but the pleasure of fucking does not render me too blind to discuss the interests of the different nations. In strong souls the torch of passions lights the torches both of Venus and Minerva; by the light of the former, I fuck like your sister-in-law (Marie-Antoinette of France) and by the beams of the latter, I think and speak like Montesquieu and Hobbes."

Faced with this self-portrait, in which humor adds to the sublime, one can well imagine that poor Ferdinand remains nonplused:

> "By heaven, I don't understand too much of that," replied this utter fool. "I fuck, I eat macaroni without a cook, I build houses without an architect, I collect medals without an antique dealer, I play billiards like a footman, I drill my cadets like a sergeant; but I never speak of politics, religion, customs or government, because I know nothing at all about them."

The principal quality of this utter fool is that he shows to best advantage the extraordinarily successful creation that is Sade's Juliette. To the point of caricature, Ferdinand is everything that she is not. By means of a reversal peculiar to Sade, the man finds himself thrown back into his organic state of wretchedness, enslaved by social puppetry, while a woman finds within herself the strength — hitherto inconceivable — to free herself from her long-standing fate.

Once again, it is hard not to think of Rimbaud and his now famous prophecy:

> When the unending servitude of woman is at an end, when she lives for and by herself, when man — who until now, has been abominable — when man has given her freedom, she, too, will be a poet! She will seek out the unknown! Will her mental world be different from ours? She will find strange things, unfathomable, revolting and delightful things; we shall take them, we shall understand them.

Again, one cannot help wondering why Rimbaud and Sade — both despising women trapped in feminine roles, if not women altogether — have both given female forms to their images of freedom? One thinks, too, of Jarry, announcing without preamble that "We don't like women at all, but if we ever loved one, we would want her to be our equal, which is no minor thing!" Yet the most liberated character Jarry ever created is young Ellen in *The Supermale*. This gives us further cause to wonder about the nature of the poetic wager born with Juliette, and which gives rise to the most disturbing thoughts of our modernity. For it is nonetheless surprising that Sade, Rimbaud and Jarry, distant as they were from women, unite in betting on the future of the female form. What, in terms of choice, have female forms to do with freedom?

The answer is, of course: everything, precisely because female forms have always been considered hopelessly foreign to freedom. And because, in seeking it, one risks taking an enormous detour through the labyrinth of bodies. It may even be a double, triple or infinitely repeated detour, since this body can produce so many labyrinths. If Sade, Rimbaud and Jarry all chose the female form, which is naturally capable of creating other forms like itself, it is first of all because it constitutes the greatest challenge to the artifice of thought, having in its power to invent an infinite number of improbable beings. Because through the female form, and violently at that, it is possible to represent the inevitable rivalry of nature and thought which true poetry always manages to evoke. Because in the female form, representing as it does a double challenge — one issued by nature to thought, one issued by thought to nature — the enigma of human freedom receives its full expression.

Sade was the first to choose an exquisite female body and make it into a scene of poetic confrontation between natural fatality and the artifice of thought. It was as if he wanted to propagate this confrontation throughout the universe. For these reasons, his is certainly the most prestigious of poetic minds. We owe him the power of discovering, across erotic energy and its infinite transformations, *the material character of freedom.* I'm not sure we yet know what that is.

On one particularly tender day, Sade wrote a letter to his wife, beginning with the words: "Fresh piglet of my thoughts." I hope that one day there will be a woman who can dream of receiving a love letter that begins as well, for the whole world is thereby laid at her feet, and freedom — real freedom, freedom as lived by Juliette — is rolled out before her like a carpet. I shall not discuss Sade's letters here. I recommend only that you read them when very much alone.

And Now . . .

I make no claims, especially concerning the objectivity of this review. That is why, in ending it, I should like to make quite clear that I do realize the peculiarity of my approach. I should be deceiving myself greatly if I did not know that this is just *one* look brought to bear on Sade, at just *one* moment of my life. There is nothing extraordinary in that. But, unlike all the others, I say so and accept the consequences.

First of all, there are, of course, the innumerable aspects of Sade's thought with which I have not dealt. But even had I done so, even if others do so, Sade would — will still — remain this crystal block of chasm, because Sade is he who pushes people into the abyss and who offers, as the one way out, an unforgiving thought. A thought which, through having returned to its origins at the point where it is confused with desire, forgives nothing. A thought which, for the first time, gives thought the strength to be a measure for what is and measureless for what is not. Or again, to be immeasurable for what is, and a measure of what is not.

It is a terrible thought, a thought of first innocence. The tricks played by our minds make us both its authors and its victims, and work constantly to keep us at a distance from it. Hence the critical violence I have shown with respect to certain of Sade's critics. At the same time, however, I was well aware that without them — that is, without the readings of Bataille, Paulhan, and Blanchot — I would have found it harder to advance in the enigmatic world of Sade. Without Eugène Dühren, Maurice Heine and also Gilbert

Lely, whose enthusiasm and patience have succeeded in revealing the scope of Sade's work, clearing it out from under the debris of fear and stupidity. Without the poets — especially Apollinaire, Breton, Eluard, and Mandiargues — whose voices, like an echo ringing forth from isle to isle, succeeded in conveying what a superb and formidable volcano had risen on our horizon, what flames were burning in the depths of the mind, what a trajectory, until then unthinkable, we could follow with our mind's eye. Without Jean-Jacques Pauvert, who committed his whole destiny to this endeavor and took the risk of making Sade's thought live for other men.

Thanks to all of the above, I was able to write this book quickly, very quickly, with that speed which no mere deadline could have spurred me to maintain, had I not obeyed some curious inner haste. Determined at the outset to confront the unresolved questions which sprang up all around Sade, I gradually perceived that I tended to pause longest over those which concerned Sade's *coherence,* as if that coherence was the most important aspect, and as if a certain balance were dependent on it— as if our own coherence were dependent on it. This explains the inner haste from which I never escaped, not even for an instant, discovering, while Sade's silhouette grew slowly clearer to me, that in tracing it, one encountered all the blind spots of our landscape.

They occur where literature proliferates, where atheism collapses, wherever ideology takes root, where representation grows congested, the subject disappears, the body is deficient, machines grind out meaning; where negativity obstructs the exits, and where freedom is conceived as an abstraction. Little by little I came to see that Sade's coherence could constitute a very forceful criticism of our incoherent modernity. For against this modern thought, illusory to the point of having actually turned its critical existence into a mythology, and of no longer functioning save as a myth of criticism, one could oppose his total atheism. Only this was capable of demystifiying this thought of doubt, born of disbelief, but subsequently grown into thought of systematic suspicion concerning everything outside itself. Only Sade's definitive atheism was capable of canceling this crisis of a representation concerned only with representing the crisis. Only Sade's vital atheism could preserve us from the deception of a thought originally designed for unmasking, but which had subsequently turned into an ideology of remasking. For a process of questioning the working of the world had been transformed, through interposed structuralism, into a spectacle of functioning, at the expense of any other perspective, until it had deprived us of the possibility of meaning springing forth.

This, indeed, is the imposture of a deadly process of abstraction, of which Sade, and he alone, postulating the body as a unique cornerstone, brings us to measure the disturbing scope. Especially as Sade also shows us that as we dismiss the body, we thereby lose all possibility of gaining access to the truth, or more exactly, of avoiding lies. So much for the accommodations we make with whatever ideology we find so essential, for these accommodations are actually disguises which prevent us from watching ourselves dying.

Perhaps this is why, in reaching the end of this journey through Sade's thought, I wanted to disappear — not in a tragic sense, just disappear. Had this long and intense period of time spent with Sade succeeded, on that day, in effacing all ideology? It's possible. Wandering about Paris, the whole day long, I experienced an intense feeling of having no more limits, of not being in this world, of actually being the world or rather, of sinking into everything that I was not. But what more could I hope for, when Sade had foreseen that Juliette's death would make her "disappear from the stage of the world, just as everything that shines on earth normally must vanish"? How could I not be grateful to him for having shown me that within every forceful thought lies an intense wish to be nothing?

FOR JEAN-JACQUES PAUVERT

There, everything is happening as if the journey had reached an end. Without you, it would never have taken place, and so I would simply like its outcome to be on a par with what you expected when you first proposed it.

I have tried to rid myself of all encumbrances — ideas, feelings and perhaps a kind of happiness — to venture into that huge devastated region that Sade left us for our one horizon. I don't know if I succeeded. However, I do know that you played a part in this. To ignite something as yet inexistent, to give a spark of life to something that will soon exist, that is perhaps a publisher's job; but there are very few who are as adept as yourself in this species of manipulation.

For anyone even slightly acquainted with you, and who knows you were behind some of the most disturbing meteorological revolutions of our time, this is not terribly surprising. What is surprising is your bond with Sade, which goes beyond mere publishing. Unless, of course, publishing is what you made of it for Sade: a formidable machine against time and death, against solitude, true solitude, which is the implacable awareness of both. But that is saying too little when your entire life has been spent in attending to Sade, despite the spectacular reactions on all sides which rewarded your boldness and your courage in being his first publisher.

For perhaps we should remember — and remind you — that, without you, it is entirely possible that Sade would still be inaccessible to us; at the very least, we should not be able to read him, without the customary precautions, and in his entirety. Your role in this was considerable, for you set about publishing his complete works in defiance of the law (this publication cost you innumerable appearances in court); in defiance of your interests as a publisher (Sade did not sell); and despite certain Sadians who felt it preferable to make selections of his writings. It is to you, too, that we owe the happy thought of persuading thinkers of all kinds to introduce these texts, forestalling, by these diverse points of view, any attempt to take possession of a work at once so forceful and so threatened.

That is perhaps what is most moving in your relationship with Sade: ever since you first read him at the age of seventeen, you've been protecting him. You never stop protecting him. Even today, at a time when others find it more expedient to disseminate his thought, you decided to reintegrate his texts. You are one of the very few who understands the extreme fragility of any powerful thought. I would even say, you are one of the very few who are physically aware of it. Hence, you build up books like barricades to protect these thoughts; thoughts so powerful that they subvert the order of things without anybody noticing; thoughts so fragile that everything inside us strives to prevent them from dragging us beyond ourselves. I would even venture to think that for this reason you became a publisher, when so few are aware of this paradoxical fragility, which comes from the fact that reality immediately becomes opaque as soon as one wishes to pass through it — although this is only our fear, preventing us from thinking in the full awareness of our nudity. The stronger this thought is, the more fragile it becomes; but the stronger it is, the more brutally it drags us to the truth inscribed across the nothingness of bodies.

This, indeed, is what will never be forgiven Sade, and what fascinates you in him: that he dared point out this organic bond between truth and the body. That he dared point out a truth henceforth as perishable as the body that endows it with form, a truth which is definitively intolerable to human pride. Is not the quest for this unstable, trembling, haggard truth, as pursued through bodies, exactly what you yourself incessantly pursue in your passionate curiosity for eroticism? And that is why, instinctively, you have always known the inestimable value of Sade's naked gaze, knowing, too, that we need this gaze to live, and to avoid being crushed beneath the weight of those overwhelming impostures from which you managed to save Sade, *despite everything.*

For all these reasons, I wanted to dedicate this long reflection to you. At the same time, I found it perplexing that a work devoted to Sade should not belong to him entirely. Furthermore, you know as well as I do that one writes only for oneself. And so, I should have found it distasteful to offer you a second-hand present. But if I did not write this text for you, I certainly cannot say I wrote it without you.

One day, many other tributes will most certainly be paid you; my one ambition is that this one be the truest.

Annie Le Brun

November 28, 1985, or exactly two hundred years after Sade finished writing *The One Hundred and Twenty days of Sodom,* on November 28, 1785.

BIBLIOGRAPHY

Bataille, Georges. *Erotism: Death & Sensuality.* Translated by
Mary Dalwood, San Francisco: City Lights Books, 1986.
———. *Literature and Evil.* Translated by Alastair Hamilton.
London: Calder and Boyers, 1972.
———. *The Tears of Eros.* Translated by Peter Connor. San
Francisco: City Lights Books, 1989.
Foucault, Michel. *Madness and Civilization: A History of Insanity
in the Age of Reason.* Translated by Richard Howard. New
York: Random House, 1965.
Lely, Gilbert. *The Marquis de Sade: a Biography.* Translated by
Alec Brown. New York: Grove Press, 1962.
Sade, Marquis de. *The Complete Justine, Philosophy in the
Bedroom & Other Writings.* Compiled and translated by
Richard Seaver and Austryn Wainhouse. Introductions by
Jean Paulhan ("The Marquis de Sade and His
Accomplice") and Maurice Blanchot ("Sade"). Includes
Chronology, *Seven Letters, Note Concerning My Detention,
Last Will and Testament, Dialogue Between a Priest and a
Dying Man, Philosophy in the Bedroom, Eugénie de Franval,*
and *Justine, or Good Conduct Well Chastised.)* New York:
Grove Press, 1965.
———. *Eugénie de Franval and Other Stories.* Translated by
Margaret Crosland. London: Nevelle Spearman, 1965, 1968.
———. *Juliette.* Translated by Austryn Wainhouse. New York:
Grove Press, 1968.
———. *The 120 Days of Sodom and Other Writings.* Compiled
and translated by Austryn Wainhouse and Richard Seaver.
Introductions by Simone be Beauvoir ("Must We Burn

Sade?") and Pierre Klossowski ("Nature as Destructive Principle"). (Includes *Les Crimes de l'amour, Reflections on the Novel, Florville and Courval, or the Works of Fate, The 120 Days of Sodom, Oxtiern, or the Misfortunes of Libertinage,* and *Ernestine, a Swedish Tale).* New York: Grove Press, 1966.

———. *Les Ouevres Complètes,* vol. I-XV (in progress). Paris: Jean-Jacques Pauvert et Societé Nouvelle des Editions Pauvert, 1985-19–.

———. *Selected Letters.* Preface by Gilbert Lely. Translated by W. J. Strachen. Edited by Margaret Crosland. London: Peter Owen, 1965.